Artificial Neural Networks: Advanced Principles

Artificial Neural Networks: Advanced Principles

**Edited by
Jeremy Rogerson**

www.willfordpress.com

Published by Willford Press,
118-35 Queens Blvd., Suite 400,
Forest Hills, NY 11375, USA

ISBN: 978-1-68285-669-7

Cataloging-in-Publication Data

Artificial neural networks : advanced principles / edited by Jeremy Rogerson.
   p. cm.
Includes bibliographical references and index.
ISBN 978-1-68285-669-7
1. Neural networks (Computer science). 2. Artificial intelligence. I. Rogerson, Jeremy.
QA76.87 .A78 2019
006.32--dc23

For information on all Willford Press publications
visit our website at www.willfordpress.com

Contents

Preface

This book has been a concerted effort by a group of academicians, researchers and scientists, who have contributed their research works for the realization of the book. This book has materialized in the wake of emerging advancements and innovations in this field. Therefore, the need of the hour was to compile all the required researches and disseminate the knowledge to a broad spectrum of people comprising of students, researchers and specialists of the field.

Artificial neural networks refer to the computing systems inspired by biological neural networks. They are based on nodes or artificial neurons, which are a replica of biological neurons found in the brain of animals. This enables them to learn and thereby perform tasks by considering examples. The use of artificial neural networks is vast as they are applied in varied fields like medical diagnosis, speech recognition, computer vision, machine translation, etc. Some common variants include convolutional neural networks, deep stacking networks, deep belief networks, deep predictive coding networks, etc. The theoretical properties of artificial neural networks are capacity, generalization and statistics, computational power, convergence, etc. This book is a valuable compilation of topics, ranging from the basic to the most complex advancements in the field of artificial neural networks. The book attempts to assist those with a goal of delving into this field. The various studies that are constantly contributing towards advancing technologies and evolution of this field are examined in detail.

At the end of the preface, I would like to thank the authors for their brilliant chapters and the publisher for guiding us all-through the making of the book till its final stage. Also, I would like to thank my family for providing the support and encouragement throughout my academic career and research projects.

Editor

Preface

A Continuous-Time Recurrent Neural Network for Joint Equalization and Decoding – Analog Hardware Implementation Aspects

Mohamad Mostafa, Giuseppe Oliveri,
Werner G. Teich and Jürgen Lindner

Additional information is available at the end of the chapter

Abstract

Equalization and channel decoding are "traditionally" two cascade processes at the receiver side of a digital transmission. They aim to achieve a reliable and efficient transmission. For high data rates, the energy consumption of their corresponding algorithms is expected to become a limiting factor. For mobile devices with limited battery's size, the energy consumption, mirrored in the lifetime of the battery, becomes even more crucial. Therefore, an energy-efficient implementation of equalization and decoding algorithms is desirable. The prevailing way is by increasing the energy efficiency of the underlying digital circuits. However, we address here promising alternatives offered by mixed (analog/digital) circuits. We are concerned with modeling joint equalization and decoding *as a whole* in a continuous-time framework. In doing so, continuous-time recurrent neural networks play an essential role because of their nonlinear characteristic and special suitability for analog very-large-scale integration (VLSI). Based on the proposed model, we show that the superiority of joint equalization and decoding (a well-known fact from the discrete-time case) preserves in analog. Additionally, analog circuit design related aspects such as adaptivity, connectivity and accuracy are discussed and linked to theoretical aspects of recurrent neural networks such as Lyapunov stability and simulated annealing.

Keywords: continuous-time recurrent neural networks, analog hardware neural networks, belief propagation, vector equalization, joint equalization and decoding

1. Introduction

Energy efficiency has been increasingly attracting more interest due to economical and environmental reasons. Mobile communications sector has currently a share of 0.2% in global carbon emissions. This share is expected to double between 2007 and 2020 due to the ever-increasing demand for wireless devices [1, 2]. The sustained interest in higher data rate transmission is strengthening this impact. While major resources are being invested in increasing the energy efficiency of digital circuits, there is, on the other hand, a growing interest pointing at alternatives to the digital realization [3], including a mixed (analog/digital) approach. In such an approach, specific energy consuming (sub)tasks are implemented in analog instead of a "conventional" digital realization. The analog implementation possesses a high potential to significantly improve the energy efficiency [4] because of the inherent parallel processing of signals that are continuous in both time and amplitude. This has been shown in the field of error correction coding with a focus on decoding of low-density parity-check (LDPC) codes. Our ongoing research on equalization reveals similar results. We do not intend "analog" for linear signal processing with all its disadvantages like component inaccuracies and susceptibility to noise and temperature dependency [5] but for *nonlinear processing* instead. The work of Mead [6] and others on *Neuromorphic analog very-large-scale integration (VLSI)* has shown that *"analog signal processing systems can be built that share the robustness of digital systems but outperform digital systems by several orders of magnitude in terms of speed and/or power consumption"* [5].

The nonlinearity makes the analog implementation of an algorithm as robust as its digital counterpart [3, 5]. This profits from the match between the needed nonlinear operations for the algorithm and the physical properties of analog devices [7].

The capability of artificial neural networks (in the following neural networks) to successfully solve many scientific and engineering tasks has been shown oftentimes. Moreover, mapping algorithms to neural network structures can simplify the circuit design because of the regular (and repetitive) structure of neural networks and their limited number of *well-defined* arithmetic operations. Digital implementations can be considered precise (reproducibility of results under similar circumstances) but accurate (closeness of a result to the "true" value) *only* to the extent to which they have enough digits to represent [8]. This means, accuracy in digital implementations is achieved at the cost of efficiency (e.g., relatively larger chip area and more power consumption) [9]. An analog implementation is usually efficient in terms of chip area and processing speed [9], however, at the price of an inherent lack of the reproducibility of results [8] (because of a limited accuracy of the network components as an example [9]). However, by exploiting the distributed nature of neural structures the precision of the analog implementation can be improved despite inaccurate components and subsystems [8][1]. In other words, it is the distributed massively parallel nonlinear collective behavior of an analog implementation (of neural networks) which offers the possibility to make it as robust as its digital counterpart but more energy efficient[2] (additionally to smaller chip area). Particularly for *recurrent* neural networks (the class we focus on when considered as nonlinear dynamical systems), the robustness can be additionally achieved by exploiting "attracting" equilibrium points. In the light of this discussion, we map in this chapter a joint equalization and decoding algorithm into a novel *continuous-time* recurrent neural network structure. This class of neural networks has been attracting a lot of interest because of their widespread applications. They can be either trained for system identification [10], or they can be considered as dynamical

---

[1]For a clear distinction between *accuracy* and *precision* when used in hardware implementation context, we refer to [8].
[2]Energy efficiency is defined later as appropriate.

systems (dynamical solver). In the latter case, there is *no need* for a computationally complex and time-consuming training phase. This relies on the ability of these networks (under specific conditions) to be Lyapunov stable.

Equalization and channel decoding (together, in the following detection) are processes at the receiver side of a digital transmission. They aim to provide a reliable and efficient transmission. Equalization is needed to cope with the interference caused by multipath propagation, multiusers, multisubchannels, multiantennas and combinations thereof [11]. Channel (de)coding is applied for further improving the power efficiency. Equalization and decoding are nonlinear discrete optimization problems. The optimum solutions, in general, are computationally very demanding. Therefore, suboptimum solutions are applied, often soft-valued iterative schemes because of their good complexity-performance trade-off.

For high data rates, the energy consumption of equalization and decoding algorithms is expected to become a limiting factor. The need for floating-point computation and the nonlinear and iterative nature of (some of) these algorithms revive the option of an analog electronic implementation [12, 13], embedded in an essentially digital receiver. This option has been strengthened since the emergence of the "soft-valued" computation in this context [4] since soft-values are a natural property of analog signals. In contrast to analog decoding, analog equalization did not attract that amount of attention.

Furthermore, *joint* equalization and decoding (a technique where equalizer and decoder exchange their *local* available knowledge) further improves the efficiency of the transmission as an example in terms of lower bit error rates, however, at the cost of more computational complexity [14]. Most of the work related to joint equalization and decoding is limited to the discrete-time realization. One of the very few contributions focusing on continuous-time joint equalization and decoding is given in [13]. The consideration in [13] is not "neural networks-based". Stability and convergence are observed but not "deeply" considered.

We introduce in this chapter a novel continuous-time joint equalization and decoding structure. For this purpose, continuous-time single-layer recurrent neural networks play an essential role because of their nonlinear and recursive characteristic, special suitability for analog VLSI and since they serve as promising computational models for analog hardware implementation [15]. Both, equalizer and decoder are modeled as continuous-time recurrent neural networks. An additional proper feedback between equalizer and decoder is established for joint equalization and decoding. We also review individually, both continuous-time equalization and continuous-time decoding based on recurrent neural network structures. No training is needed since the recurrent neural network is serving as a dynamical solver or a computational model [15, 16]. This means, transmission properties are used to define the recurrent neural network (number of neurons, weight coefficients, activation functions, etc.) such that no training is needed. In addition, we highlight challenges emerging from the analog hardware implementation such as adaptivity, connectivity and accuracy. We also introduce our developed circuit for analog equalization based on continuous-time recurrent neural networks [3]. Characteristic properties of recurrent neural networks such as stability and convergence are addressed too. Based on the introduced model, we show by simulations that the superiority of joint equalization and decoding can be preserved in the analog "domain".

The main motivation for performing joint equalization and decoding in analog instead of using conventional digital circuits is to improve the energy efficiency and to minimize the area consumption in the VLSI chips [17]. The proposed continuous-time recurrent neural network serves as a promising computational model for analog hardware implementation.

The remainder of this chapter is organized as follows: In Section 2, we describe the block transmission model. Sections 3 and 4 are dedicated to the equalization process, the application of continuous-time recurrent neural networks and the analog circuit design and its corresponding performance and energy efficiency. Sections 5 and 6 are devoted to the channel decoding and the application of continuous-time recurrent neural networks for belief propagation (a decoding algorithm for LDPC codes). For both equalization and decoding cases, analog hardware design aspects and challenges and the behavior of the continuous-time recurrent neural network as a dynamical system are discussed. The continuous-time joint equalization and decoding based on recurrent neural networks is presented in Sections 7 and 8. Simulation results are shown in Section 9. We finish this chapter with a conclusion in Section 10.

Throughout this chapter, bold small and bold capital letters designate vectors (or finite discrete sets) and matrices, respectively.[3] All nonbold letters are scalars. $\text{diag}_m\{B\}$ returns the matrix B where the nondiagonal elements are set to zeros. $\text{diag}_v\{b\}$ returns a matrix where the vector b is put on the diagonal. $\mathbf{0}_N$ is the all-zero vector of length N. $\mathbf{0}, \mathbf{1}$ and I represent the all-zero, all-one and the identity matrix of suitable size, respectively. We consider column vectors. $(\cdot)^H$ represents the conjugate transpose of a vector or a matrix, whereas $(\cdot)^T$ represents the transpose. $z_r = \mathfrak{R}(z)$, $z_i = \mathfrak{I}(z)$ returns the real and imaginary part of the complex-valued argument $z = z_r + \iota z_i$, respectively. $\iota = \sqrt{-1}$. t and l are designated to the continuous-time variable and the discrete-time index, respectively.

2. Block transmission model

The block transmission model for linear modulation schemes is shown in **Figure 1**. For details, see [18]:

- **SRC (SNK)** represents the digital source (sink). **SRC** repeatedly generates successive streams of k bits, i.e., $q_1, q_2, \cdots, q_M$.

- $q\,(\hat{q}) \in \{0,1\}^k$ is the vector of source (detected) bits of length k.

- $q_c \in \{0,1\}^n$ is the vector of encoded source bits of length $n > k$. For an *uncoded* transmission $q_c = q$ (and thus $k = n$).

- COD performs a bijective map from q to q_c where $n > k$ (adding redundancy). We consider in this chapter binary LDPC codes. Only 2^k combinations of n bits out of overall 2^n

---

[3]Except for L, $\check{L}$ and L_{ch} which are vectors.

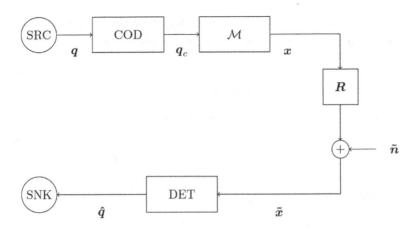

Figure 1. Block transmission model for linear modulation schemes. **SRC (SNK)** represents the digital source (sink). DET is the detector. COD performs the encoding process (adding redundancy). $\mathcal{M}$ maps encoded bits to complex-valued symbols. R is the block transmit matrix.

combinations are used. The set of the 2^k combinations represent the code book $\mathcal{C}$. $r_c = k/n$ is the code rate.

- $x \in \psi^N$ is the transmit vector of length N.

- N is the block size. Successive transmit vectors are separated by a guard time to avoid interference between different blocks. Thus, **Figure 1** describes the transmission for a single block and stays valid for the next block (possibly with a different R).

- $\psi = \{\psi_1, \psi_2, ..., \psi_{2^m}\}$, $m \in \mathbb{N}/\{0\}$ is the symbol alphabet. There exist $2^{m \cdot N}$ possible transmit vectors. The set of all possible transmit vectors is χ. The mapping from q_c to x is performed by $\mathcal{M}$. Each symbol ψ represents m bits. A special class of symbol alphabets are the so-called *separable* symbol alphabet $\psi^{(s)}$ [19, 20].

- $\tilde{x}$ is the receive vector of length N. In general $\tilde{x} \in \mathbb{C}^N$.

- We distinguish:

  - For an uncoded transmission $M \times k = m \times N$.

  - For a coded transmission and $N < n/m$: One codeword lasts over many transmit blocks.

  - For a coded transmission and $N = n/m$: One codeword lasts exactly over a single transmit block.

  - For a coded transmission and $N = M \times n/m$: M codewords are contained in a single transmit block.

- $R = \{r_{ij} : i, j \in \{1, 2, \cdots, N\}\}$ is the block transmit matrix of size $N \times N$. R is hermitian and positive semidefinite. The block transmit matrix R contains the whole knowledge about the transmission scheme (transmit and receive filters) and the physical propagation channel between transmitter(s) and receiver(s) [18].

- $\tilde{n}$ is a sample function of an additive Gaussian noise vector process of length N with zero mean and covariance matrix $\boldsymbol{\Phi}_{\tilde{n}\tilde{n}} = \frac{N_0}{2} \cdot \boldsymbol{R}$ where $\frac{N_0}{2}$ is the double-sided noise power spectral density.

- DET is the detector including equalization and decoding.

The model in **Figure 1** is a general model and fits to different transmission schemes like orthogonal frequency division multiplexing (OFDM), code division multiple access (CDMA), multicarrier CDMA (MC-CDMA) and multiple-input multiple-output (MIMO). The relation with the original continuous-time (physical) model can be found in [11, 18]. The model in **Figure 1** can be described mathematically as follows [11]:

$$\tilde{x} = R \cdot x + \tilde{n}. \tag{1}$$

By decomposing R into a diagonal part $R_d = \text{diag}_m\{R\}$ and a nondiagonal part $R_{\setminus d} = R - R_d$, Eq. (1) can be rewritten as:

$$\tilde{x} = \underbrace{R_d \cdot x}_{\text{signal}} + \underbrace{R_{\setminus d} \cdot x}_{\text{interference}} + \underbrace{\tilde{n}}_{\text{additive noise}}. \tag{2}$$

For the j-th element of the receive vector $j \in \{1, 2, \cdots, N\}$ Eq. (2) can be expressed as

$$\tilde{x}_j = r_{jj} \cdot x_j + \sum_{\substack{m=1 \\ m \neq j}}^{N} r_{jm} \cdot x_m + \tilde{n}_j. \tag{3}$$

We notice from Eqs. (2), (3) that the nondiagonal elements of R describe the interference between the elements of the transmit vector at the receiver side. For interference-free transmission $R_{\setminus d} = 0$. For an interference-free transmission over an additive white Gaussian noise (AWGN) channel $R = I$.

Figure 2 shows the channel matrix for a MIMO transmission scheme for different number of transmit/receive antennas. **Figure 3** shows the channel matrix for OFDM with/without spreading. **Figure 4** shows the channel matrix for MIMO-OFDM. In **Figures 2–4**, the darker the elements, the larger the absolute values of the entries of the corresponding matrix R, and hence larger the interference [21].

Remark 1. For a clear distinction between *channel matrix* and *block transmit matrix*, we refer to [11, 18]. Generally speaking, the block transmit matrix R is a block diagonal matrix of "many" channel matrices.

The detector DET in **Figure 1** has to deliver a vector $\hat{q}$ with a minimum bit error rate compared to q (conditional to the available computational power) given that COD, $\mathcal{M}$ and R are known at the receiver side. The optimum detection (maximum likelihood detection) for realistic cases is often infeasible. Therefore, suboptimum schemes are used, mainly based on separating the detection into an equalization EQ (to cope with interference caused by $R_{\setminus d}$) and a decoding DEC (to utilize the redundancy added by COD). In this case, we distinguish between separate

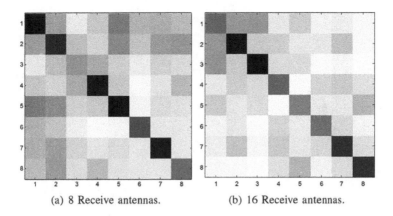

(a) 8 Receive antennas. (b) 16 Receive antennas.

Figure 2. Visualization of the channel matrix for a MIMO transmission scheme with eight transmit antennas and different receive antennas.

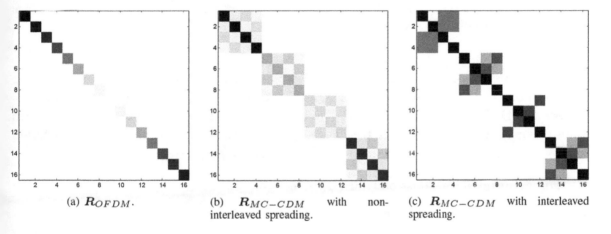

(a) R_{OFDM}. (b) R_{MC-CDM} with non-interleaved spreading. (c) R_{MC-CDM} with interleaved spreading.

Figure 3. Visualization of the channel matrix for OFDM with 16 subcarriers and spreading over four subcarriers with/without interleaving.

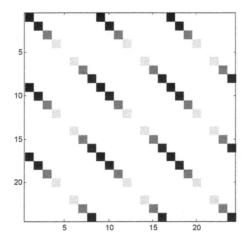

Figure 4. Visualization of the channel matrix for a MIMO-OFDM transmission scheme with eight subcarriers and three transmit antennas.

and joint equalization and decoding, cf. **Figure 5**. The superiority of the latter one is widely accepted: The separate equalization and decoding as in **Figure 5(a)** in general leads to a performance loss since the equalizer does not utilize the knowledge available at the decoder [14]. Each of the components DET, EQ and DEC can be seen as a pattern classifier. By separating the detection into equalization and decoding, an optimum detection in general cannot be achieved anymore (even if optimum equalization and optimum decoding are individually applied). Nevertheless, this is a common practice.

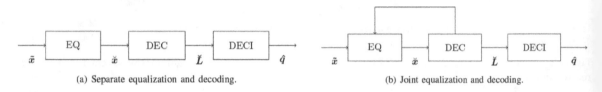

(a) Separate equalization and decoding.   (b) Joint equalization and decoding.

Figure 5. Detection: EQ is the equalizer, DEC is the decoder, DECI is a hard decision function. Notice the feedback from the decoder to the equalizer in (b), i.e., the turbo principle.

DECI in **Figure 5** is a hard decision function. For a coded transmission, DECI is a unit step function. For an uncoded transmission, COD and DEC are removed from **Figure 1** and **Figure 5**, respectively. DECI in this case is a stepwise function depending on the symbol alphabet ψ which maps the (in general complex-valued) elements of the equalized vector $\breve{x}$ to the vector of detected symbols $\hat{x} \in \psi^N$ cf. **Figure 8**. The map from $\hat{x}$ to $\hat{q}$ is then straightforward. In summary

- For an uncoded transmission DECI: $\mathbb{C}^N \to \psi^N$.

- For a coded transmission DECI: $\mathbb{R}^k \to \{0, 1\}^k$.

3. Vector equalization

For an uncoded transmission, the detection DET reduces to a vector equalization EQ as shown in **Figure 6**.

The optimum vector equalization rule (the maximum likelihood one) is based on the minimum Mahalanobis distance and is given as [21]

$$\hat{x}_{\mathrm{ML}} = \arg \min_{\xi \in \chi} \left\{ \frac{1}{2} \cdot \xi^H \cdot R \cdot \xi - \Re\{\xi^H \cdot \tilde{x}\} \right\}. \tag{4}$$

For each receive vector $\tilde{x}$, the optimum vector equalizer calculates the Mahalanobis distance Eq. (4) to *all* possible transmit vectors χ of cardinality $2^{m \cdot N}$ and decides in favor of that possible transmit vector $\hat{x}_{\mathrm{ML}}$ with the minimum Mahalanobis distance to the receive vector $\tilde{x}$, i.e., exhaustive search is required in general. This can be performed for small $2^{m \cdot N}$ which is usually

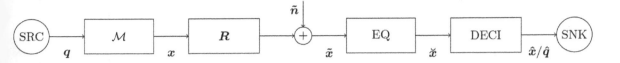

Figure 6. Uncoded block transmission model. Neither encoding at the transmitter nor decoding at the receiver. The detection reduces to a vector equalization EQ.

not the case in practice. Therefore, suboptimum equalization schemes are applied, which trade-off performance against complexity.

4. Continuous-time single-layer recurrent neural networks for vector equalization

The dynamical behavior of continuous-time single-layer recurrent neural networks of dimension N', abbreviated in the following by RNN[4], is given by the state-space equations [22]:

$$\Upsilon_e \cdot \frac{d\boldsymbol{u}(t)}{dt} = -\boldsymbol{u}(t) + \boldsymbol{W} \cdot \boldsymbol{v}(t) + \boldsymbol{W}_0 \cdot \boldsymbol{e},$$

$$\boldsymbol{v}(t) = \boldsymbol{\varphi}(\boldsymbol{u}(t)) = [\varphi_1(u_1(t)), \ \varphi_2(u_2(t)), \ \cdots, \ \varphi_{N'}(u_{N'}(t))]^T. \tag{5}$$

In Eq. (5), Υ_e is a diagonal and positive definite matrix of size $N' \times N'$. $\boldsymbol{v}(t)$ is the output, $\boldsymbol{u}(t)$ is the inner state, $\boldsymbol{e}$ is the external input. $\boldsymbol{v}, \boldsymbol{u}, \boldsymbol{e} \in \mathbb{C}^{N'}$. $\varphi_j(\cdot): j \in \{1, 2, ..., N'\}$ is the j-th activation function. $\boldsymbol{W} = \{w_{jj'}: j, j' \in \{1, 2, \cdots, N'\}\} \in \mathbb{C}^{N' \times N'}$, $\boldsymbol{W}_0 = \text{diag}_v\{[w_{10}, w_{20}, \cdots, w_{N'0}]^T\} \in \mathbb{R}^{N' \times N'}$ are the weight matrices. The real-valued RNN (all variables and functions in Eq. (5) are real-valued) is shown in **Figure 7**, which is known as "additive model" or "resistance-capacitance model" [23]. In this case, $w_{jj'} = \frac{R_j}{R_{jj'}}$ is the weight coefficient between the output of the j'-th neuron and the input of the j-th neuron, $w_{j0} = \frac{R_j}{R_{j0}}$ is the weight coefficient of the j-th external input. We also notice that the feedback $\boldsymbol{W} \cdot \boldsymbol{v}$ in Eq. (5) and **Figure 7** is a linear function of the output $\boldsymbol{v}$. Moreover, Υ_e can be given in this case as $\Upsilon_e = \text{diag}_v\{[R_1 \cdot C_1, R_2 \cdot C_2, ..., R_{N'} \cdot C_{N'}]^T\}$.

As a nonlinear dynamical system, the stability of the RNN is of primary interest [16]. This has been proven under specific conditions by Lyapunov's stability theory in [24] for real-valued RNN and in [22, 25] for complex-valued ones, among others. The RNN in Eq. (5) represents a general purpose structure. Based on N', φ, $\boldsymbol{W}$, $\boldsymbol{W}_0$ a wide range of optimization problems can be solved. First and most well-investigated applications of the RNN include the content addressable memory [24, 26], analog-to-digital converter (ADC) [27] and the traveling salesman problem [28]. In all these cases, no training is needed since the RNN is acting as a dynamical solver. This feature is desirable in many engineering fields like signal processing, communications, automatic control, etc., and has first been exploited by Hopfield in his

---

[4]The abbreviation RNN in this chapter inherently includes the continuous-time and the single-layer properties.

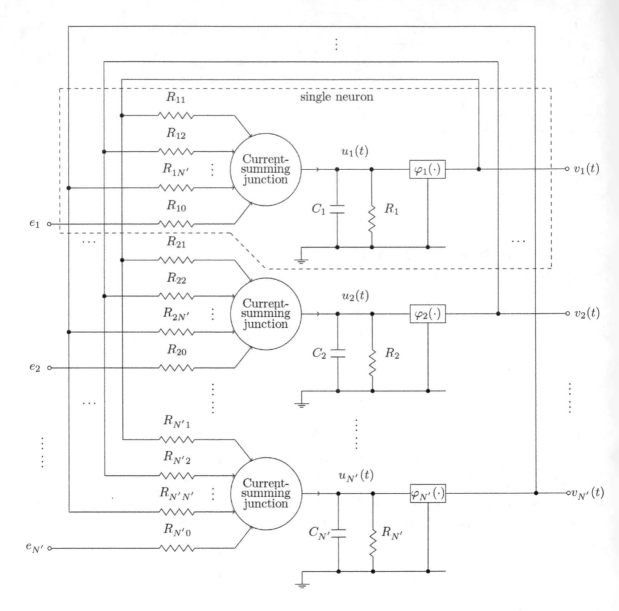

Figure 7. Continuous-time single-layer real-valued recurrent neural network. $v(t)$ is the output, $u(t)$ is the inner state, e is the external input and $\varphi(\cdot)$ is the activation function. This model is known as "additive model" or "resistance-capacitance model" [23].

pioneering work [24, 29], where information has been stored in a dynamically stable RNN. We focus in the following on the vector equalization.

Remark 2. The dimension of a real-valued RNN is the same as the number of neurons.

Remark 3. Two real-valued RNNs each of N' neurons are required to represent one complex-valued RNN (with dimension N'). This is possible by separating Eq. (5) into real and imaginary parts. However, this doubles in general the number of connections per neuron (and hence the number of multiplications) because of the required connections (represented by W_i) between the two real-valued RNNs as it can be seen from the following equation:

$$\Upsilon_e \cdot \frac{\mathrm{d}}{\mathrm{d}t} \begin{bmatrix} u_r(t) \\ u_i(t) \end{bmatrix} = -\begin{bmatrix} u_r(t) \\ u_i(t) \end{bmatrix} + \begin{bmatrix} W_r & -W_i \\ W_i & W_r \end{bmatrix} \cdot \begin{bmatrix} v_r(t) \\ v_i(t) \end{bmatrix} + \begin{bmatrix} W_0 & 0 \\ 0 & W_0 \end{bmatrix} \cdot \begin{bmatrix} e_r \\ e_i \end{bmatrix}. \tag{6}$$

Υ_e in this case is a diagonal positive definite matrix of size $2 \cdot N' \times 2 \cdot N'$ and

$$\begin{aligned} u(t) &= u_r(t) + \iota u_i(t) & , & e &= e_r + \iota e_i \\ v(t) &= v_r(t) + \iota v_i(t) & , & W &= W_r + \iota W_i. \end{aligned}$$

A. Vector equalization based on RNN

The usage of the RNN for vector equalization became known for multiuser interference cancellation in CDMA environments [30, 31]. However, this was limited to the binary phase-shift keying (BPSK) symbol alphabet $\psi = \{-1, +1\}$. This has been generalized to complex-valued symbol alphabets in [21] by combining the results of references [20, 22, 32][5]. Based thereon, it has been proven that the RNN ends in a *local* minimum of Eq. (4) if the following relations are fulfilled [21], cf. Eqs. (1), (2), (5) and **Figures 6** and **7**.

$$\begin{aligned} e &= \tilde{x} & v &= \check{x} & N' &= N \\ W_0 &= R_d^{-1} & W &= I - R_d^{-1} \cdot R & \varphi(\cdot) &= \theta^{(opt)}(\cdot) \end{aligned} \tag{7}$$

and therefore $\hat{x} = \mathrm{DECI}(v)$. **Figure 8** shows an example of an eight quadrature amplitude modulation (8 QAM) symbol alphabet and its corresponding DECI function. The relations in Eq. (7) are obtained by the comparison between the maximum likelihood function of the vector equalization and the Lyapunov function of the RNN.

The dynamical behavior of the vector equalization based on RNN can be given as, cf. Eqs. (1), (5), (7)

$$\begin{aligned} \Upsilon_e \cdot \frac{\mathrm{d}u(t)}{\mathrm{d}t} &= -u(t) + \check{x}(t) + R_d^{-1} \cdot R \cdot [x - \check{x}(t)] + R_d^{-1} \cdot \tilde{n}, \\ \check{x}(t) &= \theta^{(opt)}\left(u(t)\right) = [\theta_1^{(opt)}\left(u_1(t)\right), \theta_2^{(opt)}\left(u_2(t)\right), \cdots, \theta_N^{(opt)}\left(u_N(t)\right)]^T. \end{aligned} \tag{8}$$

The locally asymptotical stability of Eq. (8) based on Lyapunov functions has been proved in [21] (based on [22]) for separable symbol alphabets $\psi^{(s)}$. When Eq. (8) reaches an equilibrium point u_{ep}, i.e., $\frac{\mathrm{d}u(t)}{\mathrm{d}t} = 0_N \Rightarrow u = u_{ep}$, Eq. (8) can be rewritten as

$$u_{ep} = \check{x}_{ep} + R_d^{-1} \cdot R \cdot [x - \check{x}_{ep}] + R_d^{-1} \cdot \tilde{n}. \tag{9}$$

If additionally, a correct equalization is achieved, i.e., $\check{x}_{ep} = x$, the inner state is

---

[5]For *discrete-time* single-layer recurrent neural networks for vector equalization, we refer to references [19, 33].

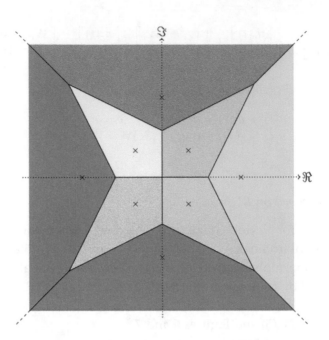

Figure 8. An example of an 8 QAM symbol alphabet and its corresponding DECI function. Each element of the symbol alphabet (marked with ×) has its own "decisions region" visualized by different colors. The function DECI delivers that element of the symbol alphabet, where the input argument lies in its corresponding decision region.

$$u_{ep} = x + \underbrace{R_d^{-1} \cdot \tilde{n}}_{n_e} . \tag{10}$$

Thus, the RNN as vector equalizer, Eq. (8) acts as "analog dynamical solver" and there is no need for a training. The covariance matrix of n_e is $\boldsymbol{\Phi}_{n_e n_e} = \frac{N_0}{2} \cdot R_d^{-1} \cdot R \cdot R_d^{-1}$. We define

$$\boldsymbol{\Sigma}_{n_e} = \mathrm{diag}_v\{[\sigma_1^2, \sigma_2^2, \cdots, \sigma_N^2]^T\} = \mathrm{diag}_m\{\boldsymbol{\Phi}_{n_e n_e}\} = \frac{N_0}{2} \cdot R_d^{-1}. \tag{11}$$

In Eq. (7), $\theta^{(opt)}(\cdot)$ is the optimum activation function and depends on the symbol alphabet ψ. For BPSK (a real-valued case)

$$\theta^{(opt)}(u) = \tanh\left(\frac{u}{\sigma^2}\right). \tag{12}$$

where σ^2 is given in Eq. (11).

Remark 4. For separable symbol alphabets, $\psi = \psi^{(s)} \Rightarrow \theta^{(opt)}(u = u_r + \iota u_i) = \theta_r^{(opt)}(u_r) + \iota \theta_i^{(opt)}(u_i)$ [19].

B. Analog hardware implementation aspects: equalization

The analog signal processing as a matter of topical importance for modern receiver architectures was recognized in [34], where an analog vector equalizer—designed in BiCMOS technology—was considered as a promising application for the analog processing of baseband signals. The equalizer accepts sampled vector symbols in analog form with an advantage that the equalizer does not require an ADC at the input interface. At very high data rates, the exclusion of an ADC softens the trade-off between chip area requirement and overall power consumption. We discuss in the following section the main features/challenges of the analog implementation of the vector equalizer based on RNN.

Structure: An RNN of dimension N' (in general $2 \cdot N'$ neurons) is capable to act as a vector equalizer as long as the block size at the transmitter side N (over all possible symbol alphabets, coding schemes and block sizes) is as maximum as N', i.e., $N \leq N'$.

Activation function: The definition of the optimum activation function $\theta^{(opt)}(\cdot)$ is not general, but depends on the symbol alphabet under consideration. Different symbol alphabets need different activation functions. However, we have proven in [20] that for square QAM symbol alphabets—the most relevant ones in practice—$\theta^{(opt)}(\cdot)$ can be approximated as a sum of a limited number of shifted and weighted hyperbolic tangent functions. Square QAM symbol alphabets are separable ones, cf. Remark 4. The analog implementation of the hyperbolic tangent well befits the large-signal transfer function of transconductance stages based on bipolar differential amplifiers [3, 34].

Adaptivity: A vector equalizer must be capable to adapt to different and time-variant interference levels. The adaptivity is regulated by the measurement of the block transmit matrix R, a task performed by a "channel estimation unit" (CEU). The weight matrices W and W_0 are then computed as in Eq. (7) and forwarded to the RNN (**Figure 9**). Thus, the weight matrices W and W_0 are *not* the outcome of any training algorithm but related directly to R, cf. Eq. (7). This represents a typical example for the mixed-signal integrated circuit, where the weight coefficients are (obtained and) stored digitally, converted into analog values, later used as weight coefficients for the analog RNN [8].

For the j-th neuron in the additive model **Figure 7**, the ratio between two resistors R_j and $R_{jj'}$ (R_j and R_{j0}) is used to configure each weight coefficient $w_{jj'}$ (w_{j0}). According to the additive

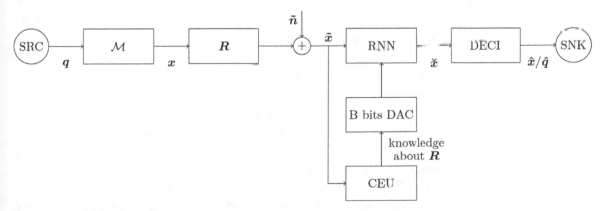

Figure 9. Uncoded block transmission model. The detection reduces to a vector equalization EQ. The channel estimation unit (CEU) estimates the block transmit matrix R.

model, $R_{jj'}$ and R_{j0} can assume both positive and negative values, and the absolute value theoretically extends from R_j to infinite (for $w_{jj'} \in [-1, +1]$). This puts serious limitations to the direct implementation of the model. In [3], we showed how this difficulty can be overcome by using a Gilbert cell as a four-quadrant analog multiplier. A Gilbert cell [35] is composed of two pairs of differential amplifiers with cross-coupled collectors, and is controlled by a differential voltage input G_{ji} applied at the base gate of the transistors. When biased with a differential tail current $I_{ji} = I_{ji}^+ - I_{ji}^-$, the differential output current $I_{ji,w} = I_{ji,w}^+ - I_{ji,w}^-$ is a fraction w of the tail current I_{ji}, as a function of the input voltage G_{ji}:

$$I_{ji,w} = I_{ji,w}^+ - I_{ji,w}^- = f_{Gc}(I_{ji} = I_{ji}^+ - I_{ji}^-, G_{ji}) = w \cdot I_{ji} \in [-I_{ji}, +I_{ji}]. \tag{13}$$

Accuracy: Locally asymptotical Lyapunov stability can be guaranteed for the RNN in Eqs. (5), (8) if, among others, the hermitian property is verified for the weight matrix W (the symmetric property in the real-valued case). Inaccuracies in the weights' representation may jeopardize the Lyapunov stability and impact the performance of the vector equalizer. The first cause of weights' inaccuracy may arise from the limited accuracy of the analog design in terms of components' parasitics, devices' mismatch, process variation, just to name a few. Those inaccuracies (if modest) are expected to slightly degrade the performance without causing a catastrophic failure, thanks to the high nonlinearity of the equalization algorithm. Moreover, it has been shown in [8, 36] that in some cases, they produce beneficial effects: These imperfections incorporate some kind of simulated annealing which enables escaping local minima by allowing occasionally "uphill steps" since the Lyapunov stable RNN is a gradient-like system. This feature is emulated in discrete-time by *stochastic* Hopfield networks [23]. Non-precision of the weights may also arise from an insufficient resolution of the digital-to-analog converter (DAC) (**Figure 9**). On the other hand, an overzealous DAC design increases the chip area, the power consumption and adds complexity to the interface between the analog vector equalizer and the digital CEU. In this case, a conservative approach suggests to use a DAC with enough resolution to match the precision used by the CEU.

Interneuron connectivity and reconfigurability: Scaling the architecture of an analog VLSI design is not straightforward. A vector equalizer based on recurrent neural networks is composed by the repetition of equal sub-systems, i.e., the neurons. Using a bottom-up approach, the first step to scale the system involves the redesign of the single neuron in order to handle more feedback inputs. In a successive step, the neurons are connected together and a system-level simulation is performed to check the functionality of the system. However, several design choices must be made during the process and it is not guaranteed that the optimum architecture for a certain number of neurons is still the best choice when the number of neurons changes. For large N, the block transmit matrix R, defining the weight matrix W, is usually sparse. If a maximum number of nonzero elements over the rows of R is assumed, the requirement for a full connectivity between the neurons in **Figure 7** can be relaxed, and only a maximum number of connections per neuron will be necessary. In this case, however, in addition to the "adaptivity", the RNN must be reconfigured according to the position of the nonzero elements in R. The hardware simplification given by the partial connectivity may be counterbalanced by the necessity of a further routing (e.g., multiplexing/demultiplexing) of the feedback. For special cases, where the block transmit matrix can be reordered around the diagonal, more independent RNNs can be simply used in parallel. In **Figures 3(b)** and **3(c)**, four independent RNNs, each of dimension four, can be used in parallel. Additionally, for specific transmission schemes such as MIMO-OFDM in **Figure 4**, the connectivity can be assumed limited (number of transmit antennas minus one) and fixed (crosstalk only between *same* subcarriers, when used simultaneously on different transmit antennas).

Example 1. In **Figure 4**, eight RNNs (number of subcarriers) each of dimension of three (number of transmit antennas) can be used in parallel. Each neuron has two feedback inputs.

C. Circuit design

We review here the main features of the analog circuit design of an RNN as vector equalizer working with the BPSK symbol alphabet and composed of four neurons. Detailed explanation can be found in reference [3]. The RNN is realized in IHP 0.25 µm SiGe BiCMOS technology (SG25H3). A simplified schematic of a neuron is shown in **Figure 10**. Schematics of gray boxes are presented in **Figure 11**.

The dynamical behavior of the circuit in **Figures 10** and **11** is described as [3]

$$
\begin{aligned}
\mathbf{\Upsilon} \cdot \frac{\mathrm{d}\mathbf{u}'(t)}{\mathrm{d}t} &= -\mathbf{u}'(t) + \mathbf{W} \cdot \mathbf{v}'(t) + \mathbf{W}_0 \cdot \mathbf{e}', \\
\frac{R \cdot I_t}{N-1} \cdot \tanh\left(\frac{\mathbf{u}'(t)}{2 \cdot V_t}\right) &= \mathbf{v}'(t), \\
\tau \cdot \mathbf{I} &= \mathbf{\Upsilon}.
\end{aligned}
\tag{14}
$$

which is equivalent to Eq. (5). $\tau = R \cdot C$ is the time constant of the circuit. R is shown in **Figure 10** and C is a fictitious capacitance between the nodes and u_j^+ and u_j^-. V_t is the thermal voltage and I_t is the tail current in **Figure 11**. The circuit is fully differential and the differential currents and voltages are denoted as, cf. **Figures 10** and **11**:

$$
\begin{aligned}
I_{ji} &= I_{ji}^+ - I_{ji}^- & I_j &= I_j^+ - I_j^- & I_o &= I_o^+ - I_o^-, \\
I_{ji,w} &= I_{ji,w}^+ - I_{ji,w}^- & u_j' &= u_j^+ - u_j^- & e_j' &= c_j^+\ e_j^-
\end{aligned}
\tag{15}
$$

(1) Performance: Simulation results based on the above described analog RNN are shown in **Figure 12**. The interference is described by the channel matrix $\mathbf{R}_{test}$.

$$
\mathbf{R}_{test} =
\begin{bmatrix}
1 & 0.24 & -0.34 & -0.57 \\
0.24 & 1 & 0.32 & 0.29 \\
-0.34 & 0.32 & 1 & 0.25 \\
-0.57 & 0.29 & 0.25 & 1
\end{bmatrix}
$$

The black dashed line shows the bit error rate (BER) for a BPSK symbol alphabet in an AWGN channel (an interference-free channel). Performance achieved by the maximum likelihood

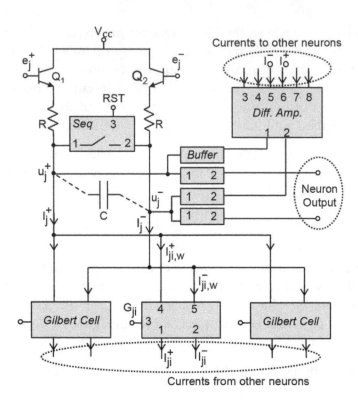

Figure 10. A simplified schematic of a single neuron as a part of a (four neurons) RNN analog vector equalizer. u'_j is the inner state, e'_j is the external input and G_{ji} is used for adapting the weight coefficient w_{ji} from the output of the i-th neuron to the input of the j-th neuron. The circuit is fully differential [3].

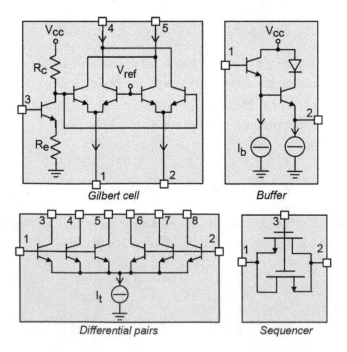

Figure 11. Details of the circuit building blocks. Gilbert cell used as a four-quadrant analog multiplier, buffer stages, BJT differential pairs for the generation of the hyperbolic tangent function and a metal-oxide-semiconductor field-effect transistor (MOSFET) switch used as a sequencer [3].

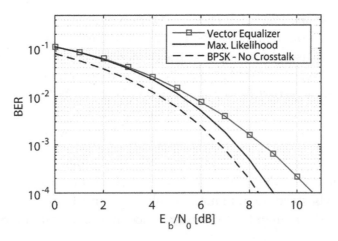

Figure 12. BER vs. E_b/N_0 for the analog RNN vector equalizer. Evolution time equals $10 \cdot \tau$. BPSK symbol alphabet and channel matrix $\mathbf{R}_{test}$.

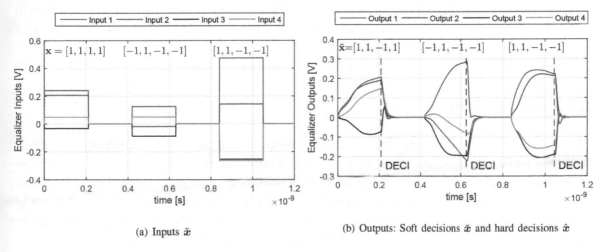

(a) Inputs $\tilde{x}$

(b) Outputs: Soft decisions $\hat{x}$ and hard decisions $\check{x}$

Figure 13. An example of a transient simulation for the analog RNN vector equalizer. (a) Inputs $\tilde{x}$ (b) Outputs: soft decisions $\hat{x}$ and hard decisions $\check{x}$.

algorithm in Eq. (4) is included as a solid black line. The performance of the analog RNN vector equalizer[6] is presented in a solid red line with square markers. Compared to the optimum algorithm, the signal-to-noise ratio (SNR) loss for the analog RNN vector equalizer can be quantified in approximately 1.7 dB at a BER of 10^{-4}. This loss in SNR emphasizes the suboptimality of the RNN as vector equalizer and depends on the channel matrix. **Figure 13** shows an example of a transient simulation for the analog RNN vector equalizer. The time constant is approximately $\tau = 40$ ps. The SNR ratio is set to 2 dB and a series of three receive vectors are equalized in sequence. Because of the channel matrix and noise, the sampled vectors at the input of the equalizer $\tilde{x}$ present different signs and values, compared to the sent

---

[6]Analog RNN vector equalizer refers to the described analog hardware-implemented RNN for vector equalization.

vectors x (shown in square brackets). The equalization of each receive vector lasts $10 \cdot \tau$. First half of this interval (evolution time) is used to reach a stable state, while the second half of the interval (reset time) is used to return to a predefined inner state (all-zero state) before the equalization of a new vector starts. At the end of the evolution time, a decision is made based on the sign of the output vector (the decision function DECI for BPSK is a sign function). In our example, a comparison between the sent and the recovered bits shows an error of one bit out of twelve, equivalent to a BER$\approx\frac{1}{12}$, a result in line with the BER shown in **Figure 12**.

Remark 5. The evolution and reset times are the two limiting factors for the maximum throughput of the analog RNN vector equalizer. However, they cannot be unlimitedly minimized since the RNN needs a minimum evolution time to reach an equilibrium point representing a local minimum of the Lyapunov function, i.e., a local minimum of Eq. (4).

(2) Energy efficiency: The energy efficiency of a hardware "architecture" is the ratio between the power requirement (Watt) of the architecture and its achievement in a given time period. In our case, the throughput of the equalizer represents the achievement. Combining the value of τ and the power consumption, the abovementioned analog vector equalizer is expected to win the competition versus common digital signal processing, thanks to three to four orders of magnitude better energy efficiency [3].

5. Channel coding

Channel coding (including encoding at the transmitter side COD and decoding at the receiver side DEC) aims to enable an error-free transmission over noisy channels with maximum possible transmit rate. This is done by adding redundancy (extra bits) at the transmitter side, i.e., the bijective map from q to q_c (**Figure 14,**) such that the codewords q_c are sufficiently distinguishable at the receiver side even if the noisy channel corrupts some bits during the transmission. **Figure 14** shows a coded transmission over an AWGN channel.

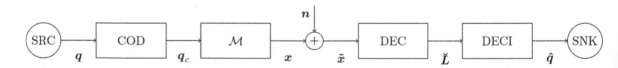

Figure 14. Coded transmission over an BER channel.

For every received codeword, the optimum decoding (the maximum likelihood one) needs to calculate the distance between the received codeword and all possible codewords $\mathcal{C}$, which makes it infeasible for realistic cases (except for convolutional codes which are not considered here). We focus on binary LDPC codes and their corresponding suboptimum decoding algorithm: the *belief propagation* with BPSK symbol alphabet. LDPC codes [37] belong to the class of binary linear block codes and have been shown to achieve an error rate very close to the Shannon limit (a performance lower bound) for the AWGN channel and have been implemented in many practical systems such as the satellite digital video broadcast (DVB-S2)

[38]. A binary linear block code is characterized by a binary parity check matrix H of size $(n-k) \times n$ for $n > k$.

6. Continuous-time single-layer high-order recurrent neural networks for belief propagation

One of the largest drawbacks of RNNs is their quadratic Lyapunov function [39]. Optimization problems associated with cost functions of higher degree cannot be solved "satisfactorily" by RNNs. Increasing the order of the Lyapunov function leads to a nonlinear feedback in the network. In doing so, we obtain the single-layer high-order recurrent neural network, named differently in literature, depending on the nonlinear feedback [39–42].

Remark 6. High-order recurrent neural networks are in the literature exclusively real-valued.

Figure 15 shows the continuous-time single-layer high-order recurrent neural network, abbreviated in the following by HORNN[7].

The dynamical behavior is given by

$$
\begin{aligned}
\Upsilon_d \cdot \frac{\mathrm{d}\check{u}(t)}{\mathrm{d}t} &= -\check{u}(t) + \check{W} \cdot \check{f}\left(\check{v}(t)\right) + \check{W}_0 \cdot \check{e}, \\
\check{v}(t) &= \check{\varphi}\left(\check{u}(t)\right) = \left[\check{\varphi}_1\left(\check{u}_1(t)\right), \check{\varphi}_2\left(\check{u}_2(t)\right), \cdots, \check{\varphi}_{\check{n}}\left(\check{u}_{\check{n}}(t)\right)\right]^T, \\
\Upsilon_d &= \mathrm{diag}_v\left\{\left[\check{R}_1 \cdot \check{C}_1, \check{R}_2 \cdot \check{C}_2, \ldots, \check{R}_{\check{n}} \cdot \check{C}_{\check{n}}\right]^T\right\}.
\end{aligned}
\tag{16}
$$

The parameters in Eq. (16) can be linked to **Figure 15** in the same way as Eq. (5) linked to **Figure 7**. $\check{f}(\check{v})$ is a real-valued continuously differentiable vector function. In addition, $\check{f}(\mathbf{0}_{\check{n}}) = \mathbf{0}_{\check{n}}$. It is worth mentioning that the term "high-order" in this case refers to the interconnections between the neurons rather than the degree of the differential equation describing the dynamics. As for RNNs, this is still of first order, cf. Eq. (16).

Remark 7. In the special case $\check{f}(\check{v}) = \check{v}$, the HORNN reduces to the (real-valued) RNN.

In order to apply HORNNs to solve optimization tasks, their stability has to be investigated. A property without which the behavior of dynamical systems is often suspected [39]. This was the topic of many publications [39–42]. A common denominator of the locally asymptotical stability proof of the HORNN based on Lyapunov functions is

- $\check{\varphi}(\cdot)$ is continuously differentiable and a strictly increasing function.

- The right side of the first line of Eq. (16) can be rewritten as a gradient of a scalar function.

---

[7]The abbreviation HORNN in this chapter inherently includes the continuous-time, single-layer and real-valued properties.

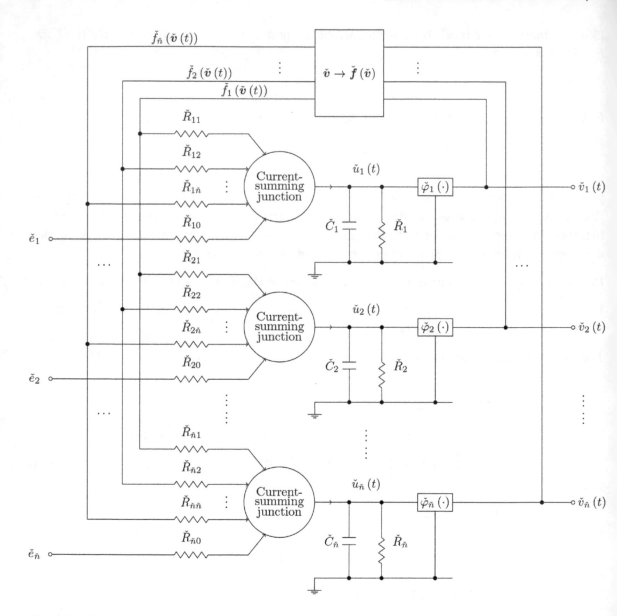

Figure 15. Continuous-time single-layer real-valued high-order recurrent neural network. $\check{v}(t)$ is the output, $\check{u}(t)$ is the inner state, $\check{e}$ is the external input and $\check{\varphi}(\cdot)$ is the activation function. $\check{f}(\check{v})$ is a real-valued continuously differentiable vector function with $\check{f}(\mathbf{0}_{\check{n}}) = \mathbf{0}_{\check{n}}$ [21].

A. Belief propagation based on HORNN

Originally proposed by Gallager [37], belief propagation is a suboptimum graph-based decoding algorithm for LDPC codes. The corresponding graph is bipartite (n parity nodes and $n - k$ check nodes) and known as Tanner graph [43]. This is shown in **Figure 16** for the Hamming code with the parity check matrix H_{Hamming} Eq. (17) where $n = 7$, $k = 4$. The belief propagation algorithm iteratively exchanges "messages" between parity and check nodes.

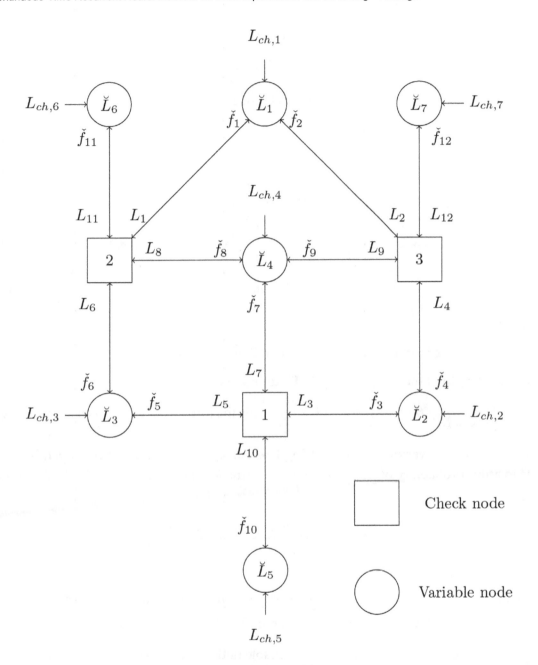

Figure 16. Tanner graph of the systematic Hamming code $n = 7$ and $k = 4$.

$$H_{\text{Hamming}} = \begin{bmatrix} 0 & 1 & 1 & 1 & 1 & 0 & 0 \\ 1 & 0 & 1 & 1 & 0 & 1 & 0 \\ 1 & 1 & 0 & 1 & 0 & 0 & 1 \end{bmatrix} \tag{17}$$

For every binary linear block code characterized by the binary parity check matrix H of size ($n - k$) × n for $n > k$, three *binary* matrices $P_{n_h \times n_h}$, $S_{n_h \times n_h}$ and $B_{n_h \times n}$ can be uniquely defined [44, 45] such that Eq. (16) and **Figure 15** perform continuous-time belief propagation if the following relations are fulfilled:

$$\check{u} = L, \tag{18a}$$

$$\check{e} = B \cdot L_{ch}, \tag{18b}$$

$$\check{\varphi}(\cdot) = \tanh\left(\frac{\cdot}{2}\right), \tag{18c}$$

$$\check{v} = \check{\varphi}(L), \tag{18d}$$

$$\check{W} = P, \tag{18e}$$

$$\check{W}_0 = I_{n_h \times n_h}, \tag{18f}$$

$$\check{f}_j = 2 \cdot \operatorname{atanh}\left\{ \prod_{j' \in \operatorname{pos}[S(j,:)=1]} \check{v}_{j'} \right\} \quad \text{for } j, j' \in \{1, 2, \dots, n_h\}, \tag{18g}$$

$$\check{n} = n_h. \tag{18h}$$

In Eq. (18)[8],

- k is the length of the information word (q in **Figures 1** and **14**).

- n is the length of the codeword (q_c in **Figures 1** and **14**).

- $n_h = \mathbf{1}^T_{\left(1 \times (n-k)\right)} \cdot H \cdot \mathbf{1}_{(n \times 1)} \in [k+1, n \cdot (n-k)]$ is the number of nonzero elements in H.

- $L_{ch,(n \times 1)}$ is the vector of intrinsic log-likelihood ratio (LLR), which depends on the transition probability of the channel. For $q_{c,j}$ (the j-th element of q_c for $j \in \{1, 2, \cdots, n\}$) it is given as

$$L_{ch,j} = \ln \frac{p(\dot{x}_j = \tilde{x}_j | q_{c,j} = 0)}{p(\dot{x}_j = \tilde{x}_j | q_{c,j} = 1)}. \tag{19}$$

In the last relation, $\dot{x}_j$ is the variable of the conditioned probability density function $p(\dot{x}_j | q_{c,j})$. $\ln(\cdot)$ is the natural logarithm. For an AWGN channel, $\mathcal{N}(0, \sigma_n^2) : L_{ch,j} = \frac{\tilde{x}_j}{2 \cdot \sigma_n^2}$.

- $L_{(n_h \times 1)}$ is the "message" sent from the variable nodes to the check nodes.

- $\check{f}_{(n_h \times 1)}$ is the "message" sent from check nodes to variable nodes.

- $I_{(n_h \times n_h)}$ is an identity matrix of size $n_h \times n_h$.

- $\operatorname{pos}[S(j, :) = 1]$ delivers the positions of the nonzero elements in the j-th row of the matrix S.

---

[8] L, $\check{L}$ and L_{ch} are vectors.

The dynamical behavior of belief propagation can be described based on Eqs. (16), (18) and **Figures 14, 15,** and **16** [45]

$$\Upsilon_d \cdot \frac{\mathrm{d}\boldsymbol{L}(t)}{\mathrm{d}t} = -\boldsymbol{L}(t) + \boldsymbol{P} \cdot \check{\boldsymbol{f}}\Big(\check{v}(t)\Big) + \boldsymbol{B} \cdot \boldsymbol{L}_{ch},$$
$$\check{v}(t) = \tanh\left(\frac{\boldsymbol{L}(t)}{2}\right), \qquad (20)$$
$$\check{\boldsymbol{L}}(t) = \boldsymbol{B}^T \cdot \check{\boldsymbol{f}}\Big(\check{v}(t)\Big) + \boldsymbol{L}_{ch}.$$

$\check{\boldsymbol{L}}(t)$ is the soft-output of the decoding algorithm, cf. **Figures 5** and **14**. The discrete-time description is given as [44]

$$\boldsymbol{L}[l+1] = \boldsymbol{P} \cdot \check{\boldsymbol{f}}(\check{v}[l]) + \boldsymbol{B} \cdot \boldsymbol{L}_{ch},$$
$$\check{v}[l] = \tanh\left(\frac{\boldsymbol{L}[l]}{2}\right), \qquad (21)$$
$$\check{\boldsymbol{L}}[l] = \boldsymbol{B}^T \cdot \check{\boldsymbol{f}}(\check{v}[l]) + \boldsymbol{L}_{ch}.$$

B. Dynamical behavior of belief propagation

In a series of papers, Hemati *et. al.* [12, 17, 46–49] also modeled the dynamics of analog belief propagation as a set of first-order nonlinear differential equations Eq. (20). This was motivated from a circuit design aspect, where Υ_d (the same is valid for Υ_e) can be seen as a bandwidth limitation of the analog circuit, realized taking advantage of the low-pass filter behavior of transmission lines **Figure 17**. We have shown in [45] that the model in **Figure 17** also has important dynamical properties when compared with the discrete-time belief propagation Eq. (21) [44]. Particularly, the equilibrium points of the continuous-time belief propagation of Eq. (20) coincide with the fixed points of the discrete-time belief propagation of Eq. (21). This has been proved in [45]. In both cases

$$\boldsymbol{L}_{ep} = \boldsymbol{P} \cdot \check{\boldsymbol{f}}\left(\tanh\left(\frac{\boldsymbol{L}_{ep}}{2}\right)\right) + \boldsymbol{B} \cdot \boldsymbol{L}_{ch}. \qquad (22)$$

The absolute stability of belief propagation Eqs. (20), (21) was proven for repetition codes (one of the simplest binary linear block codes) in [44, 45]. In this case

$$\check{\boldsymbol{L}}_{ep} = \boldsymbol{1}_{(n \times n)} \cdot \boldsymbol{L}_{ch}. \qquad (23)$$

Far away from repetition codes, it has been noticed that iterative decoding algorithms (belief propagation is one of them) exhibit depending on the SNR a wide range of phenomena associated with nonlinear dynamical systems such as existence of multiple fixed points, oscillatory behavior, bifurcation, chaos and transit chaos [50]. Equilibrium points are reached at "relatively" high SNR. The analysis in reference [50] is limited to the discrete-time case.

Remark 8. The HORNN in **Figure 15**, Eqs. (18), (20) for belief propagation acts as a computational model.

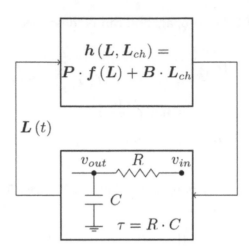

Figure 17. A simple model for analog decoding as presented in [46].

C. Analog hardware implementation aspects: decoding

Many analog hardware implementation aspects have been already mentioned in Section 4-B. We mention here only additional aspects exclusively related to the analog belief propagation based on HORNN.

Structure: In practice, different coding schemes (different parity check matrices H) with various (k, n) constellations are applied to modify the code rate $r_c = k/n$ depending on the channel state. The HORNN in **Figure 15** is capable to act as a continuous-time belief propagation (decoder) as long as the number of neurons $\check{n}$ in **Figure 15** equals (or is larger than) the maximum number of nonzero elements over all parity check matrices and all (k,n) constellations, i.e., $\check{n} \geq \max_H n_h$.

Adaptivity: No training is needed. $\check{W}_0$ and $\check{W}$ are directly related to the parity check matrix H. In contrast to the analog RNN vector equalizer, the weight coefficients are binary, i.e., the weight matrices $\check{W}_0$ and $\check{W}$ define a feedback to be either existent or not. In such a case for **Figure 15**, $\check{R}_{jj'}$, $\check{R}_{j0} \in \{\check{R}_j, \infty\}$. Moreover, there is no need for high-resolution DAC for the weight coefficients.

Interneuron connectivity: No full connection is needed since the matrix P for LDPC codes is sparse. The number of connections per neuron must equal the maximum number of nonzero elements in P row-wise over all considered coding schemes and equals $\max_H P \cdot 1_{(n_h \times 1)}$. If this is fulfilled and if interneuron connectivity control is available, the structure in **Figure 15** becomes valid for all considered coding scheme.

Vector function connectivity: For different coding schemes, the number of the arguments $\check{v}'_j$ to evaluate the function $\check{f}_j$ changes, cf. Eq. (18g). The maximum number of the arguments depends on the number of the nonzero elements in S row-wise and equals $\max_H S \cdot 1_{(n_h \times 1)}$. Thus, implementing the function $\check{f}_j$ according to this maximum number enables evaluating the function $\check{f}_j$ for all considered coding schemes.

Remark 9. For a specific coding scheme, the interneuron connectivity can be made fixed. The resulted HORNN structure in this case is valid also for all codeword lengths resulted after performing a puncturing of the original code.

Remark 10. Both, the interneuron connectivity and the weight adaptation play a significant role, in the equalization as well as in the decoding. It can safely be said that they represent the major challenge of the circuit, since the analog circuit must be capable to perform equalization and decoding for a given number of possible combinations of block size, symbol alphabet, coding scheme, etc. Particularly for the decoding, the advantage of having a non-full connectivity is counterbalanced by a double (and very complex) (de)multiplexing of the signals (once for the vector function $\check{f}$ and once for the interneuron connectivity).

7. Joint equalization and decoding

Turbo equalization is a joint iterative equalization and decoding scheme. In this case, a symbol-by-symbol maximum aposteriori probability (s/s MAP) equalizer exchanges in an iterative way reliability values L with a (s/s MAP) decoder [51, 52]. This concept is inspired from the decoding concept of turbo codes, where two (s/s MAP) decoders exchange iteratively reliability values [53]. Despite its good performance, the main drawback of the turbo equalizer is the very high complexity of the s/s MAP-equalizer for multipath channels with long impulse response (compared with symbol duration) and/or symbol alphabets with large cardinality. Therefore, a suboptimum equalization (and a suboptimum decoding) usually replace the s/s-MAP ones (**Figure 18**).

One discrete-time joint equalization and decoding approach has been introduced in [52] and is shown in **Figure 19**. $\tilde{x}$, R_d and R are as in Eq. (2) and z^{-1} is a delay unit. We notice that there are two different (iteration) loops in **Figure 19**: the equalization loop (the blue one) on symbol basis (in the sense of ψ) and the decoding loop (the dashed one) on bit basis. $a = \{1, 2, 3, \cdots\}$, $\rho \in \mathbb{N}$, i.e., after each ρ equalization loops, one decoding loop is performed. The conversion between symbol basis and bit basis (u to L_{ch}) is performed by $\theta_{S/L}(\cdot)$, the way around ($\check{L}$ to $\check{x}$) by $\theta_{L/S}(\cdot)$. The expressions for $\theta_{L/S}(\cdot)$ and $\theta_{L/S}(\cdot)$ can be found in [52]. However, for BPSK, they are given as

$$\theta_{S/L}(u) = \frac{2}{\sigma^2} \cdot u,$$
$$\theta_{L/S}(\check{L}) = \tanh\left(\frac{\check{L}}{2}\right). \tag{24}$$

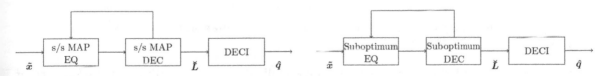

Figure 18. Two examples for joint equalization and decoding. Notice the feedback from the decoder to the equalizer, i.e., turbo principle.

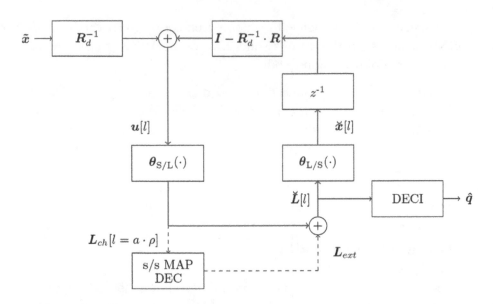

Figure 19. Joint equalization and decoding as described in [52]. L_{ext} represents the "knowledge" obtained by exploiting the redundancy of the code.

σ^2 is given in Eq. (11). If we consider *only* the equalization loop in **Figure 19**, we notice that it describes exactly the dynamical behavior of discrete-time recurrent neural networks [19, 25, 33, 54–56]

$$
\begin{aligned}
u[l+1] &= [I - R_d^{-1} \cdot R] \cdot \check{x}[l] + R_d^{-1} \cdot \tilde{x}, \\
\check{x}[l] &= \theta_{L/S}(\theta_{S/L}(u[l])).
\end{aligned}
\tag{25}
$$

Remark 11. If $\theta_{L/S}\big(\theta_{S/L}(u)\big) = \theta^{(opt)}(u)$, Eqs. (8), (25) share the same equilibrium/fixed points. For BPSK, it can be easily shown based on Eqs. (12), (24) that this is fulfilled.

8. Continuous-time joint equalization and decoding

Motivated by the expected improvement of the energy efficiency by analog implementation compared with the conventional digital one, we map in this section the joint equalization and decoding structure given in **Figure 19** to a continuous-time framework. s/s MAP DEC in **Figure 19** is replaced by a suboptimum decoding algorithm: the *belief propagation*. Moreover, equalization and decoding loops in **Figure 19** are replaced by RNN and HORNN as discussed previously in Sections 4-A and 6-A, respectively. The introduced structure serves as a computational model for an analog hardware implementation and does not need any training.

Figure 20 shows a novel continuous-time joint equalization and decoding based on recurrent neural network structures. The dynamical behavior of the whole system is described by the following differential equations:

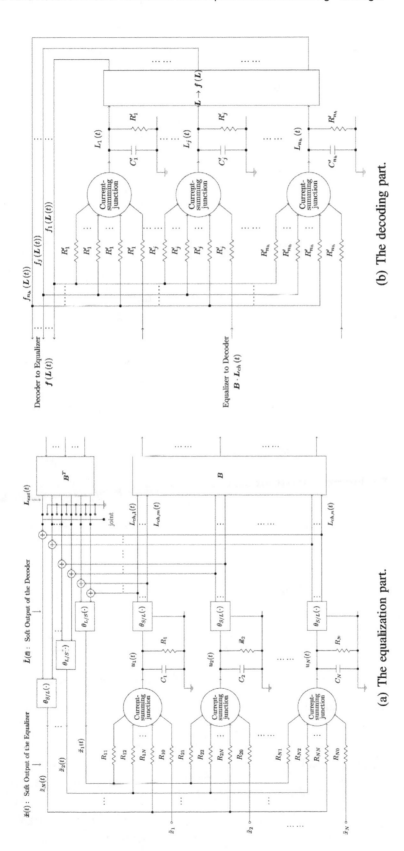

(b) The decoding part.

(a) The equalization part.

Figure 20. Continuous-time *joint* equalization and decoding based on a recurrent neural network structure for real-valued symbol alphabet (for complex-valued ones, cf. Remark 3). $\check{L}(t)$, $\check{x}(t)$ are the soft output of the decoder and the equalizer, respectively. (a) The equalization part. (b) The decoding part.

$$\Upsilon_e \cdot \frac{\mathrm{d}u(t)}{\mathrm{d}t} = -u(t) + W \cdot \check{x}(t) + W_0 \cdot \tilde{x}, \tag{26a}$$

$$L_{ch}(t) = \theta_{S/L}\Big(u(t)\Big), \tag{26b}$$

$$\Upsilon_d \cdot \frac{\mathrm{d}L(t)}{\mathrm{d}t} = -L(t) + P \cdot f\Big(L(t)\Big) + B \cdot L_{ch}(t), \tag{26c}$$

$$\check{L}(t) = \underbrace{B^T \cdot f\Big(L(t)\Big)}_{L_{ext}(t)} + L_{ch}(t), \tag{26d}$$

$$\check{x}(t) = \theta_{L/S}\Big(\check{L}(t)\Big), \tag{26e}$$

$$f_j = 2 \cdot \mathrm{atanh}\left\{ \prod_{j' \in \mathrm{pos}[S(j,\,:)=1]} \tanh\left(\frac{L_{j'}}{2}\right) \right\}. \tag{26f}$$

- Eq. (26a) and **Figure 20(a)** describe the continuous-time vector equalization, cf. Eqs. (1), (5), (7), (8).

- Eq. (26c) and **Figure 20(b)** describe the continuous-time belief propagation, cf. Eqs. (16), (18), (20).

Comparing **Figure 20** with **Figures 7** and **15**, we notice that

- The function $\varphi(\cdot)$ in **Figure 7** (the optimum activation function $\theta^{(opt)}(\cdot)$) has been split into two functions $\theta_{S/L}(\cdot)$ and $\theta_{L/S}(\cdot)$ in **Figure 20(a)**. For BPSK symbol alphabet and based on Eqs. (12), (24), it can be easily shown that $\theta^{(opt)}(u) = \theta_{L/S}\Big(\theta_{S/L}(u)\Big)$, cf. Remark 11.

- The functions $\check{\varphi}(\cdot)$ and $\check{f}(\cdot)$ in **Figure 15**, Eq. (18) have been merged to one function $f(\cdot)$ in **Figure 20(b)**, Eq. (26f) $f(L) = \check{f}\Big(\check{\varphi}(L)\Big)$. $\check{L}(t)$ and $\check{x}(t)$ are the soft output of the decoder and the equalizer, respectively.

A. Special cases

The novel structure in **Figure 20** is general and stays valid for the following cases:

- **Separate equalization and decoding**: In this case, **Figure 20(a)** is modified such that no feedback from decoder to equalizer is applied. This is shown in **Figure 21(a)**. *Only* at the end of the separate equalization and decoding process, the output is given as $\check{L} = L_{ext} + L_{ch}$. We distinguish between two cases

    1. Equalization and decoding take place separately *at the same time*.

    2. Successive equalization and decoding: *only* after the end of the equalization process, L_{ch} are forwarded to the decoder and the decoder starts the evolution. We focus on this case.

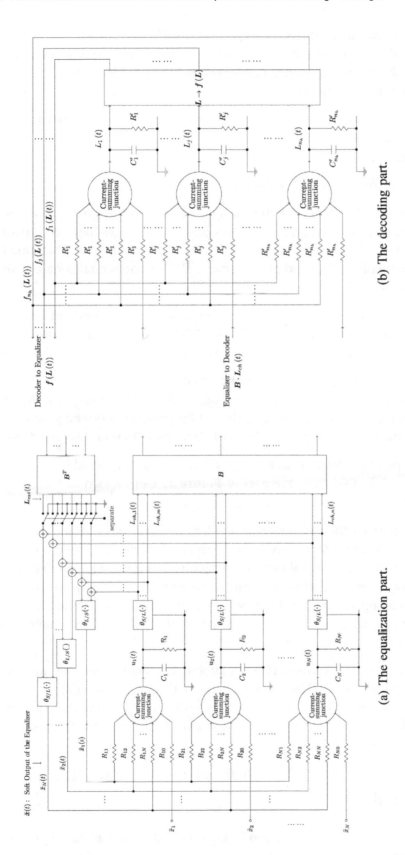

(a) The equalization part.

(b) The decoding part.

Figure 21. Continuous-time *separate* equalization and decoding based on a recurrent neural network structure for real-valued symbol alphabet (for complex-valued ones, cf. Remark 3). $\check{x}(t)$ is the soft output of the equalizer.

- **Coded transmission over an AWGN channel**: In this case, $R = I$ and hence based on Eq. (7) $W = 0$, $W_0 = I$. Under these conditions, Eq. (26a) becomes linear and can easily be solved $u(t) \to \tilde{x}$ and $L_{ch}(t)$ in Eq. (26b) becomes time independent L_{ch}. In this case, Eq. (26c) reduces to Eqs. (16), (18).

- **Uncoded transmission over an "interference-causing" channel**: In this case, $P = 0$, $B = 0$ and Eq. (26c) becomes $L = 0_{n_h}$. Under these conditions, Eq. (26a) reduces to Eqs. (5), (7), (8) (notice, however, Remark 11).

B. Throughput, asynchronicity and scheduling

The diagonal elements in Υ_d define the duration of the transient response the HORNN needs in order to converge eventually (in case of convergence). The larger they are, the longer is the transient response and consequently the less is the decoding throughput. The same is valid for Υ_e. The diagonal elements of Υ_e based on our analog RNN vector equalizer are in the range of a few tens of picoseconds.

Unequal diagonal elements in Υ_e (and Υ_d) represent some kind of continuous-time asynchronicity [46]. Asynchronicity in discrete-time RNNs is desirable since it provides the ability to avoid limit cycles, which can probably occur in synchronous discrete-time RNNs [54, 57].

Assuming $\Upsilon_d = \tau_d \cdot I$ and $\Upsilon_e = \tau_e \cdot I$, we notice that the ratio τ_e/τ_d is comparable to the scheduling problem in the discrete-time joint equalization and decoding case. More precisely, how many iterations ρ within the equalizer should be performed before a decoding process takes place, cf. **Figure 19**. This is optimized usually by simulations and is case dependent.

From a dynamical point of view, the case $\tau_e/\tau_d \ll 1$ (or $\tau_d/\tau_e \ll 1$) could be seen as a singular perturbation (in time). In this case, one part of **Figure 20** can be seen as "frozen" compared with the other part.

Remark 12. We notice that the parameters of the transmission model (block transmit matrix, symbol alphabet, block size, channel coding scheme) are utilized to define the parameters of the continuous-time recurrent neural network structure in **Figure 20** such that no training is needed. This represents in practice a big advantage especially for analog hardware. However, to enable different coding schemes and symbol alphabets, either a full connectivity or a vector and interneuron connectivity controls are needed. Both structures are challenging from a hardware implementation point of view.

Remark 13. For the ease of depiction, **Figures 20** and **21** assume that one transmitted block contains exactly one codeword. This is not necessarily the case in practice. As an example, if one transmitted block contains two codewords, one RNN and two parallel HORNNs will be needed. On the other hand, if one codeword lasts over two transmitted blocks, two parallel RNNs and one HORNN is needed.

9. Simulation results

We simulate the dynamical system as given in Eq. (26) and **Figure 20** based on the first Euler method [58]. We assume:

- BPSK modulation scheme (symbol alphabet $\psi = \{-1, +1\}$).

- Each transmitted block contains one codeword, cf. Remark 13.

- $\Upsilon_d = \Upsilon_e = \tau \cdot I$.

- Channel coding scheme: An LDPC code with $k = 204$, code rate 0.5 ($n = 408$) and column weight 3 taken from [59].

- Multipath channels [60]:

  –Proakis-a abbreviated in the following by its channel impulse response h_a leading to a small interference.

  –Proakis-b abbreviated in the following by its channel impulse response h_b leading to a moderate interference.

The impulse response of h_a and h_b are

$$h_a = [0.04 \quad -0.05 \quad 0.07 \quad -0.21 \quad -0.5 \quad 0.72 \quad 0.36 \quad 0 \quad 0.21 \quad 0.03 \quad 0.07],$$
$$h_b = [\quad 0.407 \quad 0.815 \quad 0.407 \quad].$$

The block transmission matrix R is a banded Toeplitz matrix of the autocorrelation function of the channel impulse response [61]. The following cases are considered:

- Uncoded transmission over AWGN channel. The bit error rate can be obtained analytically and is given as $\frac{1}{2} \cdot \mathrm{erfc}\left\{\frac{E_b}{N_0}\right\}$ [62]. $\mathrm{erfc}(\cdot)$ is the complementary error function and E_b is the energy per bit.

- Coded transmission over AWGN channel and continuous-time decoding at the receiver (HORNN-belief propagation).

- Uncoded transmission over (the abovementioned) multipath channels and continuous-time equalization at the receiver (RNN-equalization).

- Coded transmission over (the abovementioned) multipath channels. We distinguish between joint equalization and decoding (**Figure 20**) and separate equalization and decoding (**Figure 21**). In the latter case, equalization is performed firstly, and consequently the decoding.

The evolution time for the whole system in all cases is $20 \cdot \tau$, i.e., all simulated scenarios deliver the same throughput. For separate equalization and decoding, the evolution time of the equalization equals the evolution time of the decoding and equals $10 \ \tau$. The simulation results are shown in **Figure 22**. We notice the following:

- Joint equalization and decoding outperforms the separate one, which is a fact we know from the discrete-time case. Our proposed model in **Figure 20** is capable of "transforming" this advantage to the continuous-time case.

- For the channel h_a, the BER (for continuous-time joint equalization and decoding) is close to the coded BER curve.

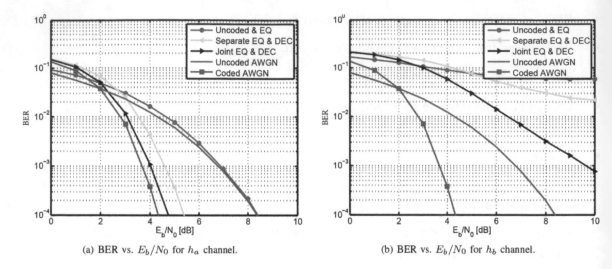

(a) BER vs. E_b/N_0 for h_a channel.   (b) BER vs. E_b/N_0 for h_b channel.

Figure 22. BER vs. E_b/N_0 for evolution time equals $20 \cdot \tau$. Continuous-time (joint) equalization and decoding. BPSK symbol alphabet.

- For the channel h_b, there exists a gap between the obtained results and the coded AWGN curve. This was expected, since h_b represents a more severe multipath channel compared with h_a.

- If only equalization performance is considered, we compare between "Uncoded & EQ" curves and "Uncoded BER" curves. In **Figure 22(a)**, the vector equalizer based on continuous-time recurrent neural networks is capable to remove already all interferences caused by the multipath channel h_a, whereas in **Figure 22(b)**, the "Uncoded & EQ" curve approaches an error floor.

Remark 14. Interleaving and antigray mapping often encountered in the context of iterative equalization and decoding can be easily integrated in the proposed model in **Figure 20**. Antigray mapping will influence the functions $\theta_{S/L}(\cdot)$ and $\theta_{L/S}(\cdot)$, whereas interleaving affects the matrix B.

10. Conclusion

Joint equalization and decoding is a detection technique which possesses the potential for improving the bit error rates of the transmission at the cost of additional computational complexity at the receiver. Joint equalization and decoding is being considered only for the discrete-time case. However, for high data rates, the energy consumption of a digital implementation becomes a limiting factor and shortens the lifetime of the battery. Improving the energy efficiency revives the analog implementation option for joint equalization and decoding algorithms, particularly taking advantage of the nonlinearity of the corresponding algorithms.

Continuous-time recurrent neural networks serve as promising computational models for analog hardware implementation and stand out due to their Lyapunov stability (the proved existence of attracting equilibrium points under specific conditions) and special suitability for analog VLSI. They have often been applied for solving optimization problems even without the need for a training. The drop of the training is particularly favorable for analog hardware implementation.

In this chapter, we introduced a novel continuous-time recurrent neural network structure, which is capable to perform continuous-time joint equalization and decoding. This structure is based on continuous-time recurrent neural networks for equalization and continuous-time high-order recurrent neural networks for belief propagation, a well-known decoding algorithm for low-density parity-check codes. In both cases, the behavior of the underlying dynamical system has been addressed, Lyapunov stability and simulated annealing are a few examples. The parameters of the transmission system (channel matrix, symbol alphabet, block size, channel coding scheme) are used to define the parameters of the proposed recurrent neural network such that *no training* is needed.

Simulation results showed that the superiority of joint equalization and decoding preserves, if this is done in analog according to our proposed model. Compared with the digital implementation, the analog one is expected to improve the energy efficiency and consume less chip area. We confirmed this for the analog hardware implementation of the equalization part. In this case, the analog vector equalization achieves an energy efficiency of a few picojoule per equalized bit, which is three to four orders of magnitude better than the digital counterparts. Additionally, analog hardware implementation aspects have been discussed. We showed as an example the importance of the interneuron connectivity, especially pointing out the challenges represented either by the hardware implementation of a massively distributed network, or by the routing of the signals using (de)multiplexers.

Author details

Mohamad Mostafa[1]*, Giuseppe Oliveri[2], Werner G. Teich[3] and Jürgen Lindner[3]

*Address all correspondence to: Mohamad.Mostafa@DLR.de

1 German Aerospace Center (DLR), Institute of Communications and Navigation, Wessling, Germany

2 Ulm University, Institute of Electron Devices and Circuits, Ulm, Germany

3 Ulm University, Institute of Communications Engineering, Ulm, Germany

References

[1] G. P. Fettweis, K.-C. Chen, and R. Tafazoli, "Green radio: Energy efficiency in wireless networks," *Journal of Communications and Networks*, vol. 12, no. 2, pp. 99–102, April 2010.

[2] C. A. Chan, A. F. Gygax, E. Wong, C. A. Leckie, A. Nirmalathas, and D. C. Kilper, "Methodologies for assessing the use-phase power consumption and greenhouse gas emissions of telecommunications network services," *Environmental Science & Technology*, vol. 47, no. 1, pp. 485–492, January 2013.

[3] G. Oliveri, M. Mostafa, W. G. Teich, J. Lindner, and H. Schumacher, "Advanced low power, high speed nonlinear analog signal processing: An analog VLSI example," in *Wireless Innovation Forum, European Conference on Communications Technologies and Software Defined Radio*, Erlangen, Germany, 5–9 October 2015.

[4] H.-A. Löliger, "Analog decoding and beyond," in *IEEE Information Theory Workshop*, 2–7 September 2001, pp. 126–127.

[5] H.-A. Löliger, F. Tarköy, F. Lustenberger, and M. Helfenstein, "Decoding in analog VLSI," *IEEE Communications Magazine*, vol. 37, no. 4, pp. 99–101, April 1999.

[6] C. Mead, *Analog VLSI and neural systems*, ser. Addison-Wesley VLSI system series. Addison-Wesley, 1989.

[7] E. A. Vittoz, "Analog VLSI signal processing: Why, where and how?" *Journal of VLSI Signal Processing Systems for Signal, Image and Video Technology*, vol. 8, no. 1, pp. 27–44, February 1994.

[8] S. Draghici, "Neural networks in analog hardware - Design and implementation issues," *International Journal of Neural Systems*, vol. 10, no. 1, pp. 19–42, February 2000.

[9] J. Misra and I. Saha, "Artificial neural networks in hardware: A survey of two decades of progress," *Neurocomputing*, vol. 74, no. 1-3, pp. 239–255, December 2010.

[10] S. L. Goh and D. P. Mandic, "A complex-valued RTRL algorithm for recurrent neural networks," *Neural Computation*, vol. 16, no. 12, pp. 2699–2713, December 2004.

[11] J. Lindner, "MC-CDMA in the context of general multiuser/multisubchannel transmission methods," *European Transactions on Telecommunications*, vol. 10, no. 4, pp. 351–367, July-August 1999.

[12] S. Hemati and A. H. Banihashemi, "Dynamics and performance analysis of analog iterative decoding for low-density parity-check LDPC codes," *IEEE Transactions on Communications*, vol. 54, no. 1, pp. 61–70, January 2006.

[13] J. Hagenauer, E. Offer, C. Méasson, and M. Mörz, "Decoding and equalization with analog non-linear networks," *European Transactions on Telecommunications*, vol. 10, no. 6, pp. 659–680, November-December 1999.

[14] M. Dangl, *Iterative estimation and detection for single carrier block transmission*. Der Andere Verlag, Dissertation, Ulm University, Institute of Information Technology, 2007.

[15] A. Cichocki and R. Unbehauen, *Neural networks for optimization and signal processing*. John Wiley & Sons Ltd. & B. G. Teubner, Stuttgart, 1993, ch. 2.

[16] H. Tang, K. C. Tan, and Z. Yi, "Various computational models and applications," in *Neural networks: Computational models and applications*, ser. Studies in computational intelligence, J. Kacprzyk, Ed. Springer-Verlag Berlin Heidelberg, 2007, vol. 53, ch. 5, pp. 57–79.

[17] S. Hemati and A. Yongacoglu, "Dynamics of analog decoders for different message representation domains," *IEEE Transactions on Communications*, vol. 58, no. 3, pp. 721–723, May 2010.

[18] W. G. Teich, M. A. Ibrahim, F. Waeckerle, and R. F. H. Fischer, "Equalization for fiber-optic transmission systems: Low-complexity iterative implementations," in *17th ITG-Fachtagung Photonische Netze*, Leipzig, Germany, May 2016.

[19] A. Engelhart, *Vector detection techniques with moderate complexity*. VDI Verlag GmbH, Dissertation, Ulm University, Institute of Information Technology, 2003.

[20] M. Mostafa, W. G. Teich, and J. Lindner, "Approximation of activation functions for vector equalization based on recurrent neural networks," in *6th International Symposium on Turbo Codes and Iterative Information Processing*, Bremen, Germany, 18-22 August 2014, pp. 52–56.

[21] M. Mostafa, *Equalization and decoding: A continuous-time dynamical approach*. Der Andre-Verlag, Dissertation, Ulm University, Institute of Communications Engineering, 2014, ch. 1 & 3.

[22] K. Kuroe, N. Hashimoto, and T. Mori, "On energy function for complex-valued neural networks and its applications," in *9th International Conference on Neural Information Processing*, vol. 3, 18-22 November 2002, pp. 1079–1083.

[23] S. Haykin, *Neural networks: A comprehensive foundation*. USA: Macmillan college publishing company, Inc., 1994.

[24] J. J. Hopfield, "Neurons with graded response have collective computational properties like those of two-state neurons," in *Proceedings of the National Academy of Sciences of the USA*, vol. 81, no. 10, pp. 3088–3092, May 1984.

[25] M. Yoshida and T. Mori, "Global stability analysis for complex-valued recurrent neural networks and its application to convex optimization problems," in *Complex-valued neural networks: Utilizing high-dimensional parameters*, T. Nitta, Ed. Information science reference, 2009, ch. 5, pp. 104–114.

[26] J. M. Zurada, I. Cloete, and W. van der Poel, "Generalized Hopfield networks for associative memories with multi-valued stable states," *Neurocomputing*, vol. 13, pp. 135–149, 1996.

[27] D. Tank and J. J. Hopfield, "Simple 'neural' optimization network: An A/D converter, signal decision circuit, and a linear programming circuit," *IEEE Transactions on Circuits and Systems*, vol. 33, no. 5, pp. 553–541, May 1986.

[28] J. J. Hopfield and D. W. Tank, "'Neural' computation of decisions in optimization problems," *Biological Cybernetics*, vol. 52, no. 3, pp. 141–152, 1985.

[29] J. J. Hopfield, "Neurons networks and physical systems with emergent collective computational abilities," in *Proceedings of the National Academy of Sciences of the USA*, vol. 79, no. 8, pp. 2554–2558, April 1982.

[30] G. I. Kechriotis and E. S. Manolakos, "Hopfield neural network implementation for optimum CDMA multiuser detector," *IEEE Transactions on Neural Networks*, vol. 7, no. 1, pp. 131–141, January 1996.

[31] T. Miyajima, T. Hasegawa, and M. Haneishi, "On the multiuser detection using a neural network in code-division multiple-access communications," *IEICE Transactions on Communications*, vol. E76-B, pp. 961–968, 1993.

[32] M. Mostafa, W. G. Teich, and J. Lindner, "Vector equalization based on continuous-time recurrent neural networks," in *6th IEEE International Conference on Signal Processing and Communication Systems*, Gold Coast, Australia, 12-14 December 2012, pp. 1–7.

[33] W. G. Teich and M. Seidl, "Code division multiple access communications: Multiuser detection based on a recurrent neural network structure," in *4th IEEE International Symposium on Spread Spectrum Techniques and Applications*, vol. 3, Mainz, Germany, 22-25 September 1996, pp. 979–984.

[34] H. Schumacher, A. C. Ulusoy, G. Liu, and G. Oliveri, "Si/SiGe ICs for ultra-broadband communications: The analog signal processing perspective," in *IEEE MTT-S International Microwave Symposium Digest (IMS)*, Seattle, WA, June 2013, pp. 1–4.

[35] B. Gilbert, "A precise four-quadrant multiplier with subnanosecond response," *IEEE Journal of Solid-State Circuits*, vol. 3, no. 4, pp. 365–373, December 1968.

[36] A. F. Murray and A. V. W. Smith, "Asynchronous arithmetic for VLSI neural systems," *Electronic Letters*, vol. 23, no. 12, pp. 642–643, June 1987.

[37] R. G. Gallager, "Low-density parity-check codes," *IRE Transactions on Information Theory*, vol. 8, no. 1, pp. 21–28, January 1962.

[38] "Digital video broadcasting (DVB), Second generation framing structure, channel coding and modulation systems for broadcasting, interactive services, news gathering and other broadband satellite applications; Part 1: DVB-S2," ETSI EN 302 307-1 V1.4.1, Tech. Rep., 11 2014. [Online]. Available: http://www.etsi.org/deliver/etsi_en/302300_302399/30230701/01.04.01_60/en_30230701v010401p.pdf

[39] A. Dembo, O. Farotimi, and T. Kailath, "High-order absolutely stable neural networks," *IEEE Transactions on Circuits and Systems*, vol. 38, no. 1, pp. 57–65, January 1991.

[40] M. Vidyasagar, "Minimum-seeking properties of analog neural networks with multilinear objective functions," *IEEE Transactions on Automatic Control*, vol. 40, no. 8, pp. 1359–1375, August 1995.

[41] E. B. Kosmatopoulos and M. A. Christodoulou, "Structural properties of gradient recurrent high-order neural networks," *IEEE Transactions on Circuits and Systems-II: Analog and Digital Signal Processing*, vol. 42, no. 9, pp. 592–603, September 1995.

[42] X. Xu, N. K. Huang, and W. T. Tsai, "A Generalized Neural Network Model," *Technical report*, Computer Science Department, Inst. of Technology, Univ. vol. 1, supplement 1, pp. 150, 1988.

[43] R. M. Tanner, "A recursive approach to low complexity codes," *IEEE Transactions on Information Theory*, vol. IT-27, no. 5, pp. 533–547, September 1981.

[44] B. S. Rüffer, C.-M. Kellett, P.-M. Dower, and S. R. Weller, "Belief propagation as a dynamical system: The linear case and open problems," *Control Theory & Applications, IET*, vol. 4, no. 7, pp. 1188–1200, July 2010.

[45] M. Mostafa, W. G. Teich, and J. Lindner, "Comparison of belief propagation and iterative threshold decoding based on dynamical systems," in *IEEE International Symposium on Information Theory*, Istanbul, Turkey, 7-12 July 2013, pp. 2995–2999.

[46] S. Hemati and A. H. Banihashemi, "Comparison between continuous-time asynchronous and discrete-time synchronous iterative decoding," in *IEEE Global Telecommunications Conference*, vol. 1, 29 November-3 December 2004, pp. 356–360.

[47] S. Hemati and A. H. Banihashemi, "Convergence speed and throughput of analog decoders," *IEEE Transactions on Communications*, vol. 55, no. 5, pp. 833–836, May 2007.

[48] S. Hemati and A. Yongacoglu, "On the dynamics of analog min-sum iterative decoders: An analytical approach," *IEEE Transactions on Communications*, vol. 58, no. 5, pp. 2225–2231, August 2010.

[49] S. Hemati, A. H. Banihashemi, and C. Plett, "A 0.18 μm CMOS analog min-sum iterative decoder for a (32,8) low-density paroty-check LDPC code," *IEEE Journal on Solid-State Circuits*, vol. 41, no. 11, pp. 2531–2540, November 2006.

[50] L. Kocarev, F. Lehman, G. M. Maggio, B. Scanavino, Z. Tasev, and A. Vardi, "Nonlinear dynamics of iterative decoding systems: Analysis and applications," *IEEE Transactions on Information Theory*, vol. 52, no. 4, pp. 1366–1384, April 2006.

[51] C. Douillard, M. Jézéquel, C. Berrou, A. Picart, P. Didier, and A. Glavieux, "Iterative correction of intersymbol interference: Turbo-equalization," *European Transactions on Tele-communications*, vol. 6, no. 5, pp. 507–511, 1995.

[52] C. Sgraja, A. Engelhart, W. G. Teich, and J. Lindner, "Combined equalization and decoding for BFDM packet transmission schemes," in *1st International OFDM-Workshop*, vol. 3, Hamburg, Germany, 21-22 September 1999, pp. 1–5.

[53] C. Berrou, A. Glavieux, and P. Thitimajshima, "Near shannon limit error-correcting coding and decoding: Turbo codes(1)," in *IEEE International Conference on Communications ICC*, vol. 2, Geneva, Switzerland, 1993, pp. 1064–1070.

[54] M. Mostafa, W. G. Teich, and J. Lindner, "Local stability analysis of discrete-time, continuous-state, complex-valued recurrent neural networks with inner state feedback," *IEEE Transactions on Neural Networks and Learning Systems*, vol. 25, no. 4, pp. 830–836, April 2014.

[55] A. Engelhart, W. G. Teich, J. Lindner, G. Jeney, S. Imre, and L. Pap, "A survey of multi-user/multisubchannel detection schemes based on recurrent neural networks," *Wireless Communications and Mobile Computing, Special Issue on Advances in 3G Wireless Networks*, vol. 2, no. 3, pp. 269–284, May 2002.

[56] E. Goles, E. Chacc, F. Fogelman-Soulié, and D. Pellegrin, "Decreasing energy functions as a tool for studying threshold functions," *Discrete Applied Mathematics*, vol. 12, no. 3, pp. 261–277, 1985.

[57] E. Goles, and S. Martinez, "A short proof on the cyclic behaviour of multithreshold symmetric automata," *Information and Control*, vol. 51, no. 2, pp. 95–97, November 1981.

[58] D. G. Zill, *A first course in differential equations with modeling applications*. Cengage Learning, Inc., 2009, ch. 9, pp. 340–345.

[59] T. J. C. MacKay. Encyclopedia of sparse graph codes. [Online]. Available: http://www.inference.phy.cam.ac.uk/mackay/codes/data.html

[60] J. G. Proakis, *Digital Communications*. McGraw-Hill, Inc, 1995.

[61] R. M. Gray, *Toeplitz and Circulant Matrices: A Review*, ser. Foundations and Trends in Technology. Now Publishers, 2006.

[62] J. Lindner, *Informations übertragung*. Springer-Verlag Berlin Heidelberg, 2005.

2

Zhang Neural Networks for Online Solution of Time-Varying Linear Inequalities

Dongsheng Guo, Laicheng Yan and Yunong Zhang

Additional information is available at the end of the chapter

Abstract

In this chapter, a special type of recurrent neural networks termed "Zhang neural network" (ZNN) is presented and studied for online solution of time-varying linear (matrix-vector and matrix) inequalities. Specifically, focusing on solving the time-varying linear matrix-vector inequality (LMVI), we develop and investigate two different ZNN models based on two different Zhang functions (ZFs). Then, being an extension, by defining another two different ZFs, another two ZNN models are developed and investigated to solve the time-varying linear matrix inequality (LMI). For such ZNN models, theoretical results and analyses are presented as well to show their computational performances. Simulation results with two illustrative examples further substantiate the efficacy of the presented ZNN models for time-varying LMVI and LMI solving.

Keywords: Zhang neural network (ZNN), Zhang function (ZF), time-varying linear inequalities, design formulas, theoretical results

1. Introduction

In recent years, linear inequalities have played a more and more important role in numerous fields of science and engineering applications [1–9], such as obstacle avoidance of redundant robots [1, 2], robustness analysis of neural networks [3] and stability analysis of fuzzy control systems [5]. They, including linear matrix-vector inequality (LMVI) and linear matrix inequality (LMI), have now been considered as a powerful formulation and design technique for solving a variety of problems [7–11]. Due to their important roles, lots of numerical algorithms and neural networks have been presented and studied for online solution of linear inequalities [7–17]. For example, an iterative method was presented by Yang *et al.* for linear inequalities solving [12]. In [13], three continuous-time neural networks were developed by Cichocki and Bargiela to solve the system of linear inequalities. Besides, a gradient-based neural network and a simplified neural network were investigated respectively in [10] and [11] for solving a class of LMI problems (e.g., Lyapunov matrix inequalities and algebraic Riccati matrix inequalities).

It is worth pointing out that most of the reported approaches are designed intrinsically to solve the time-invariant (or say, static) linear inequalities. In view of the fact that many systems in science and engineering applications are time-varying, the resultant linear inequalities may be time-varying ones (i.e., the coefficients are time-varying). Generally speaking, to solve a time-varying problem, based on the assumption of the short-time invariance, such a time-varying problem can be treated as a time-invariant problem within a small time period [8]. The corresponding approaches (e.g., numerical algorithms and neural networks) are thus designed for solving the problem at each single time instant. Note that, as for this common way used to solve the time-varying problem, the time-derivative information (or say, the change trend) of the time-varying coefficients is not involved. Due to the lack of the consideration of such an important information, the aforementioned approaches may be less effective, when they are exploited directly to solve time-varying problems [7–9, 17–19].

Aiming at solving time-varying problems (e.g., time-varying matrix inversion and time-varying quadratic program), a special type of recurrent neural networks termed Zhang neural network (ZNN) has been formally proposed by Zhang *et al.* since March 2001 [7–9, 17–21]. According to Zhang *et al.*'s design method, the design of a ZNN is based on an indefinite Zhang function (ZF), with the word "indefinite" meaning that such a ZF can be positive, zero, negative or even lower-unbounded. By exploiting methodologically the time-derivative information of time-varying coefficients involved in the time-varying problems, the resultant ZNN models can thus solve the time-varying problems effectively and efficiently (in terms of avoiding the lagging errors generated by the conventional approaches) [18, 19]. For better understanding and to lay a basis for further investigation, the concepts of ZNN and ZF [18] are presented as follows.

Concept 1. Being a special type of recurrent neural networks, Zhang neural network (ZNN) has been developed and studied since 2001. It originates from the research of Hopfield-type neural networks and is a systematic approach for time-varying problems solving. Such a ZNN is different from the conventional gradient neural network(s) in terms of the problem to be solved, indefinite error function, exponent-type design formula, dynamic equation, and the utilization of time-derivative information.

Concept 2. Zhang function (ZF) is the design basis of ZNN. It differs from the common error/ energy functions in the study of conventional approaches. Specifically, compared with the conventional norm-based scalar-valued positive or at least lower-bounded energy function, ZF can be bounded, unbounded or even lower-unbounded (in a word, indefinite). Besides, corresponding to a vector- or matrix-valued problem to be solved, ZF can be vector- or matrix-valued to monitor the solving process fully.

In this chapter, focusing on time-varying linear (matrix-vector and matrix) inequalities solving, we present four different ZNN models based on four different ZFs. Specifically, by defining the first two different ZFs, the corresponding two ZNN models are developed and investigated for solving the time-varying LMVI. Then, being an extension, by defining another two different ZFs, another two ZNN models are developed and investigated to solve the time-varying LMI. For such ZNN models, theoretical results and analyses are also presented to show their computational performances. Simulation results with two illustrative examples further substantiate the efficacy of the presented ZNN models for time-varying LMVI and LMI solving.

2. Preliminaries

As mentioned in Concept 2, the ZF is the design basis for deriving ZNN models to solve time-varying LMVI and LMI. Thus, for presentation convenience, in this chapter, the ZF is denoted by $E(t)$ with $\dot{E}(t)$ being the time derivative of $E(t)$. Based on the ZF, the design procedure of a ZNN model for time-varying LMVI/LMI solving is presented as follows [18, 19].

1. Firstly, an indefinite ZF is defined as the error-monitoring function to monitor the solving process of time-varying LMVI/LMI.

2. Secondly, to force the ZF (i.e., $E(t)$) converge to zero, we choose its time derivative (i.e., $\dot{E}(t)$) via the ZNN design formula (including its variant).

3. Finally, by expanding the ZNN design formula, the dynamic equation of a ZNN model is thus established for time-varying LMVI/LMI solving.

In order to derive different ZNN models to solve time-varying LMVI and LMI, the following two design formulas (being an important part in the above ZNN design procedure) are exploited in this chapter [7–9, 17–21]:

$$\dot{E}(t) = -\gamma \mathcal{F}(E(t)), \tag{1}$$

$$\dot{E}(t) = -\gamma \text{SGN}(E_0) \odot \mathcal{F}(E(t)), \tag{2}$$

where $\gamma > 0 \in R$, being the reciprocal of a capacitance parameter, is used to scale the convergence rate of the solution, and $\mathcal{F}(\cdot)$ denotes the activation-function array. Note that, in general, design parameter γ should be set as large as the hardware system would permit, or selected appropriately for simulation purposes [22]. In addition, function $f(\cdot)$, being a processing element of $\mathcal{F}(\cdot)$, can be any monotonically increasing odd activation function, e.g., the linear, power-sigmoid and hyperbolic-sine activation functions [19, 23]. Furthermore, $E_0 = E(t = 0)$

denotes the initial error, and the unipolar signum function sgn($\cdot$), being an element of SGN($\cdot$), is defined as

$$\text{sgn}(c) = \begin{cases} 1, & \text{if } c > 0, \\ 0, & \text{if } c \leq 0. \end{cases}$$

Besides, the multiplication operator $\odot$ is the Hadamard product [24] and is defined as follows:

$$U \odot V = \begin{bmatrix} u_{11}v_{11} & u_{12}v_{12} & \cdots & u_{1n}v_{1n} \\ u_{21}v_{21} & u_{22}v_{22} & \cdots & u_{2n}v_{2n} \\ \vdots & \vdots & \ddots & \vdots \\ u_{m1}v_{m1} & u_{m2}w_{m2} & \cdots & u_{mn}v_{mn} \end{bmatrix} \in R^{m \times n}.$$

Note that, as for the presented design formulas (1) and (2), the former is the original ZNN design formula proposed by Zhang *et al.* to solve the time-varying Sylvester equation [20], while the latter is the variant of such a ZNN design formula constructed elaborately for time-varying linear inequalities solving [9]. Thus, for presentation convenience and better understanding, (1) is called the original design formula, while (2) is called the variant design formula for time-varying LMVI and LMI solving in this chapter.

Remark 1. For the variant design formula (2), when the initial error $E_0 > 0$, it reduces to $\dot{E}(t) = -\gamma \mathcal{F}(E(t))$, which is exactly the original design formula (1) for various time-varying problems solving [17–21]. In this case (i.e., $\dot{E}(t) = -\gamma \mathcal{F}(E(t))$), different convergence performances of $E(t)$ can be achieved by choosing different activation function arrays [17–21, 23]. For example, (2) reduces to $\dot{E}(t) = -\gamma E(t)$ with a linear activation function array used and with $E_0 > 0$. Evidently, its analytical solution is $E(t) = \exp(-\gamma t)E_0$, which means that $E(t)$ is globally and exponentially convergent to zero with rate γ. By following the previous successful researches [17–21, 23], superior convergence property of $E(t)$ can be achieved by exploiting nonlinear activation functions, e.g., the power-sigmoid and hyperbolic-sine activation functions [23]. In addition, the convergence property can be further improved by increasing the γ value. Therefore, in the case of $E_0 > 0$, the global and exponential convergence property is guaranteed for $E(t)$. Note that, in the case of $E_0 \leq 0$, (2) reduces to $\dot{E}(t) = 0$, meaning that $E(t) = E_0$ as time t evolves. In this situation, there is no need to investigate the convergence performance of $E(t)$ with the different activation function arrays and different γ values used.

According to the presented design formulas (1) and (2), by defining different ZFs (i.e., $E(t)$ with different formulations), different ZNN models are thus developed and investigated for time-varying LMVI and LMI solving.

3. Time-varying linear matrix-vector inequality

In this section, we introduce two different ZFs and develop the resultant ZNN models for time-varying linear matrix-vector inequality (LMVI) solving. Then, theoretical results and analyses are provided to show the computational performances of such two ZNN models.

Specifically, the following problem of time-varying LMVI [7, 9] is considered in this chapter:

$$A(t)x(t) \le b(t), \tag{3}$$

in which $A(t) \in R^{n \times n}$ and $b(t) \in R^n$ are smoothly time-varying matrix and vector, respectively. In addition, $x(t) \in R^n$ is the unknown time-varying vector to be obtained. The objective is to find a feasible solution $x(t)$ such that (3) holds true for any time instant $t \ge 0$. Note that, for further discussion, $A(t)$ is assumed to be nonsingular at any time instant $t \in [0, +\infty]$ in this chapter.

3.1. ZFs and ZNN models

In this subsection, by defining two different ZFs, two different ZNN models are developed and investigated for time-varying LMVI solving.

3.1.1. The first ZF and ZNN model

To monitor and control the process of solving the time-varying LMVI (3), the first ZF is defined as follows [7]:

$$E(t) = A(t)x(t) + \Lambda^2(t) - b(t) \in R^n, \tag{4}$$

where $\Lambda^2(t) = \Lambda(t) \odot \Lambda(t)$ with the time-varying vector $\Lambda(t)$ being $\Lambda(t) = [\lambda_1(t), \lambda_2(t), \cdots, \lambda_n(t)]^T \in R^n$. In view of the fact that $\Lambda^2(t) \ge 0$, when $E(t) = 0$, then we have

$$A(t)x(t) - b(t) = -\Lambda^2(t) \le 0.$$

That is to say, time-varying LMVI (3) solving can be equivalent to solving the time-varying equation $A(t)x(t) + \Lambda^2(t) - b(t) = 0$. For further discussion, the following diagonal matrix $D(t)$ is defined:

$$D(t) = \begin{bmatrix} \lambda_1(t) & 0 & \cdots & 0 \\ 0 & \lambda_2(t) & \cdots & 0 \\ \vdots & \vdots & \ddots & \vdots \\ 0 & 0 & \cdots & \lambda_n(t) \end{bmatrix} \in R^{n \times n},$$

which yields

$$\Lambda^2(t) = D(t)\Lambda(t) \text{ and } \dot{\Lambda}^2(t) = \frac{d\Lambda^2(t)}{dt} = 2D(t)\dot{\Lambda}(t).$$

with $\dot{\Lambda}(t)$ being the time derivative of $\Lambda(t)$.

On the basis of ZF (4), by exploiting the original design formula (1), the dynamic equation of a ZNN model is established as follows:

$$A(t)\dot{x}(t) + 2D(t)\dot{\Lambda}(t) = -\dot{A}(t)x(t) + \dot{b}(t) - \gamma \mathcal{F}(A(t)x(t) + \Lambda^2(t) - b(t)), \tag{5}$$

where $\dot{x}(t)$, $\dot{A}(t)$ and $\dot{b}(t)$ are the time derivatives of $x(t)$, $A(t)$ and $b(t)$, respectively. As for (5), it is reformulated as

$$\begin{bmatrix} A(t) & 2D(t) \end{bmatrix} \begin{bmatrix} \dot{x}(t) \\ \dot{\Lambda}(t) \end{bmatrix} = \begin{bmatrix} -\dot{A}(t) & 0 \end{bmatrix} \begin{bmatrix} x(t) \\ \Lambda(t) \end{bmatrix} + \dot{b}(t) - \gamma \mathcal{F}\left(\begin{bmatrix} A(t) & D(t) \end{bmatrix} \begin{bmatrix} x(t) \\ \Lambda(t) \end{bmatrix} - b(t) \right). \tag{6}$$

By defining the augmented vector $y(t) = [x^T(t), \Lambda^T(t)]^T \in R^{2n}$, (6) is further rewritten as follows:

$$C(t)\dot{y}(t) = P(t)y(t) + \dot{b}(t) - \gamma \mathcal{F}(Q(t)y(t) - b(t)), \tag{7}$$

with $\dot{y}(t)$ being the time derivative of $y(t)$, and the augmented matrices are being defined as below:

$$C(t) = \begin{bmatrix} A^T(t) \\ 2D^T(t) \end{bmatrix}^T \in R^{n \times 2n}, P(t) = \begin{bmatrix} -\dot{A}^T(t) \\ 0 \end{bmatrix}^T \in R^{n \times 2n} \text{ and } Q(t) = \begin{bmatrix} A^T(t) \\ D^T(t) \end{bmatrix}^T \in R^{n \times 2n}.$$

In order to make (7) more computable, we can reformulate (7) to the following explicit form:

$$\dot{y}(t) = C^\dagger(t)P(t)y(t) + C^\dagger(t)\dot{b}(t) - \gamma C^\dagger(t)\mathcal{F}(Q(t)y(t) - b(t)), \tag{8}$$

where $C^{\dagger}(t) = C^{T}(t)(C(t)C^{T}(t))^{-1} \in R^{2n \times n}$ denotes the right pseudoinverse of $C(t)$ and the MATLAB routine "pinv" is used to obtain $C^{\dagger}(t)$ at each time instant in the simulations. Therefore, based on ZF (4), ZNN model (8) is obtained for time-varying LMVI solving. Besides, for better understanding and potential hardware implementation, ZNN model (8) is expressed in the ith (with $i = 1,2,\cdots,2n$) neuron form as

$$y_i = \int \sum_{k=1}^{n} c_{ik} (\sum_{j=1}^{m} p_{kj} y_j + \dot{b}_k - \gamma f(\sum_{j=1}^{m} q_{kj} y_j - b_k)) dt,$$

where y_i denotes the ith neuron of (8), $m = 2n$ and $f(\cdot)$ is a processing element of $\mathcal{F}(\cdot)$. In addition, time-varying weights c_{ik}, p_{kj} and q_{kj} denote the ikth element of $C^{\dagger}(t)$, the kjth element of $P(t)$ and kjth element of $Q(t)$, respectively. Moreover, time-varying thresholds $\dot{b}_k$ and b_k denote, respectively, the kth elements of $\dot{b}(t)$ and $b(t)$. Thus, the neural-network structure of (8) is shown in **Figure 1**.

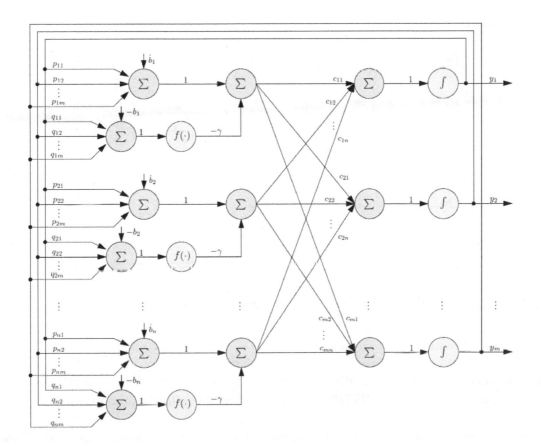

Figure 1. Structure of the neurons in ZNN model (8) for time-varying LMVI (3) solving.

3.1.2. *The second ZF and ZNN model*

Being different from the first ZF (4), the second ZF is defined as follows [9]:

$$E(t) = A(t)x(t) - b(t) \in R^n. \tag{9}$$

On the basis of such a ZF, by exploiting the variant design formula (2), another ZNN model is developed as follows:

$$A(t)\dot{x}(t) = -\dot{A}(t)x(t) + \dot{b}(t) - \gamma \mathrm{SGN}(E_0) \odot \mathcal{F}(A(t)x(t) - b(t)), \tag{10}$$

where the initial error $E_0 = E(t = 0) = A(0)x(0) - b(0)$. Therefore, based on ZF (9), ZNN model (10) is obtained for time-varying LMVI solving. Besides, for better understanding and potential hardware implementation, the block diagram of ZNN model (10) is shown in **Figure 2**, where $I \in R^{n \times n}$ denotes the identity matrix.

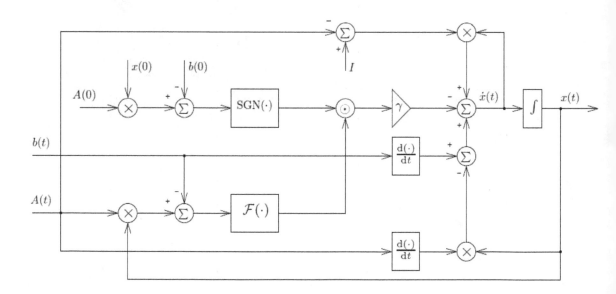

Figure 2. Block diagram of ZNN model (10) for time-varying LMVI (3) solving.

3.2. Theoretical results and analyses

In this subsection, theoretical results and analyses of the presented ZNN models (8) and (10) for solving the time-varying LMVI (3) are provided via the following theorems.

Theorem 1. Given a smoothly time-varying nonsingular coefficient matrix $A(t) \in R^{n \times n}$ and a smoothly time-varying coefficient vector $b(t) \in R^n$ in (3), if a monotonically increasing odd activation function array $\mathcal{F}(\cdot)$ is used, then ZNN model (8) generates an exact time-varying solution of the time-varying LMVI (3).

Proof: To lay a basis for discussion, we define $x^*(t)$ as a theoretical time-varying solution of (3), i.e., $A(t)x^*(t) \leq b(t)$. Then, a time-varying vector $\Lambda^*(t)$ would exist, which results in the time-varying matrix-vector equation as follows:

$$A(t)x^*(t) + \Lambda^{*2}(t) = b(t). \tag{11}$$

By differentiating (11) with respect to time t, we have

$$A(t)\dot{x}^*(t) + \dot{A}(t)x^*(t) + \dot{\Lambda}^{*2}(t) = \dot{b}(t), \tag{12}$$

with $\dot{x}^*(t)$ and $\dot{\Lambda}^{*2}(t)$ being respectively the time derivatives of $x^*(t)$ and $\Lambda^{*2}(t)$. Based on (7), (11) and (12), we further have

$$A(t)(\dot{x}(t) - \dot{x}^*(t)) + \dot{A}(t)(x(t) - x^*(t)) + \dot{\Lambda}^2(t) - \dot{\Lambda}^{*2}(t)$$
$$= -\gamma \mathcal{F}(A(t)(x(t) - x^*(t)) + \Lambda^2(t) - \Lambda^{*2}(t)),$$

which is rewritten as

$$\dot{\tilde{E}}(t) = -\gamma \mathcal{F}(\tilde{E}(t)), \tag{13}$$

where $\tilde{E}(t) = A(t)(x(t) - x^*(t)) + \Lambda^2(t) - \Lambda^{*2}(t) \in R^n$ with $\dot{\tilde{E}}(t)$ being the time derivative of $\tilde{E}(t)$.

As for (13), its compact form of a set of n decoupled differential equations is written as follows:

$$\dot{\tilde{e}}_i(t) = -\gamma f(\tilde{e}_i(t)), \tag{14}$$

where $i = 1, 2, \cdots, n$. To analyze (14), we define a Lyapunov function candidate $v_i(t) = \tilde{e}_i^2(t)/2 \geq 0$ with its time derivative being

$$\dot{v}_i(t) = \frac{dv_i(t)}{dt} = \tilde{e}_i(t)\dot{\tilde{e}}_i(t) = -\gamma \tilde{e}_i(t) f(\tilde{e}_i(t)).$$

Since $f(\cdot)$ is a monotonically increasing odd activation function, i.e., $f(-\tilde{e}_i(t)) = -f(\tilde{e}_i(t))$, then we have

$$\tilde{e}_i(t) f(\tilde{e}_i(t)) \begin{cases} > 0, & \text{if } \tilde{e}_i(t) \neq 0, \\ = 0, & \text{if } \tilde{e}_i(t) = 0, \end{cases}$$

which guarantees the negative definiteness of $\dot{v}_i(t)$. That is to say, $\dot{v}_i(t) < 0$ for $\tilde{e}_i(t) \neq 0$, while $\dot{v}_i(t) = 0$ for $\tilde{e}_i(t) = 0$ only. By Lyapunov theory, $\tilde{e}_i(t)$ converges to zero for any $i \in \{1,2,\cdots,n\}$, thereby showing that $\tilde{E}(t)$ is convergent to zero as well.

Besides, based on (11), we have $A(t)x^*(t) + \Lambda^{*2}(t) = b(t)$. Then, $\tilde{E}(t)$ is rewritten as $\tilde{E}(t) = A(t)x(t) + \Lambda^2(t) - b(t)$, which is equivalent to $A(t)x(t) - b(t) = -\Lambda^2(t) + \tilde{E}(t)$. Note that, as analyzed previously, $\tilde{E}(t) \to 0$ with time $t \to +\infty$. Thus, as time evolves,

$$A(t)x(t) - b(t) = -\Lambda^2(t) + \tilde{E}(t) \to -\Lambda^2(t).$$

Since $-\Lambda^2(t) \leq 0$ (i.e., each element is less than or equal to zero), then we have $A(t)x(t) - b(t) \leq 0$. This implies that $x(t)$ (being the first n elements of $y(t)$ of (8)) would converge to a time-varying vector which satisfies the time-varying LMVI (3); i.e., $x(t) \to x^*(t)$ to make (3) hold true. In summary, the presented ZNN model (8) generates an exact time-varying solution of the time-varying LMVI (3). The proof is thus completed. □

Theorem 2. Given a smoothly time-varying nonsingular coefficient matrix $A(t) \in R^{n \times n}$ and a smoothly time-varying coefficient vector $b(t) \in R^n$ in (3), if a monotonically increasing odd activation function array $\mathcal{F}(\cdot)$ is used, then ZNN model (10) generates an exact time-varying solution of the time-varying LMVI (3).

Proof: Consider ZNN model (10), which is derived from the variant design formula (2). Thus, there are three cases as follows.

1. If the randomly generated initial state $x(0) \in R^n$ is outside the initial solution set $S(0)$ of (3), i.e., $E_0 > 0$ in (10), based on Remark 1 and the previous work [9], the global and exponential convergence of the error function $E(t)$ is achieved (or say, $E(t) = A(t)x(t) - b(t) \to 0$ globally and exponentially). This also means that the neural state $x(t)$ of ZNN model (10) is convergent to the theoretical time-varying solution of the matrix-vector equation $A(t)x(t) - b(t) = 0$. Note that $A(t)x(t) - b(t) = 0$ (i.e., $A(t)x(t) = b(t)$) is a special case of $A(t)x(t) \leq b(t)$. Therefore, ZNN model (10) is effective on solving the time-varying LMVI (3), in terms of $x(t)$ being convergent to the time-varying solution set $S(t)$ of (3).

2. If $x(0)$ is inside $S(0)$ of (3), i.e., $E_0 \leq 0$ in (10), based on Remark 1, the error function $E(t)$ would remain E_0 with $t \to +\infty$. That is, $E(t) = E_0 \leq 0$, no matter how time t evolves. In this situation, ZNN model (10) is still effective on solving the time-varying LMVI (3), in terms of its neural state $x(t)$ always being inside $S(t)$ of (3).

3. If some elements of $x(0)$ are inside $S(0)$ of (3) while the others are outside $S(0)$, i.e., some elements of E_0 are greater than zero while the rest elements of E_0 are less than or equal to zero, then, (i) for the elements of $E(t)$ that have positive initial values (i.e., their initial values are greater than zero), they can be convergent to zero globally and exponentially; and (ii) for the rest elements of $E(t)$, they can be always equal to their initial values that are less than or equal to zero. In view of the fact that, as time evolves, each element of $E(t) = A(t)x(t) - b(t)$ is less than or equal to zero, ZNN model (10) is thus effective on solving the time-varying LMVI (3).

By summarizing the above analyses, the time-varying LMVI (3) is solved effectively via ZNN model (10), in the sense that such a model can generate an exact time-varying solution of (3). The proof is thus completed. $\square$

Remark 2. On the basis of two different ZFs (i.e., (4) and (9)), two different ZNN models (i.e., (8) and (10)) are obtained for online solution of the time-varying LMVI (3). Note that the former aims at solving (3) aided with equality conversion (i.e., from inequality to equation) and the original design formula (1), while the latter focuses on solving (3) directly with the aid of the variant design formula (2). The resultant ZNN model (8) is depicted in an explicit dynamics (i.e., $\dot{y}(t) = \cdots$), and ZNN model (10) is depicted in an implicit dynamics (i.e., $A(t)\dot{x}(t) = \cdots$). As analyzed above and as demonstrated by the simulation results shown in Section 5, such two ZNN models are both effective on solving the time-varying LMVI (3). In summary, two different approaches for time-varying LMVI solving have been discovered and presented in this chapter; i.e., one is based on the variant of the original ZNN design formula, and the other is based on the conversion from inequality to equation. This can be viewed as an important breakthrough on (time-varying or static) inequalities solving [7–9].

4. Time-varying linear matrix inequality

In this section, being an extension, by defining another two different ZFs, another two ZNN models are developed and investigated for time-varying linear matrix inequality (LMI) solving.

Specifically, the following problem of time-varying LMI is considered [9]:

$$A(t)X(t) \le B(t), \tag{15}$$

where $A(t) \in R^{m \times m}$ and $B(t) \in R^{m \times n}$ are smoothly time-varying matrices, and $X(t) \in R^{m \times n}$ is the unknown matrix to be obtained. Note that (15) is a representative time-varying LMI problem which is studied here. The design approaches presented in this chapter (more specifically, summarized in Remark 2) can be directly extended to solve other types of time-varying LMIs [8, 10, 11].

4.1. The first ZF and ZNN model

In order to solve the time-varying LMI (15), the first ZF is defined as follows:

$$E(t) = A(t)X(t) + \Lambda^2(t) - B(t) \in R^{m \times n}, \tag{16}$$

where $\Lambda^2(t) = \Lambda(t) \odot \Lambda(t)$ with the time-varying vector $\Lambda(t)$ being

$$\Lambda(t) = \begin{bmatrix} \lambda_{11}(t) & \lambda_{12}(t) & \cdots & \lambda_{1n}(t) \\ \lambda_{21}(t) & \lambda_{22}(t) & \cdots & \lambda_{2n}(t) \\ \vdots & \vdots & \ddots & \vdots \\ \lambda_{m1}(t) & \lambda_{m2}(t) & \cdots & \lambda_{mn}(t) \end{bmatrix} \in R^{m \times n}.$$

In addition, for matrices $\Lambda(t)$ and $\Lambda^2(t)$, we have

$$\text{vec}(\Lambda^2(t)) = D(t)\text{vec}(\Lambda(t)),$$

where operator $\text{vec}(\cdot) \in R^{mn}$ generates a column vector obtained by stacking all column vectors of a matrix together [8, 18, 19]. In addition, the diagonal matrix $D(t)$ is defined as follows:

$$D(t) = \begin{bmatrix} \tilde{\lambda}_1(t) & 0 & \cdots & 0 \\ 0 & \tilde{\lambda}_2(t) & \cdots & 0 \\ \vdots & \vdots & \ddots & \vdots \\ 0 & 0 & \cdots & \tilde{\lambda}_n(t) \end{bmatrix} \in R^{mn \times mn},$$

with the ith (with $i = 1, \cdots, n$) block matrix being

$$\tilde{\lambda}_i(t) = \begin{bmatrix} \lambda_{1i}(t) & 0 & \cdots & 0 \\ 0 & \lambda_{2i}(t) & \cdots & 0 \\ \vdots & \vdots & \ddots & \vdots \\ 0 & 0 & \cdots & \lambda_{mi}(t) \end{bmatrix} \in R^{m \times m}.$$

By defining $u(t) = \text{vec}(X(t)) \in R^{mn}$, $v(t) = \text{vec}(\Lambda(t)) \in R^{mn}$ and $w(t) = \text{vec}(B(t)) \in R^{mn}$, ZF (16) is reformulated as $E(t) = M(t)u(t) - w(t) + D(t)v(t) \in R^{mn}$, where $M(t) = I \otimes A(t) \in R^{mn \times mn}$ with $I \in R^{n \times n}$ being the identity matrix and $\otimes$ denoting the

Kronecker product [18, 19]. Thus, on the basis of (16), by exploiting the original design formula (1), we have

$$C(t)\dot{y}(t) = P(t)y(t) + \dot{w}(t) - \gamma \mathcal{F}(Q(t)y(t) - w(t)), \tag{17}$$

where the augmented vector $y(t) = [u^T(t), v^T(t)]^T \in R^{2mn}$, and $\dot{y}(t) \in R^{2mn}$ and $\dot{w}(t) \in R^{mn}$ are the time derivatives of $y(t)$ and $w(t)$, respectively. In addition, the augmented matrices are defined as

$$C(t) = \begin{bmatrix} M^T(t) \\ 2D^T(t) \end{bmatrix}^T \in R^{mn \times 2mn}, P(t) = \begin{bmatrix} -N^T(t) \\ 0 \end{bmatrix}^T \in R^{mn \times 2mn}$$

$$\text{and } Q(t) = \begin{bmatrix} M^T(t) \\ D^T(t) \end{bmatrix}^T \in R^{mn \times 2mn},$$

where $N(t) = \dot{M}(t) = I \otimes \dot{A}(t) \in R^{mn \times mn}$ with $\dot{A}(t)$ being the time derivative of $A(t)$.

Similarly, to make (17) more computable, we can reformulate (17) as the following explicit form:

$$\dot{y}(t) = C^\dagger(t)P(t)y(t) + C^\dagger(t)\dot{w}(t) - \gamma C^\dagger(t)\mathcal{F}(Q(t)y(t) - w(t)), \tag{18}$$

where $C^\dagger(t) = C^T(t)(C(t)C^T(t))^{-1} \in R^{2mn \times mn}$. Therefore, based on ZF (16), ZNN model (18) is obtained for time-varying LMI solving. Note that the neural-network structure of (18) is similar to the one shown in **Figure 1**, and is thus omitted here. Besides, as for ZNN model (18), we have the following theoretical result, with the related proof being generalized from the proof of Theorem 1 and being left to interested readers to complete as a topic of exercise.

Corollary 1. Given a smoothly time-varying nonsingular coefficient matrix $A(t) \in R^{m \times m}$ and a smoothly time-varying coefficient matrix $B(t) \in R^{m \times n}$ in (15), if a monotonically increasing odd activation function array $\mathcal{F}(\cdot)$ is used, then ZNN model (18) generates an exact time-varying solution of the time-varying LMI (15).

4.2. The second ZF and ZNN model

In this subsection, being different from the first ZF (16), the second ZF is defined as follows:

$$E(t) = A(t)X(t) - B(t) \in R^{m \times n}. \tag{19}$$

On the basis of such a ZF, by exploiting the variant design formula (2), the following ZNN model for time-varying LMI solving is developed:

$$A(t)\dot{X}(t) = -\dot{A}(t)X(t) + \dot{B}(t) - \gamma \mathrm{SGN}(E_0) \odot \mathcal{F}(A(t)X(t) - B(t)), \tag{20}$$

where the initial error $E_0 = E(t = 0) = A(0)X(0) - B(0)$. Note that, due to similarity to the block diagram of (10), the block diagram of ZNN model (20) is omitted. Besides, as for ZNN model (20), we have the following theoretical result, of which the proof is generalized from the proof of Theorem 2 (and is also left to interested readers to complete as a topic of exercise).

Corollary 2. Given a smoothly time-varying nonsingular coefficient matrix $A(t) \in R^{m \times m}$ and a smoothly time-varying coefficient matrix $B(t) \in R^{m \times n}$ in (15), if a monotonically increasing odd activation function array $\mathcal{F}(\cdot)$ is used, then ZNN model (20) generates an exact time-varying solution of the time-varying LMI (15).

5. Simulative verifications

In this section, one illustrative example is first simulated for demonstrating the efficacy of the presented ZNN models (8) and (10) for solving the time-varying LMVI (3). Then, another illustrative example is provided for substantiating the efficacy of the presented ZNN models (18) and (20) for solving the time-varying LMI (15).

Example 1 In the first example, the following smoothly time-varying coefficient matrix $A(t)$ and coefficient vector $b(t)$ of (3) are designed to test ZNN models (8) and (10):

$$A(t) = \begin{bmatrix} 3 + \sin(3t) & \cos(3t)/2 & \cos(3t) \\ \cos(3t)/2 & 3 + \sin(3t) & \cos(3t)/2 \\ \cos(3t) & \cos(3t)/2 & 3 + \sin(3t) \end{bmatrix} \in R^{3 \times 3}$$

$$\text{and } b(t) = \begin{bmatrix} \sin(3t) + 1 \\ \cos(3t) + 2 \\ \sin(3t) + \cos(3t) + 3 \end{bmatrix} \in R^3.$$

The corresponding simulation results are shown in **Figures 3** through **9**.

Specifically, **Figures 3** and **4** illustrate the state trajectories synthesized by ZNN model (8) using $\gamma = 1$ and the power-sigmoid activation function. As shown in **Figures 3** and **4**, starting from five randomly generated initial states, the $x(t)$ trajectories (being the first 3 elements of $y(t)$ in (8)) and the $\Lambda(t)$ trajectories (being the rest elements of $y(t)$) are time-varying. In addition, **Figure 5** presents the characteristics of residual error

$\| Q(t)y(t) - b(t) \|_2 = \| A(t)x(t) + \Lambda^2(t) - b(t) \|_2$ (with symbol $\| \cdot \|_2$ denoting the two norm of a vector), from which we can observe that the residual errors of ZNN model (8) (corresponding to **Figures 3** and **4**) are all convergent to zero. This means that the $x(t)$ and $\Lambda(t)$ solutions shown in **Figures 3** and **4** are the time-varying solutions of $A(t)x(t) + \Lambda^2(t) - b(t) = 0$. In view of $-\Lambda^2(t) \leq 0$, such a solution of $x(t)$ is an exact solution of the time-varying LMVI (3), i.e., $A(t)x(t) \leq b(t)$. For better understanding, the profiles of the testing error function $\varepsilon(t) = A(t)x(t) - b(t)$ (i.e., ZF (9)) are illustrated in **Figure 6**. As shown in the figure, all the elements of $\varepsilon(t)$ are less than or equal to zero, thereby meaning that the $x(t)$ solution satisfies $A(t)x(t) \leq b(t)$ (being an exact time-varying solution of (3)). These simulation results substantiate the efficacy of ZNN model (8) for time-varying LMVI solving. Besides, **Figure 7** shows the simulation results synthesized by ZNN model (8) using different γ values (i.e., $\gamma = 1$ and $\gamma = 10$) and different activation functions (i.e., linear, hyperbolic-sine and power-sigmoid activation functions). As seen from **Figure 7**, the residual errors all converge to zero, which means that ZNN model (8) solves the time-varying LMVI (3) successfully. Note that, from **Figure 7**, we have a conclusion that superior computational performance of ZNN model (8) can be achieved by increasing the γ value and choosing a suitable activation function.

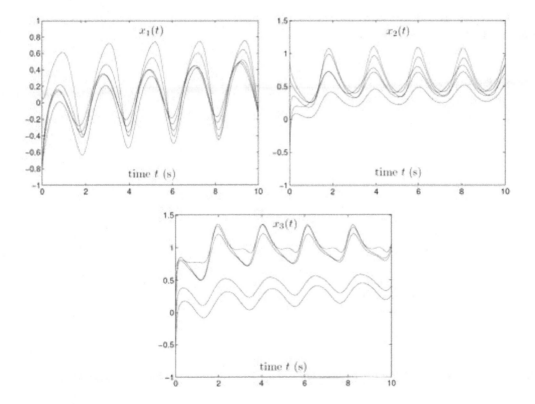

Figure 3. State trajectories of $x(t) \in R^3$ synthesized by ZNN model (8) with $\gamma = 1$ and the power-sigmoid activation function used for time-varying LMVI (3) solving.

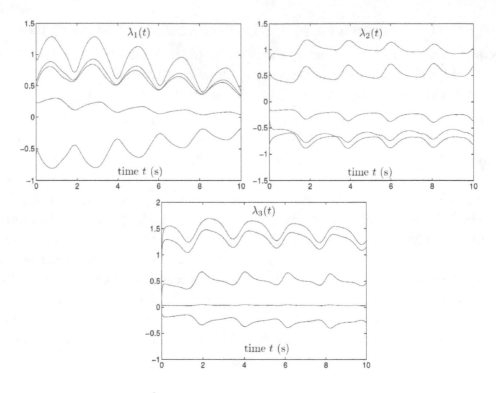

Figure 4. State trajectories of $\Lambda(t) \in R^3$ synthesized by ZNN model (8) with $\gamma = 1$ and the power-sigmoid activation function used for time-varying LMVI (3) solving.

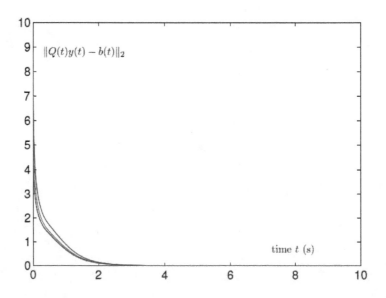

Figure 5. Residual errors $\| Q(t)y(t) - b(t) \|_2$ of ZNN model (8) for time-varying LMVI (3) solving.

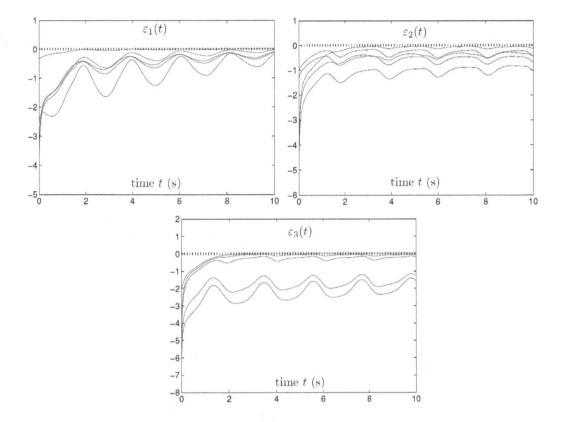

Figure 6. Profiles of $\varepsilon(t) = A(t)x(t) - b(t) \in R^3$ synthesized by ZNN model (8) with $\gamma = 1$ and the power-sigmoid activation function used for time-varying LMVI (3) solving.

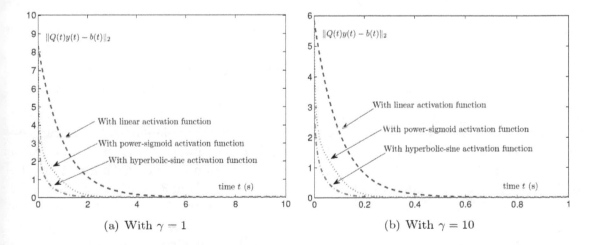

(a) With $\gamma - 1$ (b) With $\gamma = 10$

Figure 7. Residual errors $\| Q(t)y(t) - b(t) \|_2$ of ZNN model (8) with γ fixed and different activation functions used for time-varying LMVI (3) solving.

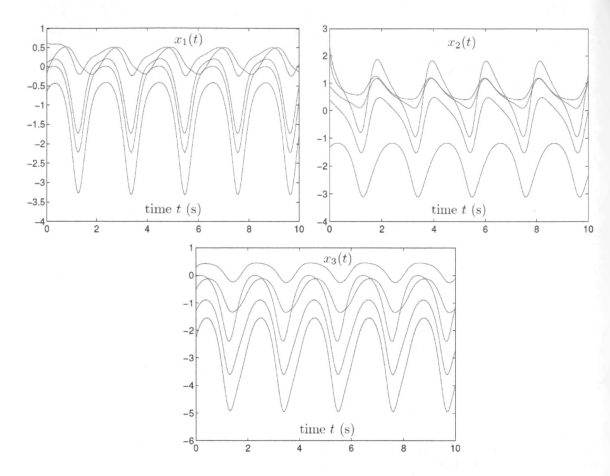

Figure 8. State trajectories of $x(t) \in R^3$ synthesized by ZNN model (10) with $\gamma = 1$ and the power-sigmoid activation function used for time-varying LMVI (3) solving.

It is worth pointing out here that, in general, it may be difficult to know whether the initial state $x(0)$ used for simulation/application is outside the initial solution set $S(0)$ of the time-varying LMVI (3) or not. Thus, as for ZNN model (10), we focus on investigating its computational performance when some elements of $x(0)$ are outside $S(0)$ while the others are inside $S(0)$. In this case, some elements of the initial error $E_0 = A(0)x(0) - b(0)$ are greater than zero, while the rest are less than or equal to zero. The corresponding simulation results synthesized by ZNN model (10) using $\gamma = 1$ and the power-sigmoid activation function are illustrated in **Figures 8** and **9**. As shown in **Figure 8**, starting from five randomly generated initial states, the $x(t)$ trajectories of ZNN model (10) are time-varying. Besides, from **Figure 9** which shows the profiles of the testing error function $\varepsilon(t) = A(t)x(t) \leq b(t)$, we can observe that the elements of $\varepsilon(t)$ with positive initial values are convergent to zero, while the rest elements remain at their initial values. This result implies that the $x(t)$ solutions shown in **Figure 6** are the time-varying solutions of (3), i.e., $A(t)x(t) \leq b(t)$, thereby showing the efficacy of ZNN model (10) for time-varying LMVI solving. That is, ZNN model (10) generates an exact time-varying solution of the time-varying LMVI (3). Note that the computational performance of ZNN model (10) can be improved by increasing the value of γ and choosing a suitable activation function (which is similar to that of ZNN model (8)). Being a topic of exercise, the corresponding simulative verifications of ZNN model (10) are left for interested readers.

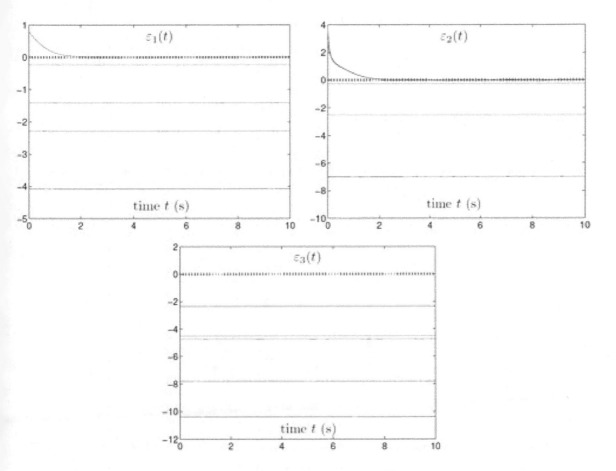

Figure 9. Profiles of $\varepsilon(t) = A(t)x(t) - b(t) \in R^3$ synthesized by ZNN model (10) with $\gamma = 1$ and the power-sigmoid activation function used for time-varying LMVI (3) solving.

In summary, the above simulation results (i.e., **Figures 3** through **9**) have substantiated that the presented ZNN models (8) and (10) are both effective on time-varying LMVI solving.

Example 2 In the second example, the following smoothly time-varying coefficient matrices $A(t)$ and $B(t)$ of (15) are designed to test ZNN models (18) and (20):

$$A(t) = \begin{bmatrix} \sin(10t) & \cos(10t) \\ -\cos(10t) & \sin(10t) \end{bmatrix} \in R^{2\times2} \text{ and }$$

$$B(t) = \begin{bmatrix} \cos(10t)+1 & \sin(10t)+1.5 \\ -\sin(10t)+1.5 & -\cos(10t)+1 \end{bmatrix} \in R^{2\times2}.$$

The corresponding simulation results are illustrated in **Figures 10** through **13**.

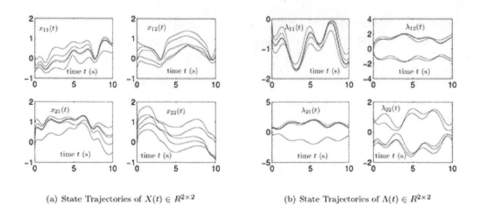

(a) State Trajectories of $X(t) \in R^{2 \times 2}$

(b) State Trajectories of $\Lambda(t) \in R^{2 \times 2}$

Figure 10. Neural states synthesized by ZNN model (18) with $\gamma = 1$ and the hyperbolic-sine activation function used for time-varying LMI (15) solving.

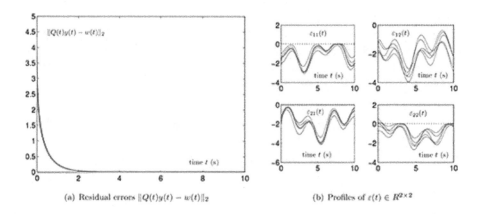

(a) Residual errors $\|Q(t)y(t) - w(t)\|_2$

(b) Profiles of $\varepsilon(t) \in R^{2 \times 2}$

Figure 11. Profiles of residual errors $\| Q(t)y(t) - w(t) \|_2$ and $\varepsilon(t) = A(t)X(t) - B(t)$ synthesized by ZNN model (18) with $\gamma = 1$ and the hyperbolic-sine activation function used for time-varying LMI (15) solving.

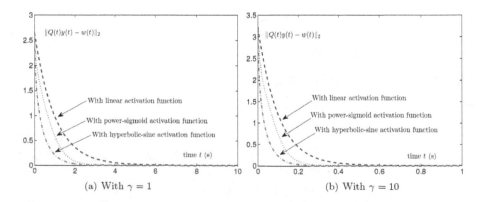

(a) With $\gamma = 1$

(b) With $\gamma = 10$

Figure 12. Residual errors $\| Q(t)y(t) - w(t) \|_2$ of ZNN model (18) with γ fixed and different activation functions used for time-varying LMI (15) solving.

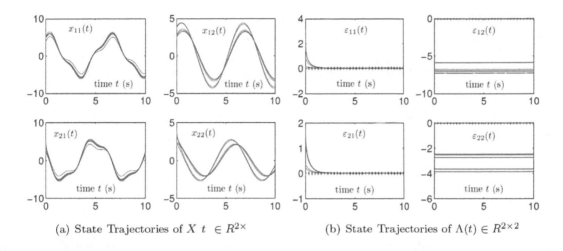

(a) State Trajectories of $X_t \in R^{2\times}$ (b) State Trajectories of $\Lambda(t) \in R^{2\times2}$

Figure 13. Simulation results synthesized by ZNN model (20) with $\gamma = 1$ and the hyperbolic-sine activation function used for time-varying LMI (15) solving.

On one hand, as synthesized by ZNN model (18) using $\gamma = 1$ and the hyperbolic-sine activation function, **Figure 10** shows the trajectories of $X(t)$ (being the first 4 elements of $y(t)$ in (18)) and $\Lambda(t)$ (being the rest elements of $y(t)$), which are time-varying. In addition, **Figure 11(a)** shows the characteristics of residual error $\| Q(t)y(t) - w(t) \|_2 = \| A(t)X(t) + \Lambda^2(t) - B(t) \|_F$ (with symbol $\| \cdot \|_F$ denoting the Frobenius norm of a matrix), from which we can observe that the residual errors of ZNN model (18) all converge to zero. This means that the solutions of $X(t)$ and $\Lambda(t)$ shown in **Figure 10** are the time-varying solutions of $A(t)X(t) + \Lambda^2(t) - B(t) = 0$. That is, $X(t)$ satisfies $A(t)X(t) = B(t) - \Lambda^2(t) \leq B(t)$, showing that such a solution is an exact time-varying solution of the time-varying LMI (15). For better understanding, **Figure 11(b)** shows the profiles of the testing error function $\varepsilon(t) = A(t)X(t) - B(t)$, from which we can observe that all the elements of $\varepsilon(t)$ are less than or equal to zero. These simulation results substantiate the efficacy of ZNN model (18) for time-varying LMI solving. Besides, **Figure 12** shows the simulation results synthesized by ZNN model (18) using different γ values and different activation functions. As seen from **Figure 12**, the residual errors all converge to zero, which means that the time-varying LMI (15) is solved successfully via ZNN model (18). Note that, as for ZNN model (18), its computational performance can be improved by increasing the γ value and choosing a suitable activation function (as shown in **Figure 12**).

On the other hand, as synthesized by ZNN model (20) using $\gamma = 1$ and the hyperbolic-sine activation function, **Figure 13** shows the related simulation results, where some elements of the initial state $X(0)$ are outside the initial solution set $S(0)$ of the time-varying LMI (15) while the others are inside $S(0)$. From **Figure 13(a)**, we can observe that the $X(t)$ trajectory of ZNN model (20) is time-varying. In addition, as shown in **Figure 13(b)**, the errors $\varepsilon_{11}(t)$ and $\varepsilon_{21}(t)$ (being the elements of the testing error function $\varepsilon(t) = A(t)X(t) - B(t)$) converge to zero, and the errors $\varepsilon_{12}(t)$ and $e_{22}(t)$ are always equal to $\varepsilon_{12}(0) < 0$ and $\varepsilon_{22}(0) < 0$. This means that the

$X(t)$ solution shown in **Figure 13(a)** is the time-varying solution of (15), i.e., $A(t)X(t) \leq B(t)$, thereby showing the efficacy of ZNN model (20). That is, ZNN model (20) generates an exact time-varying solution of the time-varying LMI (15). Besides, the investigations on the computational performance of (10) using different γ values and different activation functions are left to interested readers to complete as a topic of exercise.

In summary, the above simulation results (i.e., **Figures 10** through **13**) have substantiated that the presented ZNN models (18) and (20) are both effective on time-varying LMI solving.

6. Summary

In this chapter, by exploiting two design formulas (1) and (2), based on different ZFs (i.e., (4), (9), (16) and (19)), four different ZNN models (i.e., (8), (10), (18) and (20)) have been developed and investigated to solve the time-varying LMVI (3) and time-varying LMI (15). For such ZNN models, theoretical results and analyses have also been presented to show their computational performances. Simulation results with two illustrative examples have further substantiated the efficacy of the presented ZNN models for time-varying LMVI and LMI solving.

Acknowledgements

This work is supported by the National Natural Science Foundation of China (with number 61473323 and 61403149), and also by the Scientific Research Funds of Huaqiao University.

Author details

Dongsheng Guo[1*], Laicheng Yan[1] and Yunong Zhang[2]

*Address all correspondence to: gdongsh2008@126.com; gdongsh@hqu.edu.cn

1 College of Information Science and Engineering, Huaqiao University, Xiamen, China

2 School of Data and Computer Science, Sun Yat-sen University, Guangzhou, China

References

[1] Guo D, Zhang Y. Acceleration-level inequality-based MAN scheme for obstacle avoidance of redundant robot manipulators. IEEE Transactions on Industrial Electronics. 2014; 61:6903–6914. DOI: 10.1109/TIE.2014.2331036

[2] Guo D, Zhang Y. A new inequality-based obstacle-avoidance MVN scheme and its application to redundant robot manipulators. IEEE Transactions on Systems, Man, and Cybernetics, Part C. 2012; 42:1326–1340. DOI: 10.1109/TSMCC.2012.2183868

[3] Jing X. Robust adaptive learning of feedforward neural networks via LMI optimizations. Neural Networks. 2012; 31:33–45. DOI: 10.1016/j.neunet.2012.03.003

[4] Wang Z, Zhang H, Jiang B. LMI-based approach for global asymptotic stability analysis of recurrent neural networks with various delays and structures. IEEE Transactions on Neural Networks. 2011; 22:1032–1045. DOI: 10.1109/TNN.2011.2131679

[5] Kim E, Kang HJ, Park M. Numerical stability analysis of fuzzy control systems via quadratic programming and linear matrix inequalities. IEEE Transactions on Systems, Man, and Cybernetics, Part A. 1999; 29:333–346. DOI: 10.1109/3468.769752

[6] Xiao L, Zhang Y. Different Zhang functions resulting in different ZNN models demonstrated via time-varying linear matrix-vector inequalities solving. Neurocomputing. 2013; 121:140–149. DOI: 10.1016/j.neucom.2013.04.041

[7] Guo D, Zhang Y. ZNN for solving online time-varying linear matrix-vector inequality via equality conversion. Applied Mathematics and Computation. 2015; 259:327–338. DOI: 10.1016/j.amc.2015.02.060

[8] Guo D, Zhang Y. Zhang neural network for online solution of time-varying linear matrix inequality aided with an equality conversion. IEEE Transactions on Neural Networks and Learning Systems. 2014; 25:370–382. DOI: 10.1109/TNNLS.2013.2275011

[9] Guo D, Zhang Y. A new variant of the Zhang neural network for solving online time-varying linear inequalities. Proceedings of the Royal Society A. 2012; 468:2255–2271. DOI: 10.1098/rspa.2011.0668

[10] Lin C, Lai C, Huang T. A neural network for linear matrix inequality problems. IEEE Transactions on Neural Networks. 2000; 11:1078–1092. DOI: 10.1109/72.870041

[11] Cheng L, Hou ZG, Tan M, A simplified neural network for linear matrix inequality problems. Neural Processing Letters. 2009; 29:213–230. DOI: 10.1007/s11063-009-9105-5

[12] Yang K, Murty KG, Mangasarian OL. New iterative methods for linear inequalities. Journal of Optimization Theory and Applications. 1992; 72:163–185. DOI: 10.1007/BF00939954

[13] Cichocki A, Bargiela, A. Neural networks for solving linear inequality systems. Parallel Computing. 1997; 22:1455–1475. DOI: 10.1016/S0167-8191(96)00065-8

[14] Xia Y, Wang J, Hung DL. Recurrent neural networks for solving linear inequalities and equations. IEEE Transactions on Circuits and Systems - I. 1999; 46:452–462. DOI: 10.1109/81.754846

[15] Zhang Y. A set of nonlinear equations and inequalities arising in robotics and its online solution via a primal neural network. Neurocomputing. 2006; 70:513–524. DOI: 10.1016/j.neucom.2005.11.006

[16] Hu X. Dynamic system methods for solving mixed linear matrix inequalities and linear vector inequalities and equalities. Applied Mathematics and Computation. 2010; 216:1181–1193. DOI: 10.1016/j.amc.2010.02.010

[17] Xiao L, Zhang Y. Zhang neural network versus gradient neural network for solving time-varying linear inequalities. IEEE Transactions on Neural Networks. 2011; 22:1676–1684. DOI: 10.1109/TNN.2011.2163318

[18] Zhang Y, Guo D. Zhang Functions and Various Models. Heidelberg: Springer-Verlag; 2015. 236 p.

[19] Zhang Y, Yi C. Zhang Neural Networks and Neural-Dynamic Method. New York: Nova Science Publishers; 2011. 261 p.

[20] Zhang Y, Jiang D, Wang J. A recurrent neural network for solving Sylvester equation with time-varying coefficients. IEEE Transactions on Neural Networks. 2002; 13:1053–1063. DOI: 10.1109/TNN.2002.1031938

[21] Zhang Y, Ge SS. Design and analysis of a general recurrent neural network model for time-varying matrix inversion. IEEE Transactions on Neural Networks. 2005; 16:1477–1490. DOI: 10.1109/TNN.2005.857946

[22] Mead C. Analog VLSI and Neural Systems. Boston, USA: Addison-Wesley, Reading; 1989. 371 p.

[23] Li Z, Zhang Y. Improved Zhang neural network model and its solution of time-varying generalized linear matrix equations. Expert Systems with Applications. 2010; 37:7213–7218. DOI: 10.1016/j.eswa.2010.04.007

[24] Liu S, Trenkler G. Hadamard, Khatri-Rao, Kronecker and other matrix products. International Journal of Cooperative Information Systems. 2008; 4:160–177.

3

Artificial Neural Network as a FPGA Trigger for a Detection of Neutrino-Induced Air Showers

Zbigniew Szadkowski, Dariusz Głas and Krzysztof Pytel

Additional information is available at the end of the chapter

Abstract

Neutrinos play a fundamental role in the understanding of the origin of ultrahigh-energy cosmic rays (UHECR). They interact through charged and neutral currents in the atmosphere generating extensive air showers. However, the very low rate of events potentially generated by neutrinos is a significant challenge for detection techniques and requires both sophisticated algorithms and high-resolution hardware. We developed the FPGA trigger which is generated by a neural network. The algorithm can recognize various waveform types. It has been developed and tested on ADC traces of the Pierre Auger surface detectors. We developed the algorithm of artificial neural network on a MATLAB platform. Trained network that we implemented into the largest Cyclone V E FPGA was used for the prototype of the front-end board for the Auger-Prime. We tested several variants, and the Levenberg–Marquardt algorithm (trainlm) was the most efficient. The network was trained: (a) to recognize 'old' very inclined showers (real Auger data were used as patterns for both positive and negative markers: for reconstructed inclined showers and for triggered by time over threshold (ToT), respectively, (b) to recognize 'neutrino-induced showers'. Here, we used simulated data for positive markers and vertical real showers for negative ones.

Keywords: FPGA, trigger, cosmic rays, detection, neural network, neutrino, inclined showers, Pierre Auger Observatory

1. Introduction

The study of ultrahigh-energy cosmic rays (UHECR) of energy 10^{18}–10^{20} eV significantly speeds up both understanding and activities in both experimental as well as theoretical fields of astroparticle physics [1]. Although many mysteries remain unsolved, such as the origin of the UHECRs, their production mechanism and composition, we are aware that it would be very difficult to explain the production of these energetic particles without associated fluxes of ultrahigh-energy neutrinos (UHEvs) [2, 3].

Generally, we can classify astrophysical models as: 'bottom-up' and 'top-down'. In the first one, protons and nuclei are accelerated from low to higher energies, while pions are produced in interactions of cosmic rays with matter or radiation at the source [4]. The 'top-down' models (based on Grand Unified Theories or Super-symmetries) consider that quark and gluon fragmentations of very heavy particles are a source of protons and neutrons, with an excess of pions compared with nucleons [5]. However, the Pierre Auger Observatory (**Figure 1**) rather disqualifies 'top-down' models because an observed photon stream is much lower than expected from the models [6]. From the other side, the Pierre Auger Observatory [7, 8] confirms the Greisen–Zatsepin–Kuzmin (GZK) cutoff [9, 10] observed also by Fly's Eye [11].

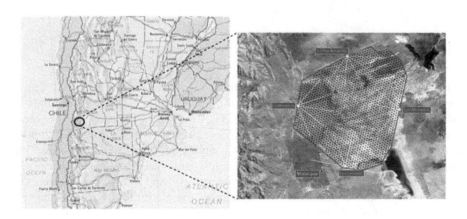

Figure 1. Location of the Southern part of the Pierre Auger Observatory.

In the downward-going channels, neutrinos of all flavours (generated via both charged and neutral current interactions) can develop extensive air showers in the entire path in the atmosphere, also very close to the ground [12].

In the Earth-skimming channel, showers can be induced by products of lepton decays after the interaction of an upward-going inside the Earth [13]. The surface detector of the Pierre Auger Observatory has potentially capabilities to detect neutrino-origin showers (for both the Earth-skimming and downward-going channels) from showers induced by regular cosmic rays for a large zenith angle ($\theta \geq 70°$) [14].

In the bottom-up scenarios, protons and nuclei are accelerated in astrophysical shocks, while pions are produced by cosmic ray interactions with matter or radiation at the source. In the top-down models, protons and neutrons are produced from quark and gluon fragmentations with a production of many more pions than nucleons.

The UHECR flux above ~5×10^{19} eV is significantly suppressed according to expectations based on the UHECRs interaction with the cosmic microwave background (CMB) radiation. For primary protons, the photo-pion production is responsible for the GZK effect; thus, UHEvs are produced from decayed charged pions. However, their fluxes are doubtful and if the primaries are heavy nuclei, the UHEvs should be strongly suppressed [15].

Neutrinos can directly show sources of their production because there is no deflection in magnetic fields. Unlike photons, they travel inviolate from the sources and may give hints for production models. UHEvs can be detected with arrays of detectors at ground level that are currently being used to measure extensive showers produced by cosmic rays [16]. The main challenge is an extraction from the background, induced by regular cosmic rays showers initiated by neutrinos. Due to a very small neutrino cross section for interactions, a higher probability of a detection is at high zenith angles because a bigger atmosphere slant depth provides a thicker target for neutrino interactions. Inclined showers that begin their development deep in the atmosphere can be a signature of neutrino events.

2. Surface detector in the Pierre Auger Observatory

One of the most frequently used detection techniques is a ground array of water Cherenkov tanks, scintillator, calorimeters, utilizing water, liquid or solid plastics, lead as radiators, etc. The parameters of such a ground array (altitude, surface area, spacing between the detector stations) must be adapted to the energy range aimed for. The water Cherenkov tanks are filled by de-ionized water. Ultra-relativistic secondary from extensive air showers (EAS) passing through the water emits Cherenkov light. The light is converted by the PMTs into an electric signal for further processing. The tank is lined with the high-performance DuPont™ Tyvec® protective material (usually used as in a weather-resistant barrier) as a diffuse reflector on the walls. The reflector and high transparency of the super-pure water, with large attenuation length, assure multiple photon reflections and in consequence long electric signal as a response to the light excitation (**Figure 2**).

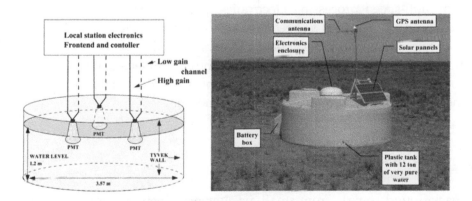

Figure 2. Water Cherenkov tank schematics. Each tank contains 12 tons of water as a radiator. The light is detected by three PMT, and each connected to a high- and a low-gain channel in the local station electronics.

EAS on the ground level hit usually several tanks. The number of hit tanks depends on the energy of the shower and the angle of arrival. The response of the surface detectors to EAS allows an estimation of the energy of the primary cosmic ray. This is obtained through the calculation of the integrated signal at the given distance from the shower axis. The distance is usually chosen to minimize shower-to-shower fluctuations (1000 m in the Pierre Auger Observatory). This signal, called hereafter S(1000) and expressed in vertical equivalent muon (VEM) units, is interpolated after a fit of a lateral distribution function to the observed signals in a given event. Simulations show that it does not depend much on the choice of the lateral distribution function. Calculation of the primary energy from S(1000) by simulation is an advanced topic and may depend on the modelling. The estimation of the primary energy from S(1000) by comparison with simulations is not a sufficient technique. The energy of showers is calculated from the SD data but calibrated from the FD data.

One of the crucial measured parameters allowing inferring characteristics of EAS is the timing of registered signals. 'Time shape' of a signal tells about the size of EAS and on a distance from the core, sharpness of rising edge enriches information on the muon composition, relative timing between neighbouring detectors determines the geometrical configuration and arrival direction of the shower. Time resolution should be good enough not to lose important time-dependent structure.

Muons tend to arrive earlier than electrons and photons and to create shower with relatively flat front, because they suffer much less scattering and so have more direct paths to the ground. Signal differences between muon and electron/photon components of EAS increases with the showers age. Inclined and deeply penetrating showers are muon rich. Muon flat front gives in PMTs a short, sharp response (electric spike). Electrons and photons give much smooth PMT signal profiles, which spread over longer interval. 'Rise time' measurements are the most robust diagnostics of composition for the surface array. Iron showers, which are both muon rich and develop higher in the atmosphere relative to proton showers, have a signal, arriving in a shorter time than that from a proton shower with the same total energy.

A practical realization of very high time resolution system meets significant difficulties. Digitalization of very wide range of signals with high speed requires not only expensive FADC but also very high-speed processing electronics. The measurement system should fetch a reasonable compromise between a speed and performance needed from the physics point of view and the costs, a level of complication, power consumption, longevity and reliability from the point of view of the practical implementation. The current technology provides a sampling of the analogue signals with the speed 40–100 Msps, with reasonable costs, high component integrity and expected reliability in long-term operation.

3. Triggers in the surface detector

The large background coming from small air showers, electronic noise and random coincidences imposes special constraints on triggers, which have to select EAS. Triggers have been accomplished in a hierarchical way both in hardware and in software to select possible interesting events and verify their structure in the consecutive levels. A splitting of triggers on hardware and software implementation is a consequence of the compromise between the speed (the processing of high-rate signals possible by hardware only) and the performance of relatively complicated algorithms investigating timing and relationships between neighbouring detectors (a software realization, possible due to much lower event rate and not necessarily too complicated for a hardware implementation).

The cosmic ray particle flux generates ~2.5 kpps event rate in the water Cherenkov tank. PMT noise adds next few kpps rate. The total background rate (single muon + small showers + PMT dark noise) is estimated on the level ~5 kpps per station. The first level-trigger selects potentially interesting data from an uncorrelated background of several kpps to ~100 pps. The main tasks of the first-level trigger are clipping muon signals to reduce both: the trigger sensitivity to the primary composition and bias from small showers close to the detector, from which the signal is spread over relatively short time. The first function is motivated by the strong dependence of the muon content on the primary species, and the muon content of the shower providing the best handles of the primary composition. The second function is motivated by the increase in the time duration of the signal farther from the shower core. The first-level trigger reduces the contribution of muons to the trigger sum by truncating the pulse height at the programmable threshold and integrating the signal below the clip level. The integration of the truncated signal biases the trigger against nearby small showers, with energy deposit over short time interval. The parallel implementation accepts events with large energy deposition and neglecting their time structure, coming from close to the core of large showers.

The trigger/memory circuit registers and analyses the set of FADC samples in six channels corresponding to the profile of showers. The only high-gain sub-channel generates the trigger. The low-gain channel provides additional information, if the high-gain channel is saturated. The gain tuning of both sub-channels assures 15-bit dynamic range (each channel provides 10-bit dynamic range, with 5-bit overlapping).

Each surface detector generates two-level triggers (T1 and T2). T1 trigger works in two modes:

- a simple threshold trigger (TH) requiring threefold coincidences of three PMTs each above 1.75 I_{peak}^{VEM}. The TH rate is dynamically set on ~100 Hz by the adjustment of high voltages on PMTs. This trigger suppresses an atmospheric muons dependence. It is used to select large signals that are not necessarily spread in time.

- the 'time over threshold' (ToT), which needs at least 13 bins in 120 ADC-bins of a sliding window of 3 μs being above 0.2 I_{peak}^{VEM} threshold in coincidence in 2 out of 3 PMTs. This trigger is especially efficient for small signals spread in time, for example low-energy showers with a dominated EM component or for high-energy showers but far from the detector (**Figure 3**).

The T1 triggers start DAQ in each surface detector: event data are stored on a local memory for 10 s waiting for a possible T3 to be transferred to central data acquisition system (CDAS). T3 trigger is generated by CDAS, when there are spatial and temporal correlations between the local triggers.

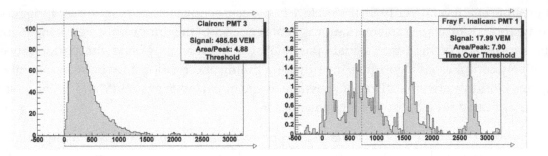

Figure 3. Sample of signals from the same event (#01307007). Signals from Clairon suggest that the shower core passed very close to this tank (Threshold trigger). Signals from Fray F. Inalican relatively weak and spread in time suggest far distance of this tank from the shower core time over threshold trigger).

4. Signal waveform analysis

In very inclined 'old' showers, the EM component is suppressed to a negligible level relatively early in a shower development. On a detection level, only the muon component survives as a muon 'pancake' of ~1 m thick. Such 'pancake' generates a very short signal in surface detectors with a very fast rising edge. These types of ADC traces (very fast jump from a pedestal level with an exponential attenuation tail) are relatively easy to recognize, especially by the algorithm based on the discrete cosine transform. The DCT trigger was already tested on the SD test detector in Malargüe (Argentina). The algorithm precisely can recognize signals of predefined shapes. The ANN algorithm is an alternative approach.

'Young' showers are spread in time over hundreds of nanoseconds. They contain also a part of EM component, which extends the signal waveforms in time. Nevertheless, the muonic component of 'young' showers overtakes the EM one and gives an early bump. The rising edge of the bump is softer than the 'old' showers, but this signal is also relatively quickly attenuated, till the EM component starts to give its own contribution. The ANN approach focuses on the early bump, to select traces potentially generated by neutrinos. Simulations of showers in CORSIKA and a calculation of the response of the surface detectors in offline showed that for neutrino showers (initiated either by ν_μ or ν_τ) for relatively big zenith angle (i.e. >70°) and low altitude (<9 km) give relatively short signal waveforms and they can be analysed also by 16-point pattern engines.

5. CORSIKA and offline simulations

5.1. Artificial neuron network: data preparation

The main motivation of an ANN implementation as a shower trigger is that up to now, and the entire array did not register any neutrino-induced event. Our idea was to use the ANN approach as a pattern recognition technique. The input data for the ANN are simulated traces of protons and muon neutrinos, which hit the atmosphere at high zenith angles—80°, 85° and 89°, respectively. The chosen energies of primary particles are 3×10^8, 10^9, 3×10^9 and 10^{10} GeV, respectively. The distances from the place of the first interaction to the detector used for simulations are dependent of the angle and the type of particle (**Table 1**). We decided not to simulate protons that are very close to the detector, because the probability that the protons will not interact to detector is very low. Additionally, traces produced by this kind of interactions may also include the electromagnetic part of the shower. These traces would look completely different than the rest and may significantly decrease the efficiency of the ANN.

		500	1000	2000	3000	4000	5000	10,000
80°	p			YES	YES	YES		
	ν	YES	YES	YES	YES	YES		
85°	p			YES	YES	YES	YES	
	ν	YES	YES	YES	YES	YES	YES	
89°	p			YES	YES	YES	YES	YES
	ν	YES	YES	YES	YES	YES	YES	YES

All distances are in g/cm². Distances are correlated with an angle.

Table 1. Distances from the place of the first interaction to detector for proton and muon neutrinos in dependence of zenith angle.

We investigated 120 different categories of events (30 active categories from **Table 1** × 4 energies). These categories are used as input by the CORSIKA simulation platform. The CORSIKA program simulates the cosmic ray shower initiated by the specific particle. The result of this simulation is the distribution of the position and energies of the particles on the level of the detector. Simulations are relatively fast. The simulated cosmic ray showers are the input for the offline package, which provides a response to the water Cherenkov detector and generates the ADC traces (signal waveforms). These simulations are very time-consuming. As a result, we obtained simulated traces from the photo-multipliers, as if they were triggered by a standard T1 trigger. We have proven that a 16-point input is sufficient for the ANN pattern recognition [17] (**Figure 4**). The next step was to find in the 16-point trace, which corresponds

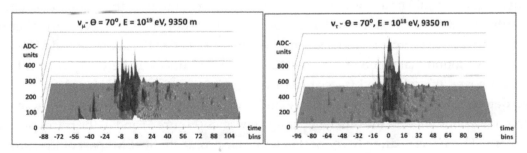

Figure 4. Simulated signal waveforms for 10^{19} and 10^{18} eV for initial ν_μ and ν_τ, respectively, at 9350 m and 70° zenith angle.

to triggered events. To see the beginning of the event clearly, we decided that first two points should be on the pedestal level. Afterwards, we subtracted the pedestal level from all used data.

5.2. Training and testing steps

For a training procedure, we decided to use half of the data available for the testing procedure. We arranged the data, to have proton and neutrino traces alternately. The proton traces were treated as negative signals ('0' for the ANN), and the neutrino traces were treated as positive ones ('1' for the ANN). This step allowed the ANN to be taught faster and to have fewer errors while training. The testing procedure consisted of assigning a specific value to the trace. This value depends on the coefficients of the trained ANN. If the value is greater than the threshold, the trace is treated as a neutrino trace; otherwise, it is treated as a proton trace. The efficiency of the neutrino recognition with a specific threshold level can be defined as the number of neutrino traces recognized correctly divided by the number of all neutrino traces. The proton mistakes level is defined as the number of proton traces treated as neutrino traces divided by the number of all proton traces.

The testing procedure was divided into two stages. First, we wanted to find out if we could use the data from the specific category to distinguish muon neutrinos and protons for all the angles or all the energies. Simulated data contains only three different angles: 80°, 85° and 89°, respectively, but we did not expect the zenith angle of the particle to be exactly like them. If the ANN trained on the specific category with an angle of 85° can also distinguish neutrinos and protons for 89° and 80° with acceptable efficiency, we assumed it could also distinguish protons and neutrinos for a full angle range: 80°–89°. The same assumptions have been established for energies. The ANN had been also trained by the data of the specific energy, and it was then tested on the other values of the chosen parameter. The second step of the testing procedure consisted of training the ANN by the randomly taken data from all categories.

5.3. Increasing the efficiency

The efficiency of the ANN strongly depends on the data used for training. The positive and negative signals should be as different as possible in order to increase the distinction of proton and neutrino traces. Our first results have shown that ANN does not work properly. There was no separation between protons and neutrinos. When we looked at the data we used for teaching the ANN, we found that some of the neutrino and proton traces looked very similar to each other. Moreover, the simulated traces produced by neutrino showers with various distances to the detector, but with the same energy and angle, and were diametrically different. We observed the same effect in the other angles and energies (**Figure 5**) and in the traces produced by protons. This effect is directly connected to the electromagnetic (EM) part of the shower. If the distance to the detector is short, the EM part of the shower gives a second component in the traces, in addition to the standard muonic one.

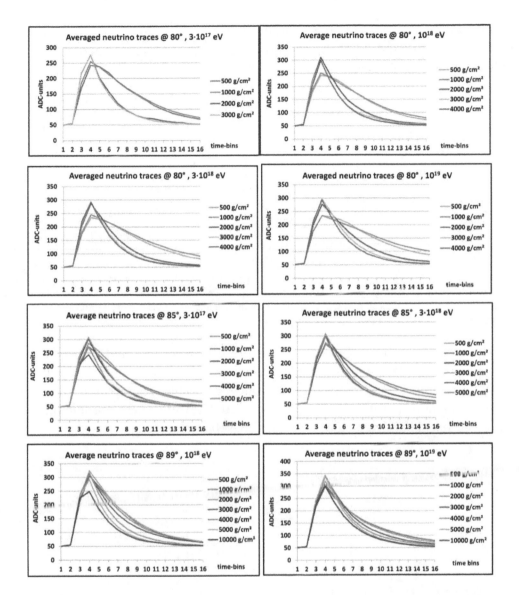

Figure 5. Plots contain averaged muon neutrino signal waveforms (ADC traces) for various angles, energies and initialization points. The exponents of the traces at distances 500 and 1000 g/cm² are different than on the rest of distances. This effect does not depend on the energy and slightly depend on the angle.

At high zenith angles, the proton showers should not have the EM component, because it should disappear after 2000–3000 g/cm². Old neutrino showers looked like old proton–neutrino showers, so we decided to separate the data and focus on recognizing only the young neutrino showers, where the EM component was still visible. We also decided to remove proton showers with a visible EM component, because the traces that they generated looked similar to traces generated by young neutrino showers.

Moreover, for these showers, the probability of occurrence at this angle was low. The data we decided to keep were for all neutrino traces with distances 500 and 1000 g/cm², and all proton traces with two maximal distances for each angle.

Figure 6 shows the average traces for data at 80 after the separation. Neutrino and proton traces have completely different shapes, so it should be easier to recognize the neutrino traces when ANN is learned and tested based on this data.

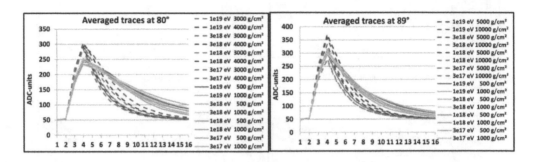

Figure 6. Plots show the differences between the traces produced by old proton showers (without markers) and young neutrino showers (with markers). Traces can be recognized on a base of exponential attenuation factors especially for relatively low angles (80°). Graphs show that for large zenith angles and very wide energy ranges, 'old' proton showers are attenuated faster than 'young' neutrino showers.

Figure 7 shows the histogram of the average exponents of rejected and accepted proton and neutrino categories. We can see that the exponents of the rejected neutrino categories correspond with exponents of the accepted proton categories. This was probably the main reason for the low distinction of protons and neutrinos by ANN. Additionally, the average exponents of the accepted proton and neutrino categories are separated.

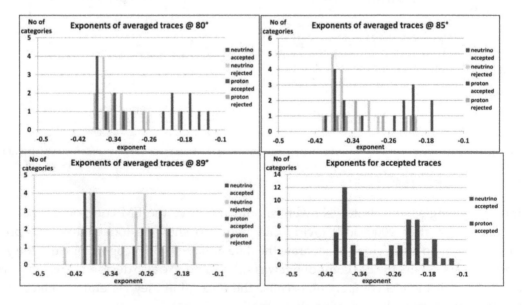

Figure 7. Histograms of exponents of rejected and accepted traces for protons and neutrinos. The accepted neutrino traces exponents are separated from the accepted proton traces exponents.

The rejected neutrino traces look very similar to traces made by old proton showers. This may cause problems with ANN training and may increase the level of the proton traces recognized as neutrino traces by the ANN. Nevertheless, the last graph shows that a proton–neutrino pattern recognition seems to be possible. Training by patterns for only 'old' proton showers and 'young' neutrino showers seems to be justified as protons start their interactions just in the beginning of the atmosphere, while the probability of neutrino interactions high in the atmosphere is negligible.

6. MATLAB analysis

Figure 8 shows the ANN efficiency versus angles and energies. If all data from simulation, independently of the origin point (of old and young, and of both proton and neutrino events), are taken for teaching, the network recognitions is poor. Proton background (spuriously recognized) is relatively high, and the efficiency of the neutrino event recognition is also poor. However, if in the teaching process we use dedicated young neutrino and old proton patterns the recognition efficiency significantly increases. The ANN tested on non-separated traces has problems distinguishing the proton and neutrinos on every level of the threshold. The efficiency of a recognition of neutrino traces and the level of proton mistakes differ only slightly. The ANN, tested on the separated traces, can recognize protons and neutrinos with acceptable efficiency. The proton mistakes level is much lower than the recognition efficiency of neutrino traces; moreover, the efficiency of finding neutrino traces is higher than in the previous case.

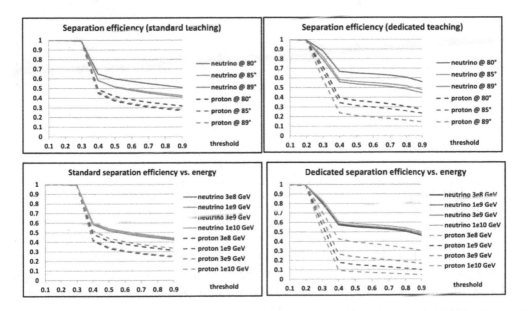

Figure 8. The graphs show the separation efficiency of the neutrino events from the proton background as a function of the threshold for various angles and energies of the initial particle. The 'standard' graphs show the efficiency for a network teaching on the basis of a wide range of initial points of the first interaction. The 'dedicated' graphs show the efficiency when the network is trained by patterns corresponding to 'young' neutrino events and 'old' proton ones. A higher level of the proton background (spuriously recognized) for lower angles (80°) comes with a higher probability of the EM.

Right graph on **Figure 8** shows our choice for future tests. The efficiency of neutrino recognition is independent of energy and on a relatively high level (0.5–0.6), while proton spuriously recognized events are on a low level especially for low energies: 3×10^8–10^9 GeV. For higher energies, signals are generally stronger, and there is a much higher probability of their recognition by a standard threshold triggers.

Preliminary results show that more complicated networks do not improve a pattern recognition on a level that justified an increment of structure complication, resources occupancy, or, finally, of much greater requirements for a budget. We did not notice that the structure from **Figure 9a** was superior over **Figure 9b**. Moreover, the much more complicated networks, 24-16-1 and 36-24-1 showed minimal improvement in comparison with a much simpler network, 12-8-1. The networks 24-16-1, and especially 36-24-1, require a huge amount of FPGA resources (especially DSP blocks). The biggest chip 5CEA9F31I7 from the low-cost FPGA family Cyclone® V contains 684 of 18 × 18 DSP embedded multipliers, while the biggest chip 5AGXB7 from the Arria® V family contains 2312 of 18 × 18 DSP blocks (the biggest chip 10AT115 from the Arria® 10 medium-cost FPGA family contains 3036 of 18 × 19 multipliers). However, the prices of Arria FPGAs are unacceptable for a mass production of the front-end boards (**Figure 12**).

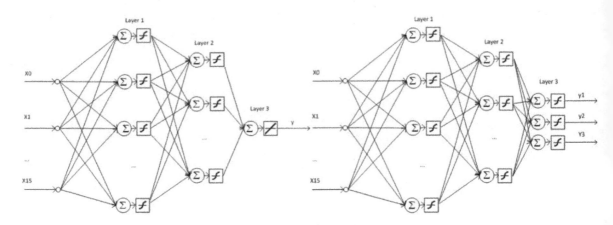

Figure 9. An internal structure of an FPGA neuron network with tansig function scaling output neuron data between consecutive layers. This right net contains more advanced last layer, which tries to separate patterns with higher efficiency.

Independently of the FPGA prices, the crucial factor becomes power consumption. Mid-size FPGAs (Arria® V or 10 as well as Stratix® IV or V families) are optimized for maximum performance, while a power budget is not a priority. Nevertheless, our estimations show that more complicated networks 24-16-1 or 36-24-1 minimally improve a neutrino–proton separation; a significantly higher cost for the implementation these networks with a much more expensive FPGA is not justified (**Figure 11**).

For training of the neural networks, we used real Auger ADC traces triggered either by the TH-T1 or by the ToT trigger [14] (**Figure 10**). Due to relatively high thresholds, the TH-T1 trigger trespasses relatively strong signals. We know that up to now the Pierre Auger Observatory did not register any event potentially generated by neutrinos. The reason may be the configuration of the standard trigger (threefold coincidence in a single time slot), which does not take into account a de-synchronization of signals [18]. The probability of de-synchronization increases for higher sampling frequencies. The Cherenkov light can simultaneously reach all PMT only for specific conditions of the angle and the input position of the trespassing ultra-relativistic particle due to a geometry of the surface detector (<8%).

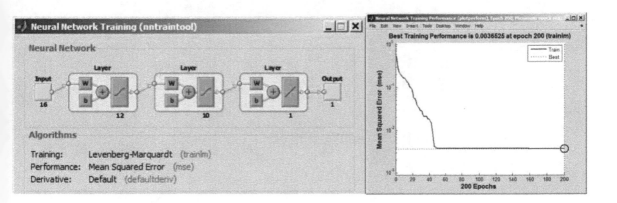

Figure 10. The MATLAB neural network tool used for teaching according to Levenberg-Marquardt algorithm (left). The right graph shows a convergence during training.

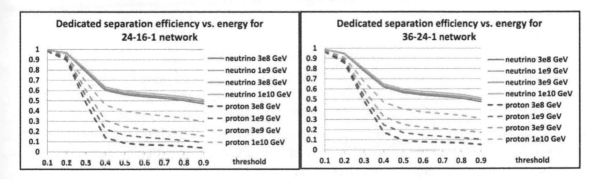

Figure 11. Efficiency of neutrino-proton separation for 24-16-1 and 36-24-1 neural networks.

Practically only twofold coincidences can give events of very inclined showers. A reflected light reaches the third PMT with a delay 'firing' the PMT in later time slots and also too low amplitude of signals for low energetic initial particles maybe the reason. We were teaching the network to recognize patterns with decreased amplitudes. The database was artificially extended by the real signal waveforms with reduced amplitudes by factors of 0.67, 0.5 and 0.25, respectively, keeping the same pedestals and shapes.

Figure 12. The front-end board with Cyclone V E FPGA used for high-resolution tests in the Pierre Auger Engineering Array.

7. FPGA implementation

Figure 9 shows an internal structure of an FPGA neuron network with tansig function scaling output neuron data between consecutive layers. Each neuron (**Figure 13**) output (before a connection to the next layer) has to be scaled by a neural transfer function to focus a response on a most important data region. Typically, the transfer function is a hyperbolic tangent sigmoid (tansig—**Figure 14**). The constant coefficients were implemented in the ROM (**Figure 17**). We selected dual-port memory (two addresses inputs and two independent data outputs by the same content) to reduce a resource occupancy.

The fundamental algorithm for each neuron is as follows:

$$Neuron_{out} = \sum_{k=0}^{n-1} ADC_k \times C_{k,layer} + bias_{k,layer} \tag{1}$$

We implemented 16,384-word dual-port ROM with 14-bit output in order to keep a sufficient accuracy with a reasonable size of the embedded memory

$$f_{index} = \frac{2}{1 + e^{-2\frac{index-8192}{sf}}} - 1 \tag{2}$$

The ADC output is connected to 12-bit shift registers whose sequential outputs drive neuron inputs. A teaching process of MATLAB generates a set of coefficients represented by 'double' variables. An implementation of floating point coefficients in the FPGA slows down significantly a register performance and dramatically increases resource occupancy. Practically, the accuracy in a fixed-point approach is absolutely sufficient. There is no need to calculate an individual neuron response in a very high precision due to general uncertainties in this estimation process.

At least two embedded DSP multipliers have to be used for a single multiplication of 12-bit input data. If we select 32-bit data width, the maximal width of the coefficients is 20-bit.

Figure 14 shows shapes of tansig function for various parameterizations. For our training data, the best scaling factor is sf = 1536, which corresponds to the range of (−5.33,…,+5.33).

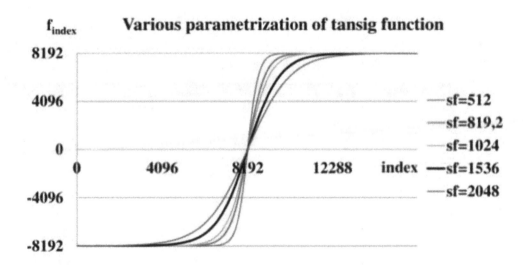

Figure 13. Altera IP floating-point procedures. A multiplication of 64-bit variables requires at least five clock cycles, a summation at least seven clock cycles, respectively.

A floating-point variables in the FPGA contain from sign bit (MSB), mantisa and exponent. Double variables require 64-bit representations (52-bit mantisa and 11-bit exponent). Summation and multiplication require at least seven and five clock cycles latency, respectively (**Figure 13**).

Signed variables in the FPGA logic require two-component representation. Altera provides fixed-point IP-core routine (ALTMULT_ADD) for four parallel multiplications and partial results summation (**Figure 15**). In order to keep 32-bit output size, coefficients must be 18-bit only (**Figure 16**).

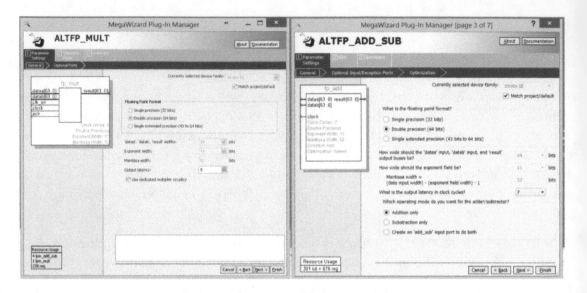

Figure 14. Tested parameterizations of tansig function for the best optimization.

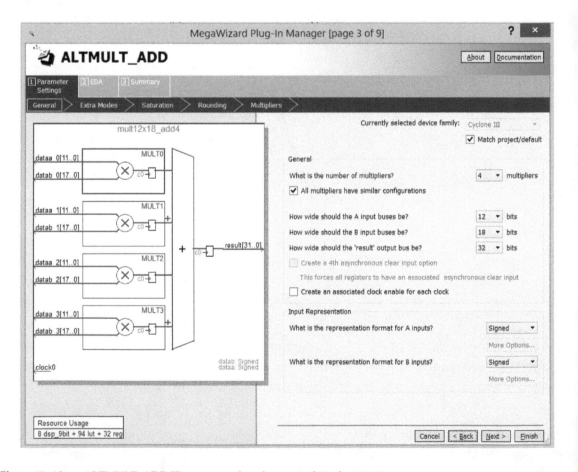

Figure 15. Altera ALTMULT_ADD IP-core procedure for a neural implementation.

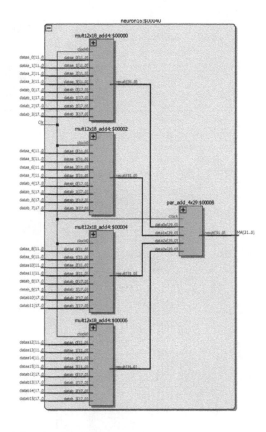

Figure 16. An internal structure of the 16-point FPGA neuron.

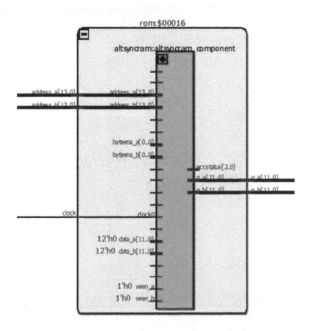

Figure 17. An implementation of the tansig function into ROM (above).

Layer	SFS	SFL	SFX	SFB	SHP	SHN
1	2	131,072	8	524,288	–	6
2	4	32,768	8	32,768	14	1
3	2	32,768	2	32,768	13	1

Table 2. Scaling, suppression and shift factors.

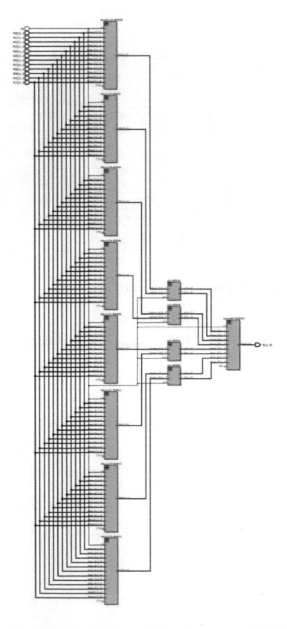

Figure 18. A structure of connections in two last layers: eight 12-input neurons + 4 ROM blocks with tansig functions + the last 8-input neuron (left graph).

Table 2 shows all factors for scaling, suppressions and finally shifts of data. At first, coefficients (coeff and bias) calculated by MATLAB are suppressed [by the factors SFS and SFX, respectively, to get a range (−1.0,…+1.0)]. Next, they are scaled by factors SFL and SFB, respectively.

$$coeff_{k,layer,fixed-point} = coeff_{k,layer} \frac{SFL}{SFS} \tag{3}$$

$$bias_{k,layer,fixed-point} = bias_{k,layer} \frac{SFB}{SFX} \tag{4}$$

The 32-bit signed output of neuron (starting from the second layer) is shifted right before a summation with the bias due to very large values from the tansig transfer function (mostly either ~−8192 or ~8191).

$$P = \left(\sum_{k=0}^{n-1} ADC_k \times C_{k,layer} \right) \rangle\rangle SHP \; address_{k,layer} = (P \rangle\rangle SHP) + 8192 \tag{5}$$

Addresses for tansig function are additionally optimized to use the most sensitive function response region. The highest bits from the neuron are neglected as irrelevant for a big argument of the tansig transfer function. Addresses are cropped to the range 0,…,16,383 (**Figure 18**).

8. Simulations for the FPGA

A relatively old tool—the Quartus simulator was used for simulations as much faster than currently recommended ModelSim. The structure of the neuron network has been implemented into several FPGA families: Cyclone III, Stratix III and Cyclone V. A response of neural network on trained patterns was verified for 16-point inputs with fixed coefficients calculated in MATLAB.

Figure 19 show Quartus simulations of selected traces. Inclined showers correspond to positive markers, and vertical showers correspond to negative markers. A recognition of selected patterns is on very high level. We simulated 160 events (totally 122,880 samples). One hundred and sixty one patterns were recognized as positive markers: 160 inclined showers and only a single false event. Among 160 vertical showers used as reference ones (with negative markers), the network recognized 39 events faulty; however, 12 with high amplitudes, which should be detected also by a standard trigger.

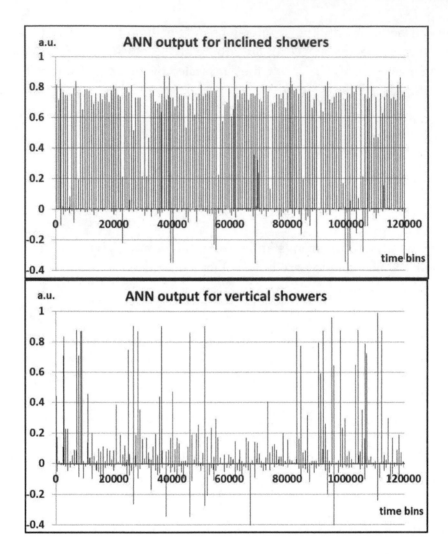

Figure 19. Graphs show the output of 12-8-1 neural network for positive-marked inclined showers (upper graph) and negative-marked vertical showers. Each graph shows 122,880 samples (768 samples/event). Outputs from the third neural layer are scaled to a range (−1,…,+1).

9. Conclusion

We simulated several showers initialized by ν_μ and ν_τ using the CORSIKA package. Output CORSIKA data (particles energies, momentum, coordinates, etc.) calculated for 1450 m a.s.l (a level of the Pierre Auger Observatory) were used offline package for simulations of a surface detector response, that is shape of ADC traces after a digitization of PMTs Cherenkov light-induced signals. These ADC waveforms were the patterns for a training process of the neural network. Analysis of results for Cyclone V E FPGA 5CEFA7F31I7 is very promising. It shows that the ANN algorithm can recognize neutrino events that are at present neglected by the standard Auger triggers.

The recognition efficiency of the neutrino traces by the ANN algorithm strongly depends on the differences between the data used for the ANN training. If we teach the ANN with the data containing only traces produced by young neutrino and old proton cosmic air showers, we can reach an acceptable level of recognition. Moreover, we can distinguish protons and neutrinos, which means that the ANN works on a very promising level.

Acknowledgements

This work is supported by the National Science Centre (Poland) under NCN Grant No. 2013/08/M/ST9/00322. The authors would like to thank the Pierre Auger Collaboration for an opportunity of using the CORSIKA and offline simulation packages.

Author details

Zbigniew Szadkowski*, Dariusz Głas and Krzysztof Pytel

*Address all correspondence to: zszadkow@kfd2.phys.uni.lodz.pl

Department of Physics and Applied Informatics, University of Łódź, Łódź, Poland

References

[1] M. Nagano, A. Watson. Observations and implications of the ultrahigh-energy cosmic rays. Rev. Mod. Phys. 2000;72(3):689–732. doi:10.1103/RevModPhys.72.689

[2] V. S. Berezinsky, A. Y. Smirnov. Cosmic neutrinos of ultrahigh energies and detection possibility. Astrophys. Space Sci. 1975;32(2):461482. doi:10.1007/BF00643157[2]

[3] F. Halzen, D. Hooper. High-energy neutrino astronomy: the cosmic ray connection. Rep. Progr. Phys. 2002;65(7):1025. doi:10.1088/0034-4885/65/7/201

[4] J. K. Becker. High-energy neutrinos in the context of multi-messenger astrophysics. Phys. Rep. 2008;458(4–5):173246. doi:10.1016/j.physrep.2007.10.006

[5] P. Bhattacharjee, G. Sigl. Origin and propagation of extremely high-energy cosmic rays. Phys. Rep. 2000;327(3–4):109–247. doi:10.1016/S0370-1573(99)00101-5

[6] J. Abraham et al. [Pierre Auger Collaboration]. Upper limit on the cosmic-ray photon fraction at EeV energies from the Pierre Auger Observatory. Astropart. Phys. 2009;31:399–406. doi:10.1016/j.astropartphys.2009.04.003

[7] J. Abraham et al. [Pierre Auger Collaboration]. Properties and performance of the prototype instrument for the Pierre Auger Observatory. Nucl. Instrum. Methods. 2004;A523(1–2):5095. doi:10.1016/j.nima.2003.12.012

[8] J. Abraham et al. [Pierre Auger Collaboration]. Observation of the suppression of the flux of cosmic rays above 4×10^{19} eV. Phys. Rev. Lett. 2008;101(6):061101. doi:10.1103/PhysRevLett.101.061101

[9] K. Greisen. End to the cosmic-ray spectrum. Phys. Rev. Lett. 1966;16:748–750. [9] doi:10.1103/PhysRevLett.16.748

[10] G. T. Zatsepin, V. A. Kuzmin. Upper limit of the spectrum of cosmic rays. Pisma v Zhurnal Eksperimentalnoi i Teoreticheskoi Fiziki. 1966;4:114. WOS:A19668298400011

[11] R. U. Abbasi et al. [Hi-Res Fly's Eye Collaboration]. First observation of the Greisen–Zatsepin–Kuzmin suppression. Phys. Rev. Lett. 2008;100(10):101101. [11] doi:10.1103/PhysRevLett.100.101101

[12] K. S. Capelle, J. W. Cronin, G. Parente, E. Zas. On the detection of ultra high energy neutrinos with the Auger Observatory. Astropart. Phys. 1998;8(4):321328. [12] doi:10.1016/S0927-6505(97)00059-5

[13] X. Bertou, P. Billoir, O. Deligny, C. Lachaud, A. Letessier-Selvon. Tau neutrinos in the auger observatory: a new window to UHECR sources. Astropart. Phys. 2002;17(2):183193. doi:10.1016/S0927-6505(01)00147-5

[14] J. Abraham et al. [Pierre Auger Collaboration]. Trigger and aperture of the surface detector array of the Pierre Auger Observatory. Nucl. Instrum. Methods. 2010;A613:29–39. doi:10.1016/j.nima.2009.11.018

[15] K. Kotera, D. Allard, A. V. Olinto. Cosmogenic neutrinos: parameter space and detectability from PeV to ZeV. JCAP. 2010;20(10):013. doi:10.1088/1475-7516/2010/10/013

[16] E. Zas. Neutrino detection with inclined air showers. New J. Phys. 2005;7:130. doi:10.1088/1367-2630/7/1/130

[17] Z. Szadkowski, K. Pytel. Artificial neural network as a FPGA trigger for a detection of very inclined air showers. IEEE Trans. Nucl. Sci. 2015;62(3):1002–1009. doi:10.1109/TNS.2015.2421412

[18] Z. Szadkowski. Optimization of the detection of very inclined showers using a spectral DCT trigger in arrays of surface detectors. IEEE Trans. Nucl. Sci. 2013;60(5):3647–3653. doi:10.1109/TNS.2013.2280639

4

Bayesian Regularized Neural Networks for Small *n* Big *p* Data

Hayrettin Okut

Additional information is available at the end of the chapter

Abstract

Artificial neural networks (ANN) mimic the function of the human brain and they have the capability to implement massively parallel computations for mapping, function approximation, classification, and pattern recognition processing. ANN can capture the highly nonlinear associations between inputs (predictors) and target (responses) variables and can adaptively learn the complex functional forms. Like other parametric and nonparametric methods, such as kernel regression and smoothing splines, ANNs can introduce overfitting (in particular with highly-dimensional data, such as genome wide association -GWAS-, microarray data etc.) and resulting predictions can be outside the range of the training data. Regularization (shrinkage) in ANN allows bias of parameter estimates towards what are considered to be probable. Most common techniques of regularizations techniques in ANN are the Bayesian regularization (BR) and the early stopping methods. Early stopping is effectively limiting the used weights in the network and thus imposes regularization, effectively lowering the Vapnik-Chervonenkis dimension. In Bayesian regularized ANN (BRANN), the regularization techniques involve imposing certain prior distributions on the model parameters and penalizes large weights in anticipation of achieving smoother mapping.

Keywords: artificial neural network, Bayesian regularization, shrinkage, $p \gg n$, prediction ability

1. Introduction

The issue of dimensionality of independent variables (i.e. when the number of observations is comparable to or larger than the sample size; small *n* big *p*; $p \gg n$) has garnered much attention over the last few years, primarily due to the fact that high-dimensional data are so common in up-to-date applications (e.g. microarray data, fMRI image processing, next generation sequencing, and many others assays of social and educational data). This issue is of particular interest in the field of human molecular genetics as the growing number of common single nucleotide polymorphisms (minor allele frequency > 0.01) available for assay in a single experiment, now close to 10 million (http://www.genome.gov/11511175), is quickly outpacing researchers' ability to increase sample sizes which typically number in the thousands to tens of thousands. Further, human studies of associations between molecular markers and any trait of interest include the possible presence of cryptic relationships between individuals that may not be tractable for use in traditional statistical models. These associations have been investigated primarily using a naïve single regression model for each molecular marker and linear regression models using Bayesian framework and some machine learning techniques typically ignoring interactions and non-linearity [1]. Soft computing techniques have also been used extensively to extract the necessary information from these types of data structures. As a universal approximator, Artificial Neural Networks (ANNs) are a powerful technique for extracting information from large data, in particular for $p \gg n$ studies, and provide a computational approach with the ability to optimize the learning algorithm and make discoveries about functional forms in an adaptive approach [2, 3]. Moreover, ANNs offer several advantages, including requiring less formal statistical training, an ability to perfectly identify complex nonlinear relationships between dependent and independent variables, an ability to detect all possible interactions between input variables, and the availability of multiple training algorithms [4]. In general, the ANN architecture, or "model" in statistical jargon, is classified by the fashion in which neurons in a neural network are connected. Generally speaking, there are two different classes of ANN architecture (although each one has several subclasses). These are *feedforward* ANNs and *recurrent* ANNs. Only Bayesian regularized multilayer perceptron (MLP) *feedforward* ANNs will be discussed in this chapter.

This chapter begins with introducing of multilayer feedforward architectures. The regularization using other backpropagation algorithms to avoid overfitting will be explained briefly. Then Bayesian regularization (BR) for overfitting, Levenberg-Marquardt (LM) a training algorithm, BR, optimization of hyper parameters, inferring model parameters for given value of hyper parameters, pre-processing of data will be considered. Chapter will be ended with a MATLAB example for Bayesian Regularized feedforward multilayer artificial neural network (BRANN).

2. Multilayer perceptron feedforward neural networks

The MLP feedforward neural network considered herein is the most popular and most widely used ANN paradigm in many practical applications. The network is fully connected and divided into layers as depicted in **Figure 1**. In the left-most layer, there are input variables. The input layer consists of p_i (p=4 in **Figure 1** for illustration) independent variables and covariates. Then input layer is followed by a hidden layer, which consists of S number of neurons (S=3 in **Figure 1**), and there is a bias specific to each neuron. Algebraically, the process can be represented as follows. Let t_i (the target or dependent variable) be a trait (quantitative or qualitative) measured in individual i and let $p_i = \{p_{ij}\}$ be a vector of inputs (independent variables) or any other covariate measured for each individual. Suppose there are S neurons in the hidden layer. The input into neuron k ($k=1, 2,\ldots, S$) prior to activation, as described in greater detail later in this chapter, is the linear function $w'_k\, p_i$, where $w'_k = \{w_{kj}\}$ is a vector of unknown connection strengths (slope in regression model) peculiar to neuron k, including a bias (e.g. the intercept in regression model). Each neuron in the hidden layer performs a weighted summation (n_i in **Figure 1**) of the inputs prior to activation which is then passed to a nonlinear activation function

$$f_k\left(b_k^{(1)} + \sum_{j=1}^{P} w_{kj} p_j\right).$$ Suppose the activation function chosen in the hidden layer is the

hyperbolic tangent transformation $f(x_i) = \dfrac{e^{x_i} - e^{-x_i}}{e^{x_i} + e^{-x_i}}$, where $f(x_i)$ is the neuron emission for

input variables [3]. Based on the illustration given in the **Figure 1**, the output of each neuron (shown as purple, orange, and green nodes) in the hidden layer (t_h) with hyperbolic tangent transformation are calculated as in equation (1).

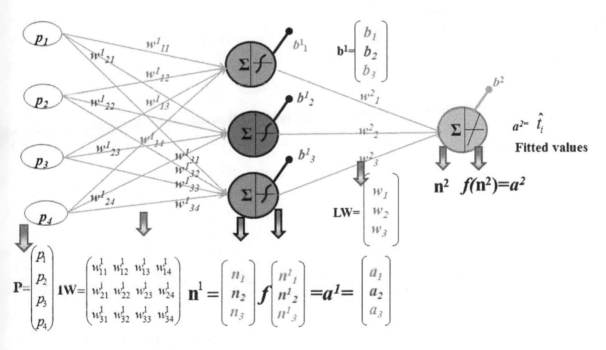

Figure 1. Artificial neural network design with 4 inputs (p_i). Each input is connected to up to 3 neurons via coefficients $w^{(l)}_{kj}$ (l denotes layer; j denotes neuron; k denotes input variable). Each hidden and output neuron has a bias parameter $b^{(l)}_j$. Here **P** = inputs, **IW** = weights from input to hidden layer (12 weights), **LW** = weights from hidden to output layer (3 weights), b^1 = Hidden layer biases (3 biases), b^2 = Output layer biases (1 bias), $n^1 = \textbf{IWP} + b^1$ is the weighted summation of the first layer, $a^1 = f(n^1)$ is output of hidden layer, $n^2 = \textbf{LW}a^1 + b^2$ is weighted summation of the second layer, and $\hat{t} = a^2 = f\left(n^2\right)$ is the predicted value of the network. The total number of parameters for this ANN is 12+3+3+1 =19.

$$t_{hidden} = \beta_0 + \beta_1 \left(\frac{\exp(b_1^1 + w_{11}^1 p_1 + w_{12}^1 p_2 + w_{13}^1 p_3 + w_{14}^1 p_4) - \exp(-b_1^1 - w_{11}^1 p_1 - w_{12}^1 p_2 - w_{13}^1 p_3 - w_{14}^1 p_4)}{\exp(b_1^1 + w_{11}^1 p_1 + w_{12}^1 p_2 + w_{13}^1 p_3 + w_{14}^1 p_4) + \exp(-b_1^1 - w_{11}^1 p_1 - w_{12}^1 p_2 - w_{13}^1 p_3 - w_{14}^1 p_4)} \right) \quad \text{ORANGE}$$

$$+ \beta_2 \left(\frac{\exp(b_2^1 + w_{21}^1 p_1 + w_{22}^1 p_2 + w_{23}^1 p_3 + w_{24}^1 p_4) - \exp(-b_2^1 - w_{21}^1 p_1 - w_{22}^1 p_2 - w_{23}^1 p_3 - w_{24}^1 p_4)}{\exp(b_2^1 + w_{21}^1 p_1 + w_{22}^1 p_2 + w_{23}^1 p_3 + w_{24}^1 p_4) + \exp(-b_2^1 - w_{21}^1 p_1 - w_{22}^1 p_2 - w_{23}^1 p_3 - w_{24}^1 p_4)} \right) \quad \text{PURPLE} \quad (1)$$

$$+ \beta_3 \left(\frac{\exp(b_3^1 + w_{31}^1 p_1 + w_{32}^1 p_2 + w_{33}^1 p_3 + w_{34}^1 p_4) - \exp(-b_3^1 - w_{31}^1 p_1 - w_{32}^1 p_2 - w_{33}^1 p_3 - w_{34}^1 p_4)}{\exp(b_3^1 + w_{31}^1 p_1 + w_{32}^1 p_2 + w_{33}^1 p_3 + w_{34}^1 p_4) + \exp(-b_3^1 - w_{31}^1 p_1 - w_{32}^1 p_2 - w_{33}^1 p_3 - w_{34}^1 p_4)} \right) \quad \text{GREEN}$$

The hidden layer outputs from neurons (orange, purple, and green) are the input of the next layer. After the activation function, the output from the hidden layer is then sent to the output layer again with weighted summation as $\sum_{k=1}^{S} w_k' f_k \left(b_k^{(1)} + \sum_{j=1}^{P} w_{kj} p_j \right) + b^{(2)}$, where w_k are weights specific to each neuron and $b^{(1)}$ and $b^{(2)}$ are bias parameters in the hidden and output layers, respectively. Finally, this quantity is again activated with the same or another activation function $g(.)$ as $g \left[\sum_{k=1}^{S} w_k' f_k(.) + b^{(2)} \right] = a^2 = \hat{t}$, which then becomes the predicted value $\hat{t}_i$ of the target variable in the training set. For instance, the predicted value $\hat{t}_i$ of the output layer based on details given in **Figure 1** and equation (1) can be calculated as,

$$\hat{t} = a^2 = g \left[\sum_{k=1}^{S} w_k' f_k(.) + b^{(2)} \right] = g \left[\begin{array}{c} \left(\frac{\exp(b_1^1 + w_{11}^1 p_1 + w_{12}^1 p_2 + w_{13}^1 p_3 + w_{14}^1 p_4) - \exp(-b_1^1 - w_{11}^1 p_1 - w_{12}^1 p_2 - w_{13}^1 p_3 - w_{14}^1 p_4)}{\exp(b_1^1 + w_{11}^1 p_1 + w_{12}^1 p_2 + w_{13}^1 p_3 + w_{14}^1 p_4) + \exp(-b_1^1 - w_{11}^1 p_1 - w_{12}^1 p_2 - w_{13}^1 p_3 - w_{14}^1 p_4)} \right) w_1^2 + \\ \left(\frac{\exp(b_2^1 + w_{21}^1 p_1 + w_{22}^1 p_2 + w_{23}^1 p_3 + w_{24}^1 p_4) - \exp(-b_2^1 - w_{21}^1 p_1 - w_{22}^1 p_2 - w_{23}^1 p_3 - w_{24}^1 p_4)}{\exp(b_2^1 + w_{21}^1 p_1 + w_{22}^1 p_2 + w_{23}^1 p_3 + w_{24}^1 p_4) + \exp(-b_2^1 - w_{21}^1 p_1 - w_{22}^1 p_2 - w_{23}^1 p_3 - w_{24}^1 p_4)} \right) w_2^2 + \\ \left(\frac{\exp(b_3^1 + w_{31}^1 p_1 + w_{32}^1 p_2 + w_{33}^1 p_3 + w_{34}^1 p_4) - \exp(-b_3^1 - w_{31}^1 p_1 - w_{32}^1 p_2 - w_{33}^1 p_3 - w_{34}^1 p_4)}{\exp(b_3^1 + w_{31}^1 p_1 + w_{32}^1 p_2 + w_{33}^1 p_3 + w_{34}^1 p_4) + \exp(-b_3^1 - w_{31}^1 p_1 - w_{32}^1 p_2 - w_{33}^1 p_3 - w_{34}^1 p_4)} \right) w_3^2 \end{array} + b^2 \right] \quad (2)$$

This can be illustrated as,

$$\hat{t}_i = \textit{fitted value} = a^2 = g(n^2) = g\left[\Sigma \right] = g\left[w_1^2 \bigcirc{-f} + w_2^2 \bigcirc{-f} + w_3^2 \bigcirc{-f} + b^2 \right]$$

The activation function applied to the output layer depends on the type of target (dependent) variable and the values from the hidden units that are combined at the output units with additional (potentially different) activation functions applied. The activation functions most widely used are the hyperbolic tangent, which ranges from 1 to 1, in the hidden layer and linear in the output layer, as is the case in our example in **Figure 1** (the sigmoidal type activation function such as tangent hyperbolic and logit in the hidden layer are used for their convenient mathematical properties and these are usually chosen as a smooth step function). If the activation function at the output layer $g(.)$ is a linear or identity activation function, the model on the adaptive covariates $f_k(.)$ is also linear. Therefore, the regression model is entirely linear. The term "adaptive" denotes that the covariates in ANN are functions of unknown parameters (i.e. the $\{w_{kj}\}$ connection strengths), so the network can "learn" the association between independent (input) variables and target (output) variables, as is the case in standard regression models [1]. In this manner, this type of ANN architecture can also be regarded as a regression model. Of course, the level of non-linearity in ANNs is ultimately dictated by the type of activation functions used.

As depicted in **Figure 1**, a MLP feed forward architecture with one hidden layer can virtually predict any linear or non-linear model to any degree of accuracy, assuming that you have a suitable number of neurons in the hidden layer and an appropriate amount of data. But adding more neurons in hidden layers to the ANN architecture offers the model the flexibility of prediction of exceptionally complex nonlinear associations. This also holds true in function approximation, mapping, classification, and pattern recognition in approximating any nonlinear decision boundary with great precision. By adding additional neurons in the hidden layer to a MLP feedforward ANN is similar to adding additional polynomial terms to a regression model through the practice of generalization. Generalization is a method of indicating the appropriate complexity for the model in generating accurate prediction estimates based on data that is entirely separate from the training data that was used in fitting the model [5], commonly referred to as the test data set.

3. Overfitting and regularization

Like many other nonlinear estimation methods in supervised machine learning, such as kernel regression and smoothing splines, ANNs can suffer from either underfitting or overfitting. In particular, overfitting is more serious because it can easily lead to predictions that are far beyond the range of the training data [6–8]. Overfitting is unavoidable without practicing any regularization if the number of observations in the training data set is less than the number of parameters to be estimated. Before tackling the overfitting issue, let us first consider how the number of parameters in multilayer feedforward ANN is calculated. Suppose an ANN with **1000** inputs, **3** neurons in hidden and **1** neuron in output layer. The total number of parameters for this particular ANN is **3*1000** (number of weights from the input to the hidden layer) + **3** (number of biases in the hidden layer) + **3** (number of weights from the hidden to the output layer) + **1**(bias in output) = **3007**. The number of parameters for the entire network, for example, increases to **7015** when **7** neurons are assigned to the hidden layer. In these examples, either 3007 or 7015 parameters need to be estimated from 1000 observations. To wit, the number of neurons in the hidden layer controls the number of parameters (weights and biases) in the network. Determination of the optimal number of neurons to be retained in the hidden layer is an important step in the strategy of ANN. An ANN with less number of neurons may fails to capture the complex patterns between input and target variables. In contrast, an ANN with excess number of neurons in hidden layer will suffer from over-parameterization, leading to over-fitting and poor generalization ability [3]. Note that if the number of parameters in the network is much smaller than the total number of individuals in the training data set, then that is of no concern as there is little or no chance of overfitting for given ANN. If data assigned to the training set can be increased, then there is no need to worry about the following techniques to prevent overfitting. However, in most applications of ANN, data is typically partitioned to derive a finite training set. ANN algorithms train the model (architecture) based on this training data, and the performance and generalizability of the model is gauged on how well it predicts the observations in the training data set.

Overfitting occurs when a model fits the data in the training set well, while incurring larger generalization error. As depicted in **Figure 2**, the upper panel (**Figure 2a** and **b**) shows a model which has been fitted using too many free parameters. It seems that it does an excellent fitting of the data points, as the difference between outcome and predicted values (error) at the data points is almost zero. In reality, the data being studied often has some degree of error or random noise within it. Therefore, this does not mean our model (architecture) has good generalizability for given new values of the target variable t. It is said that the model has a bias-variance trade-off problem. In other words, the proposed model does not reproduce the structure which we expect to be present in any data set generated by function $f(.)$. **Figure 2c** shows that, while the network seems to get better and better (i.e., the error on the training set decreases; represented by the blue line in **Figure 2a**), at some point during training (epoch 2 in this example) it truly begins to get worse again (i.e. the error on test data set increases; represented by the

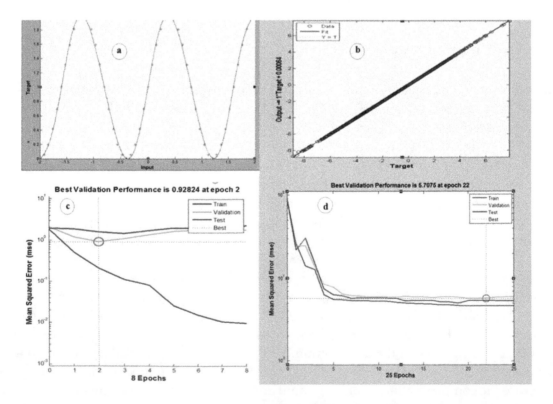

Figure 2. Function approximation of different regression models. Significant overfitting can be seen in (a)–(c).

red line in **Figure 2a**). The idealized expectation is that during training, the generalization error of the network progresses as shown in **Figure 2d**.

In general, there are two ways to deal with the overfitting problem in ANN (not considering ad hoc techniques such as pruning, greedy constructive learning, or weight sharing that reduces the number of parameters) [9]. These are **weight decay** and **early stopping**, both of which are known as *regularization* techniques. Regularization is the procedure of allowing parameter bias in the direction of what are considered to be more probable values, which reduces the variance of the estimates at the cost of introducing bias. Put in another way, regularization can be viewed as a way of compromising to minimize the objective function with regard to parameter (weights and bias) space. Next, we will briefly discuss **early stopping** before proceeding to the topic of weight decay (BR).

3.1. Early stopping

In the standard practice of backpropagation learning with early stopping, the data set is allocated into three sources: a training data set, a validation data set, and a testing data set. In most ANN practices, the biggest part of data is assigned to training data (by default a 60% of data is assigned for training in MATLAB). Each of these data sets have different task during the ANN prediction process. The training data set is used to estimate the neural network weights, while the validation data set is used to monitor the network and calculate the minimum error during the iterations till network is stopped. The last data set (test data set) is unseen data by network and task of the test data set is to decrease the bias and generate unbiased estimates for predicting future outcomes and generalizability. The test data set is used at the end of the iterative process for evaluating the performance of the model from an independently drawn sample [10]. With early stopping methods, a gradient descent algorithm is applied to the training and validation data sets. First, the training data set is used to calculate the weight and bias estimates, and then these parameter estimates are applied in the validation data set to calculate error values. The practice iterates substituting parameter estimates from the training data set into the validation data set to catch the likely smallest average error with respect to the prediction of the validation data set. Training ends when the error in the validation data set increases by certain epochs ("iterations" in statistical jargon) in order to avoid the problem of overfitting (the number of epoch is six by default in MATLAB) and then the weights at the minimum of the validation error are returned. The network parameter estimates with the best performance in the validation set are then used in analysis of the testing data to evaluate the predictive ability of the network [11].

Let the data set be $D = \{t, (p_i)_{i=1,\ldots,n}\}$, where p_i is a vector of inputs for individual i and t is a vector of target variables (input = independent and target = dependent variable in classical estimation terms in statistics). Once a set of weight values $\mathbf{w}$ is assigned to the connections in the networks, this defines a mapping from the input p_i to the output $\hat{t}_i$. Let M denote a specific network architecture (network architecture is the model in terms of numbers of neurons and choice of activation functions), then the typical objective function used for training a neural network using early stopping is the sum of squared estimation errors (E_D):

$$E_D(D \mid \mathbf{w}, M) = \sum_{i=1}^{n}\left(t_i - \hat{t}_i\right)^2 \tag{3}$$

for n input-target pairs defining D. Early stopping is effectively limiting the used weights in the network and thus imposes regularization, effectively lowering the Vapnik-Chervonenkis dimension. However, while early stopping often improves generalization, it does not do so in a mathematically well-defined way. It is crucial to realize that validation error is not a good estimate of generalization error. Early stopping regularization has a vital advantage over the usual regularized least square learning algorithm such as ridge regression (so-called penalized L_2) or Tikhonov regularization methods.

4. Bayesian regularization

The brief explanation given in the previous section described how early stopping works to deal with the overfitting issue in ANN. Another regularization procedure in ANN is BR, which is the linear combination of Bayesian methods and ANN to automatically determine the optimal regularization parameters (**Table 1**). In Bayesian regularized ANN (BRANN) models, regularization techniques involve imposing certain prior distributions on the model parameters. An extra term, E_w, is added by BRANN to the objective function of early stopping given in equation (3) which penalizes large weights in anticipation of reaching a better generalization and smoother mapping. As what happens in conventional backpropagation practices, a gradient-based optimization technique is then applied to minimize the function given in (4). This process is equal to a penalized log-likelihood,

$$F = \beta E_D(D \mid \mathbf{w}, M) + \alpha E_W(\mathbf{w} \mid M), \tag{4}$$

where $E_W(\mathbf{w} \mid M)$, is the sum of squares of architecture weights, M is the ANN architecture (model in statistical jargon), and α and β are objective function parameters (also referred to as regularization parameters or hyper-parameters and take the positive values) that need to be estimated adaptively [3]. The second term on the right hand side of equation (4), αE_W, is known as weight decay and α, the weight decay coefficient, favors small values of $\mathbf{w}$ and decreases the tendency of a model to overfit [12].

To add on a quadratic penalty function $E_W(\mathbf{w} \mid M)$, α yielding a version of nonlinear ridge regression with an estimate for $\mathbf{w}$ equivalent to the Bayesian maximum a prior (MAP) [1]. Therefore, the quadratic form (weight decay) favors small values of $\mathbf{w}$ and decreases the predisposition of a model to overfit the data. Here, in equation (4), training involves a tradeoff between model complexity and goodness of fit. If $\alpha \gg \beta$, highlighting is on reducing the extent of weights at the expense of goodness of fit, while producing a smoother network response [13]. If Bayes estimates of α are large, the posterior densities of the weights are highly concentrated around zero, so that the weights effectively disappear and the model discounts connections in the network [12, 14]. Therefore, α and β are adaptively predicted to deal with tradeoff model complexity and goodness of fit.

MATLAB Commend		Explanations
load myData		Loading data
net=newff(x,y,5,{'tansig', 'purelin'},'trainbr');		Creates a new network with a dialog box. The properties of architecture created here are: tangent sigmoid (tansig) and linear activation function (purelin) in hidden and output, respectively. The number of neuron in hidden layer is 5 and the number of neuron in output layer 1 (by default). The Bayesian regularized training algorithm (trainbr) takes play for training of data.
[net,tr]=train(net,x, y)		
randn('state',192736547)		Lets you seed the uniform random number generator.
y_t=sim(net, x)		Simulate net
net = init(net)		Reinitiate net to improve results
net = train(net,x,y)		Re-train net
net.trainParam.epochs	1000	Maximum number of epochs to train
net.trainParam.goal	0	Performance goal
net.trainParam.mu	0.005	Marquardt adjustment parameter
net.trainParam.mu_dec	0.1	Decrease factor for mu
net.trainParam.mu_inc	10	Increase factor for mu
net.trainParam.mu_max	1e10	Maximum value for mu
net.trainParam.min_grad	1e-7	Minimum performance gradient
net.trainParam.show	25	Epochs between displays (NaN for no displays)
net.trainParam. showCommandLine	False	Generate command-line output
net.trainParam. showWindow	True	Show training GUI

Table 1. Training occurs according to Bayesian regularization algorithms (trainbr) training parameters, shown here with their default values (commends given in bold face are required).

As stated in the early stopping regularization section of this chapter, the input and target data set is typically divided into three parts; the training data set, the validation data set, and the test data sets. In BRANNs, particularly when the input and target data set is small, it is not essential to divide the data into three subsets: training, validation, and testing sets. Conversely all available data set is devoted to model fitting and model comparison [15]. This implementation is important when training networks with small data sets as is thought that BR has better generalization ability than early stopping (http://www.faqs.org/faqs/ai-faq/neural-nets/part3/section-5.html).

The strength connections, **w**, of the network are considered random variables and have no meaning before training. After the data is taken, the density function for the weights can be updated according to Bayes' rule. The empirical Bayes approach in [12] is as follows. The posterior distribution of **w** given α, β, D, and M is

$$P(\mathbf{w} \mid D, \alpha, \beta, M) = \frac{P(D|\mathbf{w}, \beta, M) P(\mathbf{w}|\alpha, M)}{P(D \mid \alpha, \beta, M)}, \tag{5}$$

where D is the training data set and M is the specific functional form of the neural network architecture considered. The other terms in equation (5) are:

- $P(w|D, \alpha \beta, M)$ is the posterior probability of **w**,

- $P(D|w, \beta, M)$ is the likelihood function of **w**,

- $P(w|\alpha, M)$ is the prior distribution of weights under M, which is the probability of observing the data given **w** and

- $P(D|\alpha, \beta, M)$ is a normalization factor or evidence for hyperparameters α and β.

The normalization factor does not depend on **w** (Kumar, 2004). That is,

$$P(D \mid \alpha, \beta, M) = \int P(D|\mathbf{w}, \beta, M) P(\mathbf{w}|\alpha, M) d\mathbf{w}.$$

The weights **w**, were assumed to be identically distributed, each following the Gaussian distribution $(\mathbf{w}| \alpha, M) \sim N(0, \alpha^{-1})$. Given this, the expression of joint prior density of **w** in equation (5) is

$$p(\mathbf{w} \mid a, M) \propto \prod_{l=1}^{m} \exp\left(-\frac{\alpha w_{kj}^2}{2}\right) = \exp\left[-\frac{\alpha E_W(\mathbf{w}|M)}{2}\right].$$

After normalization, the prior distribution is then [2]

$$p(\mathbf{w} \mid \alpha, M) = \frac{\exp\left[-\dfrac{\alpha E_W(\mathbf{w}|M)}{2}\right]}{\int \exp\left[-\dfrac{\alpha E_W(\mathbf{w}|M)}{2}\right] d\mathbf{w}} = \frac{\exp\left[-\dfrac{\alpha E_W(\mathbf{w}|M)}{2}\right]}{Z_w(\alpha)}, \tag{6}$$

where $Z_W(\alpha) = \left(\dfrac{2\pi}{\alpha}\right)^{\frac{m}{2}}$.

As target variable t, is a function of input variables, $\mathbf{p}$, (the same association between dependent and independent variables in regression model) it is modeled as $t_i = f(\mathbf{p}_i) + e$, where $e \sim N(0, \beta^{-1})$ and $f(\mathbf{p}_i)$ is the function approximation to $E(t \mid \mathbf{p})$. Assuming Gaussian distribution, the joint density function of the target variables given the input variables, β and M is [2]:

$$P(\mathbf{t} \mid \mathbf{p}, \mathbf{w}, \beta, M) = \left(\frac{\beta}{2\pi} \right)^{\frac{N}{2}} \exp\left[-\frac{\beta}{2} \sum_{i=1}^{N} (t_i - f(\mathbf{p_i}))^2 \right]$$
$$= \left(\frac{\beta}{2\pi} \right)^{\frac{N}{2}} \exp\left[-\frac{\beta}{2} E_D (D \mid \mathbf{w}, M) \right] \tag{7}$$

where $E_D(D \mid \mathbf{w}, M)$ is as given in equation (3) and (4). Letting $Z_D(\beta) = \int \exp\left[-\frac{\beta}{2} E_D(D \mid \mathbf{w}, M) \right] = \left(\frac{2\pi}{\beta} \right)^{\frac{N}{2}}$, the posterior density of $\mathbf{w}$ in equation (5) can be expressed as

$$P(\mathbf{w} \mid D, \alpha, \beta, M) = \frac{\dfrac{1}{Z_W(\alpha) Z_D(\beta)} \exp\left[-\frac{1}{2} (\beta E_D + \alpha E_W) \right]}{P(D \mid \alpha\, \beta\, M)},$$
$$= \frac{1}{Z_F(\alpha, \beta)} \exp\left[-\frac{F(w)}{2} \right] \tag{8}$$

where $Z_F(\alpha, \beta) = \left[Z_W(\alpha) Z_D(\beta) P(D \mid \alpha, \beta, M) \right]$ and $F = \beta E_D + \alpha E_W$. In an empirical Bayesian framework, the "optimal" weights are those that maximize the posterior density $P(\mathbf{w} \mid D, \alpha, \beta, M)$. Maximizing the posterior density of $P(\mathbf{w} \mid D, \alpha, \beta, M)$ is equivalent to minimizing the regularized objective function F given in equation (4). Therefore, this indicates that values of α and β need to be predicted by architecture M, which will be further discussed in the next section.

While minimization of objective function F is identical to finding the (locally) maximum *a posteriori* estimates $\mathbf{w}^{MAP}$, minimization of E_D in F by any backpropagation training algorithm is identical to finding the maximum likelihood estimates $\mathbf{w}^{ML}$ [12]. Bayesian optimization of the regularization parameters require computation of the Hessian matrix of the objective function F evaluated at the optimum point $\mathbf{w}^{MAP}$ [3]. However, directly computing the Hessian matrix is not always required. As proposed by MacKay [12], the Gauss-Newton approximation to the Hessian matrix can be used if the LM optimization algorithm is employed to locate the minimum of F [16].

4.1. Brief discussion of Levenberg-Marquardt optimization

The LM algorithm is a robust numerical optimization technique for mapping as well as function approximation. The LM modification to Gauss-Newton is

$$(\mu\mathbf{I})\vDash\mathbf{J}'\mathbf{e} \tag{9}$$

and the Hessian matrix can be approximated as:

$$\mathbf{H} = \mathbf{J}'\mathbf{J}, \tag{10}$$

where $\mathbf{J}$ is the Jacobian matrix that contains first derivatives of the network errors with respect to network parameters (the weights and biases), μ is the Levenberg's damping factor, and δ is the parameter update vector. The δ indicates how much the magnitude of weights needs to be changed to attain better prediction ability. The way to calculate $\mathbf{J}$ matrix is given in equation (11). The gradient of the ANN is computed as $\mathbf{g}=\mathbf{J}'\mathbf{e}$. The μ in equation (9) is adjustable in each iteration, and guides the optimization process during ANN learning with the training data set. If reductions of the cost function F are rapid, then the parameter μ is divided by a constant (c) to bring the algorithm closer to the Gauss-Newton, whereas if an iteration gives insufficient reduction in F, then μ is multiplied by the same constant giving a step closer to the gradient descent direction (http://crsouza-blog.azurewebsites.net/2009/11/neural-network-learning-by-the-levenberg-marquardt-algorithm-with-bayesian-regularization-part-1/#levenberg). Therefore, the LM algorithm can be considered a trust-region modification to Gauss-Newton designed to serve as an intermediate optimization algorithm between the Gauss-Newton method and the Gradient-Descent algorithm [17].

The Jacobian matrix is a matrix of all first-order partial derivatives of a vector-valued function. The dimensions of the matrix are formed by the number of observations in the training data and the total number of parameters (weights + biases) in the ANN being used. It can be created by taking the partial derivatives of each output with respect to each weight, and has the form:

$$\mathbf{J} = \begin{bmatrix} \dfrac{\partial e_1(w)}{\partial w_1} & \dfrac{\partial e_1(w)}{\partial w_2} \cdots & \dfrac{\partial e_1(w)}{\partial w_n} \\ \dfrac{\partial e_2(w)}{\partial w_1} & \dfrac{\partial e_2(w)}{\partial w_2} \cdots & \dfrac{\partial e_2(w)}{\partial w_n} \\ \vdots & \vdots & \ddots & \vdots \\ \dfrac{\partial e_N(w)}{\partial w_1} & \dfrac{\partial e_N(w)}{\partial w_2} \cdots & \dfrac{\partial e_N(w)}{\partial w_n} \end{bmatrix} \tag{11}$$

The parameters at l iteration are updated as in equation (12) when the Gauss-Newton approximation of the Hessian matrix by LM in Bayesian regularized neural network (BRANN) is used.

$$w^{j+1} = w^j - \left[\mathbf{J}^T\mathbf{J} + \mu\,\mathbf{I} \right]^{-1} \mathbf{J}^T\mathbf{e} \tag{12}$$

Therefore, this approach provides a numerical solution to the problem of minimizing a nonlinear function over the parameter space. In addition, this approach is a popular alternative to the Gauss-Newton method of finding the minimum of a function (http://crsouza-blog.azurewebsites.net/2009/11/neural-network-learning-by-the-levenberg-marquardt-algorithm-with-bayesian-regularization-part-1/#levenberg). Next, let's compare the equations for some common training algorithms and use this information to decipher how parameters are updated after each iteration (epoch) in ANN: Updating the strength connection in standard backpropagation training $w^{l+1} = w^l - \alpha\dfrac{\partial E_D}{w^l}$,

updating the strength connection in Quasi-Newton training $w^{l+1} = w^l - \mathbf{H}_l^{-1}\alpha\dfrac{\partial E}{w^l}$, and

updating the strength connection in LM training $w^{l+1} = w^l - \left[\mathbf{J}^T\mathbf{J} + \mu\,\mathbf{I}\right]^{-1}\mathbf{J}^T\mathbf{e}$.

Therefore, Quasi-Newton is necessary for actual calculation of the Hessian matrix $\mathbf{H}$ while LM is used to approximate $\mathbf{H}$. The α coefficient in the first two equations is referred to as the learning rate. The performance of the algorithm is very sensitive to proper setting of the learning rate. If the learning rate is set too high, the algorithm can oscillate and become unstable. On the other hand, too low learning rate makes the network learn very slowly and converging of ANN will take a while. In gradient descent learning, it is not practical to determine the optimal setting for the learning rate before training, and in fact, the optimal learning rate changes during the training process, as the algorithm moves across the performance surface [18].

5. Tuning parameters α and β

As discussed earlier, minimizing the regularized objective function $F = \beta E_D(D\,|\,w,M) + \alpha E_W(w\,|\,M)$ in equation (4) is equivalent to maximization of the posterior density $P(\mathbf{w}\,|\,D,\,\alpha,\,\beta,\,M)$. A typical procedure used in neural networks infers α and β by maximizing the marginal likelihood of the data in equation (5). The joint probability of α and β is

$$P(\alpha, \beta \,|\, D, M) = \frac{P(D\,|\,\alpha, \beta, M)P(\alpha, \beta\,|\,M)}{P(D\,|\,M)}. \tag{13}$$

Essentially, we need to maximize the posterior probability $P(\alpha\ \beta \mid D, M)$ with respect to hyperparameters α and β which is equivalent to maximization of $P(D \mid \alpha, \beta, M)$. $P(D \mid \alpha, \beta, M)$ is the normalization factor given for the posterior distribution of $\mathbf{w}$ in equation (5).

If we apply the unity activation function in equation (5), which is the analog of linear regression, then this equation will have a closed form. Otherwise, equation (5) does not have a closed form if we apply any sigmoidal activation function, such as logit or tangent hyperbolic in the hidden layer. Hence, the marginal likelihood is approximated using a Laplacian integration completed in the area of the current value $\mathbf{w}=\mathbf{w}^{MAP}$ [3]. The Laplacian approximation to the marginal density in equation (5) is expressed as

$$\log\left[p(D \mid \alpha, \beta, M)\right] \approx K + \frac{n}{2}\log(\beta) + \frac{m}{2}\log(\alpha) - \left|F(\alpha,\beta)\right|_{w=w^{MAP}_{(\alpha,\beta)}} - \frac{1}{2}\log\|\mathbf{H}\|_{w=w^{MAP}_{(\alpha,\beta)}} \tag{14}$$

where K is a constant and $\mathbf{H} = \dfrac{\partial^2}{\partial\mathbf{w}\partial\mathbf{w}}F(\alpha,\beta)$ is the Hessian matrix as given in equation (10) and (11). A grid search can be used to locate the α, β maximizers of the marginal likelihood in the training set. An alternative approach [12, 14] involves iteration (updating is from right to left, with $\mathbf{w}^{MAP}$ evaluated at the "old" values of the tuning parameters)

$$\alpha_{new} = \frac{m}{2\left(\mathbf{w}^{MAP}{}'\mathbf{w}^{MAP} + tr\mathbf{H}^{-1}_{MAP}\right)}$$

and

$$\beta_{new} = \frac{n - m + 2\alpha_{MAP}tr\mathbf{H}^{-1}_{MAP}}{2\sum\limits_{i=1}^{n}\left(t_i - b - \sum\limits_{k=1}^{S}w_k g_k\left(b_k + \sum\limits_{j=1}^{n}a_{ij}u_j^{*[k]}\right)\right)^2\Bigg|_{w=w^{MAP}_{(\alpha,\beta)}}} \Rightarrow \beta_{new} = \frac{n - \gamma}{2E_D(\mathbf{w}^{MAP})} \tag{15}$$

The expression $\gamma = m - 2\alpha_{new}tr(\mathbf{H}^{MAP})^{-1}$ is referred to as the number of effective parameters in the neural network and its value ranges from 0 (or 1, if an overall intercept b is fitted) to m, the total number of connection strength coefficients, w, and bias, b, parameters in the network. The effective number of parameters indicates the number of effective weights being used by the network. Subsequently, the number of effective parameters is used to evaluate the model complexity and performance of BRANNs. If γ is close to m, over-fitting results, leading to poor generalization.

6. Steps in BRANN

A summary of steps in BRANN is given in **Figure 3**. Initialize α, β and the weights, w. After the first training step, the objective function parameters will recover from the initial setting.

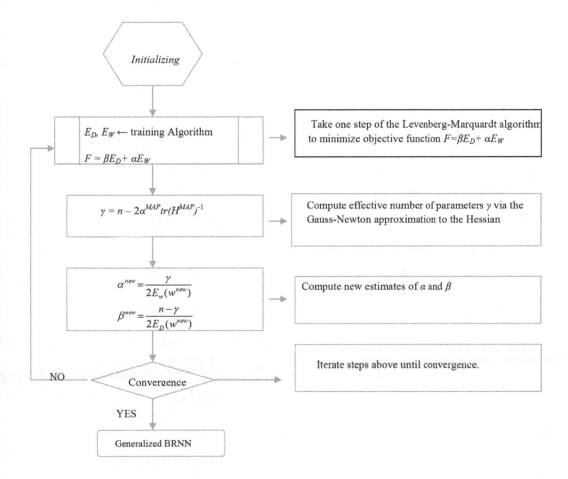

Figure 3. Flow chart for Bayesian optimization of regularization parameters α and β in the neural networks; MAP=maximum *a posteriori* [partially adapted from 16 and 2].

1. Take one step of the LM algorithm to minimize the objective function $F(\alpha,\beta)$ and find the current value of **w**.

    i.   Compute the Jacobian as given in equation (11).

    ii.   Compute the error gradient $g = J^T e$.

    iii.   Approximate the Hessian matrix using $H = J^T J$.

            Calculate the objective function as given in equation (4).

            Solve the $J'J + \mu I)\delta = J'e$.

Update the network weights **w** using **δ**.

2. Compute the effective number of parameters $\gamma = N - 2atr(\mathbf{H})^{-1}$ making use of the Gauss-Newton approximation to the Hessian matrix available from the LM training algorithm.

3. Compute updated α_{new} and β_{new} as

$$\alpha^{MAP} = \frac{\gamma}{2E_w(w^{MAP})} \quad and \quad \beta^{MAP} = \frac{m - \gamma}{2E_D(w^{MAP})} \quad ; and$$

4. Iterate steps 2-4 until convergence.

7. Practical considerations

In general, there are three steps between input and predicted values in ANN training. These are pre-processing, network object (training), and post-processing. These steps are important to make ANN more efficient as well as drive optimal knowledge from ANN. Some of these steps will be considered in the following sections.

7.1. Data cleaning

Before training, the data sets should be checked in terms of constant, corrupt, and incorrect values from the input and target data set. After checking for suspicious and improper data, the dimension of the input vector could be an important issue for efficient training. In some situations, the dimensions of the data vectors could be large, but the components in the data vectors can be highly correlated (redundant). Principal component analysis (PCA) is the most common technique for dimensionality reduction and orthogonalization.

7.2. Normalization

Normalization or scaling is not really a functional requirement for the neural networks to learn, but it significantly helps as it converts the input and target (independent and dependent variables in statistical jargon) into the data range that the sigmoid activation functions lie in (i.e. for logistic [0, 1] and tanh [−1, 1]. For example, in MLP, non-linear functions in hidden layers become saturated when the input is larger than six (exp(-6)~0.00247). Consequently, large inputs cause ill-conditioning by leading to very small weights. Further with large inputs, the gradient values become very small, and the network training will be very slow.

By default, before initiating the network processing, MATLAB Neural Network Toolbox® rescales both input and output variables such that they lie -1 to +1 range, to boost numerical stability. This task is done spontaneously in MATLAB Neural Network Toolbox® using the "mapminmax" function. To explain this, consider the simple data vector as x'=[8, 1, 5]. Here the $x_{min} = 1$ and $x_{max} = 8$. If values are to range between $A_{min} = -1$ and $A_{max} = +1$, one redefine the data vector temporarily as $x_{temp}' = [-1, 1, 5]$, so only $x_3 = 5$ needs to be rescaled to guarantee that all variables reside between -1 and +1. This is done by using the following formula:

$$x_{3,new} = A_{min} + \frac{x_3 - x_{min}}{x_{max} - x_{min}}(A_{max} - A_{min}) = -1 + \frac{5-1}{8-1}2 = -0.143.$$

When the input and target data is normalized, the network output always falls into a normalized range. The network output can then be reverse transformed into the units of the original target data when the network is put to use in the field [18].

7.3. Multiple runs

Each time a neural network is trained, the output obtained from each run can result in a different solution mainly due to: a) different initial weight and bias values, and b) different splitting of data into training, validation, and test sets (or into training and testing). As a result, function approximation using different neural network architectures trained on the same problem can produce different outputs for the same input fed into the ANN. For example, depending on the initial weights of the network, the algorithm may converge to local minima or not converge at all. To avoid local minima convergence and overtraining, improve the predictive ability of ANN, and eliminate spurious effects caused by random starting values. Several independent BRANNs, say 10, should be trained for each architecture. Results are then recorded as the average of several runs on each architecture.

7.4. Analyses and computing environment

Determination of the optimal number of neurons in the hidden layer is an essential task in ANN architectures. As stated earlier, network with only a few neurons in hidden layer may be incapable of capturing complex association between target and input variables. However, if too excessive neurons are assigned in hidden part of the network then it will follow the noise in the data due to overparameterization, leading to bad generalization and poor predictive ability of unseen data [3, 19]. Therefore, a different number of neurons in the hidden layer should be tried, and architecture performance should be assessed after each run with a certain number of neurons in the hidden layer. Because highly parameterized models are penalized in BRANN, the complexity of BRANN architectures using sum of squares weights as well as the degree of shrinkage attained by BRANN can be used to determine the optimal number of neurons. The number of parameters (weights and biases) is a function of the number of neurons. More neurons in the hidden layer imply that more parameters need to be estimated. Therefore, one criteria for model selection in complex BRANN concerns the number of weights. The more weights there are, relative to the number of training cases, the more overfitting amplifies noise in the target variables [1–3]. As demonstrated in **Figure 4**, BRANN also calculates the effective number of parameters to evaluate the degree of complexity in ANN architecture. BRANN uses the LM algorithm (based on linearization) for computing the posterior modes in BR. The penalized residual sum of squares is also used to determine the number of neurons in the hidden part of the network.

7.5. Stopping training of BRANN

In MATLAB applications, training of BRANN is stopped if:

1. The maximum number of epochs (number of iterations in statistical jargon) is reached

2. Performance of the network with the number of neurons and combinations of the activation functions has met a suitable level

3. The gradient ($J'e$) was below a suitable target

4. The LM μ parameter exceeded a suitable maximum (training stopped when it became larger than 10^{10}).

Each of these targets and goals are set as the default values in MATLAB implementation. The maximum number of iterations (called epochs) in back-propagation was set to 1000, and iteration will stop earlier if the gradient of the objective function is below a suitable level, or when there are obvious problems with the algorithm [20].

8. Interpreting the results

8.1. Degree of complexity

This example illustrates the impact of shrinkage and how regularized neural networks deal with the "curse of dimensionality". The example given here has 500 inputs and the number of neurons in the hidden layer is 5, such that the total of nominal parameters (weights and biases) is 2511. However, the effective number of parameters is 316 (**Figure 4**). In other words, the model can be explained well with only with 316 parameters when BR is used for training the networks. In practice, different architectures (different activation functions and different numbers of neurons in the hidden layer) should be explored to decide which architecture best fits the data. Hence, incremental increasing of the number of neurons from one to several is the best practice to cope with the "curse of dimensionality".

8.2. Predictive performance

The predictive correlation is 0.87 (**Figure 4**) in the given example, which is quite high, implying that the predictive ability of the model used is sufficient. However, as stated earlier, to eliminate spurious effects caused by random starting values, several independent BRANNs should be trained for each architecture and the average value of multiple runs should be reported.

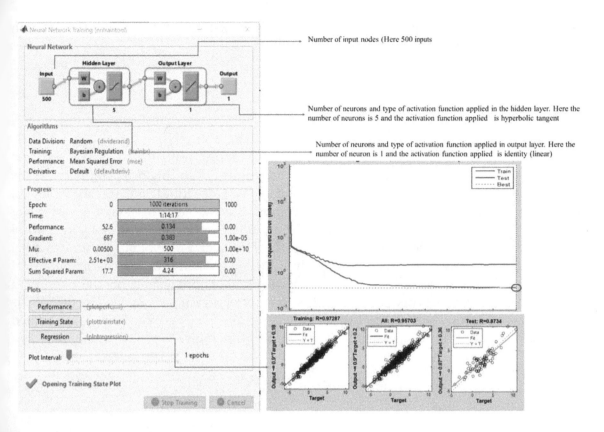

Figure 4. Output screens from MATLAB runs.

8.3. Shrinkage

The distribution of connection strengths (network parameters) in an ANN gives an evidence of the degree of regularization achieved by BRANNs. Conventionally, weight values are shrinkage with model complexity, in the same approach that estimates of network parameters become smaller in BR implementations. This is true when inputs p increase and training sample size remains constant. Moreover, the distribution of weights in any architecture is often associated with the predictive ability of network; small value weights tend to lead to better generalization for unseen data [1, 19]. **Figure 4** shows the distributions of weights for the nonlinear regularized networks with five neurons in the hidden layer. It is suggested that a linear activation function in the hidden and output layers, as well as a nonlinear activation function with different numbers of neurons in the hidden and a linear activation function in output layer should be tried. This provides a good opportunity to compare models for the extent of regularization attained. For example, the sum of squared weights for about 2500 parameters is only 4.24 in the given example (see **Figure 4**), indicating how Bayesian neural networks reduce the effective number of weights relative to what would be obtained without regularization. In other words, the method by which highly parameterized models are penalized in the Bayesian approach helps to prevent over-fitting.

9. Conclusion

Small *n and big p* (*p>>n*) is key issue for prediction of complex traits from big data sets, and ANNs provide efficient and functional approaches to deal with this problem. Because the competency of capturing highly nonlinear relationship between input and outcome variables, ANNs act as universal approximators to learn complex functional forms adaptively by using different type of nonlinear functions. Overfitting and over-parameterization are critical concerns when ANN is used for prediction in (*p>>n*). However, BRANN plays a fundamental role in attenuating these concerns. The objective function used in BRANN has an additional term that penalizes large weights to attain a smoother mapping and handle overfitting problem. Because of the shrinkage, the effective number of parameters attained by BRANN is less than the total number of parameters used in the model. Thus, the over-fitting is attenuated and generalization ability of the model is improved considerably.

Acknowledgements

Author would like to sincerely thank Jacob Keaton for his reduction, and comments.

Author details

Hayrettin Okut

Address all correspondence to: okut.hayrettin@gmail.com

Yüzüncü Yıl University, Faculty of Agriculture, Biometry and Genetic Branch, Van, Turkey

Wake Forest University, School of Medicine, Center for Diabetes Research, Center for Genomics and Personalized Medicine Research, Winston-Salem, NC, USA

References

[1] Gianola, D., Okut, H., Weigel, K., Rosa, J. G. Predicting complex quantitative traits with Bayesian neural networks: a case study with Jersey cows and wheat. BMC Genetics. 2011. 12:87.

[2] Okut, H., Gianola, D., Rosa, J. G., Weigel, K. Prediction of body mass index in mice using dense molecular markers and a regularized neural network. Genetics Research (Cambridge). 2011. 93:189–201

[3] Okut, H., Wu, X. L., Rosa, J. M. G., Bauck, S., Woodward, B., Schnabel, D. R., Taylor, F. J., Gianola, D. Predicting expected progeny difference for marbling score in Angus cattle using artificial neural networks and Bayesian regression models. Genetics Selection Evolution. 2014. 45:34. DOI: 10.1186/1297-9686-45-34.

[4] Lampinen, J., Vehtari, A. Bayesian approach for neural networks review and case studies. Neural Networks. 2001. 14:257–274.

[5] SAS® Enterprise Miner™ 14.1. Administration and Configuration Copyright©. Cary, NC: SAS Institute Inc.; 2015.

[6] Feng, N., Wang, F., Qiu, Y. Novel approach for promoting the generalization ability of neural networks. International Journal of Signal Processing. 2006. 2:131–135.

[7] Ping, G., Michael, R. L., Chen, C. L. P. Regularization parameter estimation for feed-forward neural networks. IEEE Transactions on Systems, Man, and Cybernetics—PART B: Cybernetics. 2003. 33:35–44.

[8] Wang, H. J., Ji, F., Leung, C. S., Sum, P. F. Regularization parameter selection for faulty neural networks. International Journal of Intelligent Systems and Technologies. 2009. 4:45–48.

[9] Marwala, T. Bayesian training of neural networks using genetic programming. Pattern Recognition Letters. 2007. 28:1452–1458.

[10] Matignon, R. Data Mining Using SAS Enterprise Miner. Chicago: Wiley; 2007. p. 584. ISBN: 978-0-470-14901-0. DOI: 10.1002/9780470171431

[11] Okut, H., Gianola, D., Rosa, J. G., Weigel, K. Evaluation of prediction ability of Cholesky factorization of genetic relationship matrix for additive and non-additive genetic effect using Bayesian regularized neural network. IORE Journal of Genetics. 2015. 1(1). 1–15

[12] MacKay, J. C. D. Information Theory, Inference and Learning Algorithms. Cambridge University Press, Cambridge-UK; 2008.

[13] Foresee, F. D., Hagan, M. T. Gauss-Newton approximation to Bayesian learning. Proceedings: IEEE International Conference on Neural Networks. 1997. Vol:3, 1930–1935.

[14] Titterington, D. M. Bayesian methods for neural networks and related models. Statistical Science. 2004. 19:128–139.

[15] Bishop, C. M., Tipping, M. E. A hierarchical latent variable model for data visualization. IEEE Transactions on Pattern Analysis and Machine Intelligence. 1998. 20(3):281–293.

[16] Shaneh, A., Butler, G. Bayesian learning for feedforward neural network with application to proteomic data: the glycosylation sites detection of the epidermal growth factor-

like proteins associated with cancer as a case study. In Canadian AI LNAI 4013, 2006 (ed. L. Lamontagne & M. Marchand). Berlin-Heiddelberg: Springer-Verleg; 2006. 110–121.

[17] Battiti, R. Using mutual information for selecting features in supervised neural net learning neural networks. IEEE Transactions on Neural Networks. 1994. 5(4):537–550.

[18] Demuth, H., Beale, M., Hagan, M. Neural Network ToolboxTM 6 User's Guide. Natick, MA: The MathWorks Inc.; 2010.

[19] Felipe, P.S. V., Okut, H., Gianola, D., Silva, A. M., Rosa, J. M. G. Effect of genotype imputation on genome-enabled prediction of complex traits: an empirical study with mice data. BMC Genetics. 2014. 15:149. DOI: 10.1186/s12863-014-0149-9

[20] Haykin, S. Neural Networks: Comprehensive Foundation. New York: Prentice-Hall; 2008.

5

From Fuzzy Expert System to Artificial Neural Network: Application to Assisted Speech Therapy

Ovidiu Schipor , Oana Geman ,

Iuliana Chiuchisan and Mihai Covasa

Additional information is available at the end of the chapter

Abstract

This chapter addresses the following question: What are the advantages of extending a fuzzy expert system (FES) to an artificial neural network (ANN), within a computer-based speech therapy system (CBST)? We briefly describe the key concepts underlying the principles behind the FES and ANN and their applications in assisted speech therapy. We explain the importance of an intelligent system in order to design an appropriate model for real-life situations. We present data from 1-year application of these concepts in the field of assisted speech therapy. Using an artificial intelligent system for improving speech would allow designing a training program for pronunciation, which can be individualized based on specialty needs, previous experiences, and the child's prior therapeutical progress. Neural networks add a great plus value when dealing with data that do not normally match our previous designed pattern. Using an integrated approach that combines FES and ANN allows our system to accomplish three main objectives: (1) develop a personalized therapy program; (2) gradually replace some human expert duties; (3) use "self-learning" capabilities, a component traditionally reserved for humans. The results demonstrate the viability of the hybrid approach in the context of speech therapy that can be extended when designing similar applications.

Keywords: fuzzy expert system, artificial neural network, assisted speech therapy, artificial intelligent system, hybrid expert system

1. Speech therapy: key concepts and facts

Dyslalia is a pronunciation deficiency manifested by an alteration of one or more phonemes due to several causes such as: omissions, substitutions, distortions, and permanent motor impairments. Dyslalia can be simple when it is related with only one sound (eventually in an attenuated form). An extension of pronunciation–articulation disorder related with more sounds and/or groups of syllables is called polymorphic dyslalia [1].

The existence of a dyslalia with defectological significance can be diagnosed after the age of four. Until that, dyslalia is called physiological and it is caused by the insufficient development of the speech-articulator apparatus and the neurological systems implicated in the speech process. This is the age that allows maximization of the therapeutic effects and offers a good prognosis for improvement/correction. The later the therapy begins, the weaker the effect [2].

There are many causes for dyslalia: the imitation of persons with deficient pronunciation, lack of speech stimulation, adults encouraging the preschool child to stabilize wrongful habits, defects in teeth implantation, different anomalies of the speech-articulator apparatus, cerebral deficiencies, hearing loss, weak development of phonetic hearing. Also, in severe dyslalias, heredity is considered an important factor in diagnosing and explaining this deficiency.

Impairment type		Number of subjects	Impairment frequency (%)	Overall impairment frequency (%)
Dyslalia		434	91.2	14.8
Dysarthria		–	–	–
Rhinolalia		7	1.5	0.2
Reading-writing difficulties		–	–	–
Rhythm and fluency difficulties		17	3.7	0.6
Language impairments	Selective mutism	4	0.8	0.1
	General development delays	8	1.6	0.3
Voice impairments		–	–	–
Language impairments in association with:	Autism	4	0.8	0.1
	Down syndrome	2	0.4	0.1
	Intellectual deficiencies	–	–	–
	Deafness	–	–	–
Total		476	100.0	16.2

Table 1. Speech and language impairments distribution (unpublished data from Suceava—Romania Regional Speech Therapy Centre).

In dyslalia, the sounds are not equally affected. Thus, the sounds most affected are the ones that appear later in the child's speech: vibrant—r (very important in Romanian language), affricates—c, g, t, hissing—s, z. In fact, the sounds mostly affected are the ones that require a greater effort to synchronize the elements of the phono-articulator apparatus (elements engaged in the emission of sounds: larynx, vocal cords, tongue, lips, teeth, and cheeks). Their pronunciation involves a certain position of all these elements and a certain intensity of the exhausted air jet [1].

Regarding the frequency of speech impediments and especially the frequency of dyslalia, the statistics from the Suceava Romanian Regional Speech Therapy Centre (**Table 1**; **Figure 1**) reveals the following aspects [2]: (i) Disorders that affect speech are more frequent that the ones affecting the language; (ii) Dyslalia is the most frequent pronunciation disorder, with sounds r and s most affected; (iii) the proportion of children with speech impediments:

- Decreases constantly until first grade;

- Suddenly decreases between first and second grade;

- Decreases slower and slower between second and fourth grade.

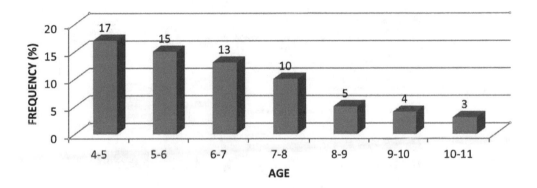

Figure 1. Evolution of speech impairments frequency across subjects' age.

The characterization of the dyslalia dynamics is of great interest also, in regard to the age of the subjects as depicted in **Figure 1**. Before age four no logopedic evaluation was conducted for children since possible speaking problems might be due to insufficient maturation of the phono-articulatory organs and of the involved cortical areas.

After this age, children with speech impairments are integrated in the speech therapy programs. The therapy determines the progressive decrease of the proportion of children with speech problems in relation to their age. At the beginning of the school, the frequency of children with speech disorders decreases suddenly, mainly because of the acquisition of writing and reading skills. Moreover, the corrective effort from the teaching community is highly emphasized. After this age, language disorders are present mainly in children with organ related disorders—structural disorders of the central or peripheral organs of speech.

The main steps of speech therapy together with the place of fuzzy expert system in therapeutic process are presented in **Figure 2**. Each therapy process contains a formative evaluation, which can be followed by the therapy within the family. After 3 months, the speech therapist can finalize the therapy or can reevaluate it [3].

The expert system incorporates information generated from social, cognitive, and affective examination, as well as from the homework reports and results' trends [4]. This allows the expert system to provide critical answers related to the length and frequency of the therapy session as well as the type of exercise to be used and its content.

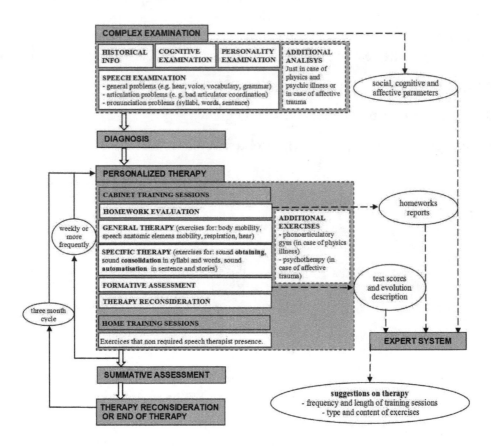

Figure 2. Speech therapy process and fuzzy expert system [3].

The therapy customization assumes a differentiated report related to the therapy stages. Thus, for each subject, there are different weights for each stage within the program structure. The therapy is generally a formative assessment because the speech therapists permanently evaluate the evolution of the patient during the exercises. The therapy is continued in familial environment during home training sessions. Thus, between the weekly sessions, family must provide the child with the adequate environment to consolidate the skills initiated at the specialty clinic.

A summative assessment is conducted every 3 months, and the child's evolution is analyzed over a longer period of time. This is the time for the reconsideration of the therapy and, eventually, for finalizing the therapeutic process.

The expert system is designed to function as a true assistant of the speech therapist. It provides suggestions based on several recordings from the integrated system. Moreover, depending on the assessments performed by the speech therapist at each session and on the homework solving, the human expert receives suggestions regarding the most appropriate exercises to recommend [5].

It is necessary for the speech therapist to have the possibility to intervene in modifying the knowledge database when the suggestion given by the expert system contradicts the speech therapist decision. The system has to self-notify the presence of a contradiction and to ask the human expert to remove the conflict. This principle is useful for the therapeutic system (in general) and for the expert system (in particular), especially in the case of the beginner speech therapist (with less practical training experience). Even if the computer decisions cannot be considered absolutely correct, they can contribute to the overall success of the therapy by raising questions which require further clarifications by consulting a human expert.

2. Expert system validation

Since 2006 we have developed Logomon, the computer-based speech therapy system (CBST) for Romanian language. The modules of the integrated system are briefly presented in **Figure 3** (modules 1,…,9). All administrative tasks are grouped in the Lab Monitor Application. The expert system takes the information it needs from the database of this module. In the first scenario, the child exercises in SLT's Lab using Lab Monitor Application.

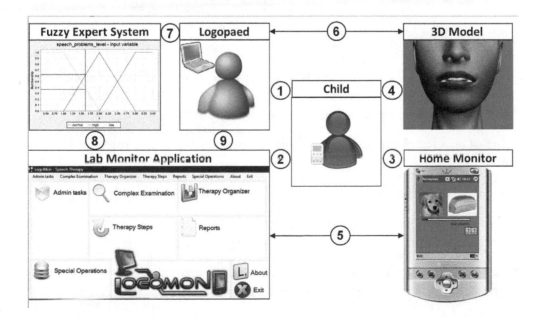

Figure 3. Architecture of Logomon CBST.

Another scenario involves the utilization of a dynamic 3D model, a module that indicates the correct positioning of elements of phono-articulator apparatus for each phoneme in Romanian language (the model can translate and rotate; the transparency of each individual elements—teeth, tongue, cheeks—can also be modified). Homework is mainly generated by the fuzzy expert system that indicates the number, the duration, and the content of home exercises. These exercises are played on a mobile device (Home Monitor), without SLT intervention [6]. The relations between input and output variables are presented in **Figure 4**.

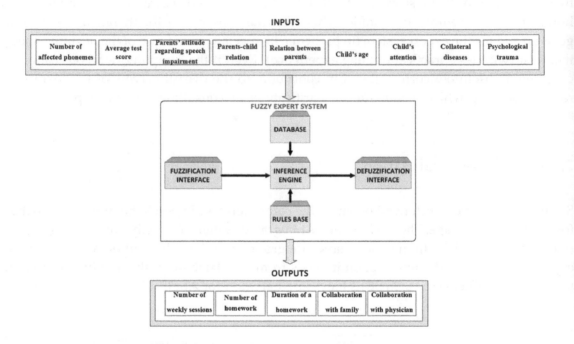

Figure 4. The relation between input and output variables.

The expert system is fed with information taken from three sources: socio-psychological parameters (Lab Monitor Application), tests scores (Lab Exercises), and homework scores (Home Monitor). These numbers are grouped in nine input variables [3].

1.   number of affected phonemes (in order to differentiate between simple and polymorphic dyslalia);

2.   average test score (indicates the intensity of impairment);

3.   parents' attitude regarding speech impairment (the parents' attitude is a key factor in therapy prognosis);

4.   parents–child relation (offer important clues regarding the importance of home training sessions);

5.   relation between parents (describes the emotional quality of familial environment);

6.   child's age (the therapeutical strategy largely vary with subject's age);

7. child's attention (this variable was taken into consideration due to increasing frequency of ADHD—attention deficit disorders—among the children);

8. collateral diseases (AIDS, Down syndrome, intellectual disabilities, nutrition diseases);

9. psychological trauma (shows the child's emotional health).

The expert system outputs five numbers that configure the personalized therapy:

1. number of weekly sessions (how many times in a week the child should encounter SLT?);

2. number of homeworks (how many homework sessions should be?);

3. duration of a homework (how long a homework should last?);

4. collaboration with family (should SLT rely on child's family support?);

5. collaboration with physician (does SLT have to collaborate with a physician?).

One major limitation of such a system is the inability to express and/or mimic emotions such as empathy and to recognize emotional states. To improve this, some studies used the human–computer interaction (HCI) model in which trained individuals reflecting a particular emotional state are used. In our previous work, we explored the possibility of adapting and integrating the classical techniques of emotion recognition in the assisted therapy for children with speech problems [6].

The fuzzy expert system is based on forward chaining of over 200 rules written in fuzzy control language (FCL). The expert system engine is coded in Java language and is integrated in our speech therapy platform. In order to adjust and validate the inferential process, we used our platform for more than 100 children from 2008 to 2015. The extension of our system using an artificial neural network (ANN) is demanding especially because it is relative hard for a SLT to change a fuzzy rule. Thus, in the case of a contradiction between human and artificial expert, an ANN could facilitate the re-training process [7, 8].

3. State of the art in fuzzy expert systems, artificial neural network and medical application

Because of the emergence of interdisciplinary technologies during the past few years, the interaction between doctors and engineers opened unprecedented opportunities, and the medical specialists are employing computerized technologies to assist in diagnosis of, and access to, related medical information.

3.1. Fuzzy expert systems for medical diagnosis

The rapid progress in computer technology plays a key role in the development of medical diagnostic tools that call for the need of more advanced intelligent and knowledge-based systems [9]. This is important since medical diagnosis is characterized by a high degree of uncertainty that can be improved through the application of fuzzy techniques that provide powerful decision support, expert systems knowledge, and enhanced reasoning capabilities in the decision-making process. Also, it provides a powerful framework for the combination of evidence and deduction of consequences based on knowledge stored in the knowledge base [9]. Therefore, fuzzy expert system (FES) can be used in applications for diagnosis, patient monitoring and therapy, image analysis, differential diagnosis, pattern recognition, medical data analysis [10–14].

The areas in which diversified applications are developed using fuzzy logic are fuzzy models for illness, heart and cardiovascular disease diagnosis, neurological diseases, asthma, abdominal pain, tropical diseases, medical analogy of consumption of drugs, diagnosis and treatment of diabetes, syndrome differentiation, diagnosis of lung and liver diseases, monitoring and control in intensive care units and operation rooms, diagnosis of chronic obstructive pulmonary diseases, diagnosis of cortical malformation, etc. The non-disease areas of applications are in X-ray mammography, interpretation of mammographic and ultrasound images, electrographic investigation of human body. Other areas for the applications of fuzzy logic are prediction of aneurysm, fracture healing, etc.

Recent research studies have contributed to the development of diagnostic techniques, quantification of medical expertise, knowledge technology transfer, identification of usage patterns, and applications of FES in practice by the medical practitioners [15]. According to [15], 21% of studies present the development of methodologies and models and 13% studies contributed to the development of neuro-fuzzy-based expert systems [9]. These studies contributed to the development of innovative diagnostic techniques, quantification of medical expertise, and application of fuzzy expert systems and their implementation in practice.

The rationale behind the decision-making process in medical diagnosis is a complex endeavor that involves a certain degree of uncertainty and ambiguity. The computer-assisted expert system that incorporates the fuzzy model has been used to aid the physician in this process [15]. As such, several computer-assisted applications for patient's diagnosis and treatments as well as web-based FES have been recently developed and include ways of handling vagueness

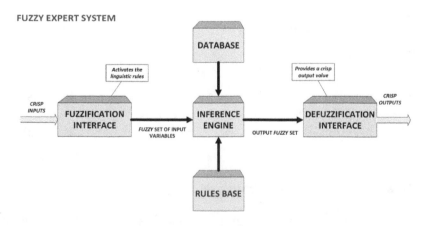

Figure 5. Fuzzy *expert* system architecture.

and complexity (**Figure 5**). Furthermore, disease-focused intelligent medical systems are rapidly emerging and are designed to handle more complex variables such as patient monitoring, predictive values, as well as taking into account assessment and performance parameters.

The architecture of a generic medical fuzzy expert system showing the flow of data through the system is depicted in **Figure 6** [9]. The knowledge base for developed medical FES contains both static and dynamic information. There are qualitative and quantitative variables, which are analyzed to arrive at a diagnostic conclusion. The fuzzy logic methodology involves fuzzification, inference engine, and defuzzification as the significant steps [9].

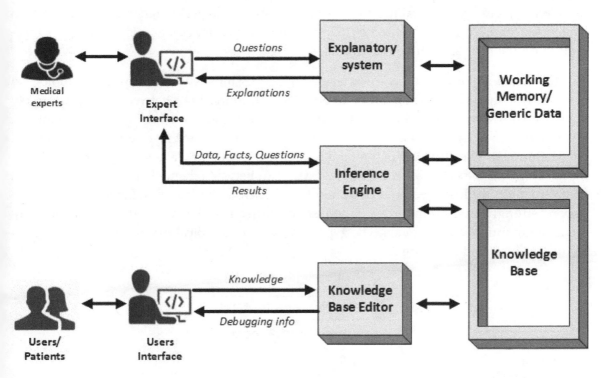

Figure 6. The architecture of a generic medical fuzzy expert system.

The FES uses both quantitative and qualitative analyses of medical data and represents a useful tool in achieving a high success rate in medical diagnosis. These computer-based diagnostic tools together with the knowledge base have proved very useful in early diagnosis of pathologies. On the other hand, the web-based applications and interfaces allow health practitioners to readily share their knowledge and know-how expertise [15].

3.2. Application of artificial neural network in medicine

An artificial neural network (ANN) is a computational model that attempts to account for the parallel nature of the human brain [16]. Analyzing approaches in different scientific procedures, the ability to learn, tolerance to data noises and capability to model incomplete data have made them unique, and once the network has been trained, new data in similar domain may be analyzed and predicted [17].

In the medical field, ANN applications that have been developed use the "classification" principle-based on which patients are assigned to a particular set of classes based on specific biological measures. For example, ANN applications have been used in the diagnosis of diabetes (using blood and urine analyses) [18, 19], tuberculosis [20, 21], leukemia [22], cardiovascular conditions [23] (such as heart murmurs [24]), liver [25], and pulmonary [26] diagnosis, as well as in urological dysfunctions [27], including expert pre-diagnosis system for automatic evaluation of possible symptoms from the uroflow results [28], and ANN applications have also been used in image analyses [29, 30] and in analysis of complicated effusion samples [31]. Finally, a neural networks-based automatic medical diagnosis system has been developed for eight different diseases [32], and in detection and diagnosis of micro-calcifications in digital format mammograms [33].

An ANN is a network of highly interconnecting processing elements (inspired by biological nervous systems—neurons) operating in parallel. The connections between elements largely determine the network function. A subgroup of processing element is a layer in the network. Each neuron in a layer is connected with each neuron in the next layer through a weighted connection [34]. The structure of a neural network is formed by layers. The first layer is the input layer, and the last layer is the output layer, and between them, there may be additional layer(s) of units (hidden layers) [16]. The number of neurons in a layer and the number of layers depend strongly on the complexity of the system studied [34]. Therefore, the optimal network architecture must be determined. The general scheme of a typical three-layered ANN architecture is illustrated in **Figure 7**.

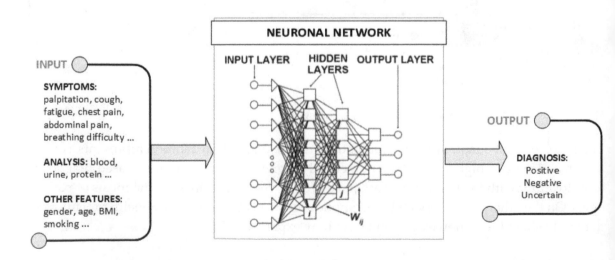

Figure 7. General structure of a neural network (modify after [34]).

Based on the way they learn, all artificial neural networks are divided into two learning categories: supervised and unsupervised. In unsupervised networks, the training procedure uses inputs only, and there are no known answers and the network must develop its own representation of the input stimuli by calculating the acceptable connection weights. On the other hand, training in the supervised learning involves both input and output patterns so that the neural weights can be changed to generate the desired output [16]. In medical applications, supervised networks may be used as alternatives to conventional response surface methodology (RSM) while the unsupervised ones can serve as alternatives to principal component analysis (PCA) in order to map multidimensional data sets onto two-dimensional spaces [17].

Models from ANNs are multifactorial models which can predict, classify, approximate function, or recognize patterns. Theoretically, ANNs are able to estimate any function and if used properly, it can be used effectively in medicine. Outputs from artificial neural networks models are generated from nonlinear combinations of input variables, and such models can be effectively employed to deal with experimental data routinely observed in medicine and to find rules governing a process from raw input data [17].

3.3. Neuro-fuzzy models

The development of intelligent systems in the health field is based on the complementarity between technologies that use the combination between fuzzy logic and neural networks models. This generated the neuro-fuzzy model that takes advantage of both the capability in modeling uncertain data by the artificial neural networks as well as of handling qualitative knowledge. The neuro-fuzzy approaches have been used in several studies to build more intelligent decision-making systems as additional supportive tools for the physicians.

For example, an application of artificial neural networks in typical disease diagnosis using a fuzzy approach was investigated in [35]. The real procedure of medical diagnosis which usually is employed by physicians was analyzed and converted to a machine implementable format. Similarly, in [16], a series of experiments were described and advantages of using a fuzzy approach were discussed.

Neuro-fuzzy (NF) computing becomes a popular framework for solving complex problems based on knowledge expressed in linguistic rules for building a FES, and on data, for learning from a simulation (training) using ANNs. For building a FES, we have to specify the fuzzy sets, fuzzy operators, and the knowledge base. For constructing an ANN for an application, the user needs to specify the architecture and the learning algorithm. Both approaches have their own drawbacks, and they should be combined when building an integrated system [36]. This way we can take advantage of the learning capabilities, which is essential for the fuzzy expert system as well as the linguistic base knowledge that constitutes part of the artificial neural networks.

Therefore, FES and ANNs have attracted the attention of many scientists, and also a huge number of successful applications of them are found in the literature, reporting problems solving in various areas of sciences, such as computing, engineering, medicine, nanotechnology, environmental science, and business.

4. Fuzzy expert system vs. neuro-fuzzy expert system

The fuzzy expert systems (FES) and artificial neuronal network (ANN) have common origin and purposes. They may carry out the logical reasoning, simulating artificial intelligence, by combining the quantitative and qualitative information and meta-knowledge. The advantages and disadvantages of these techniques are complementary. The main disadvantages of FES as regards to the acquisition of knowledge can be easily eliminated using ANN, due to its ability to learn from typical examples. On the other hand, limitations of the ANN related to the man–machine interface and capabilities to explain the reasoning leading to a certain conclusion can be theoretically compensated using the FES [10].

The FES has the following properties: (i) sequential processing; (ii) the acquisition process of knowledge takes place outside the expert system; (iii) the logic is a deducible; (iv) the knowledge is presented in the explicit form; (v) the system is based on the knowledge acquired from human experts; (vi) the rules in the chain of the rules have their origin in the logic of mathematics and fuzzy logic; and (vi) the extraction of the conclusion (implementation of the diagnosis) is done by correlating the exact amount of information and data [10].

The ANN, due to the fact that is designed according to the model of the human brain, has the ability: (i) to learn; (ii) has the advantage of a parallel processing; (iii) the acquisition of knowledge takes place inside the system; (iv) the logic is inductively; (v) the knowledge is the default and gained through examples; (vi), uses parameters and statistical methods for classification and data clustering; and (vii) the extraction of the learned conclusion is made by the approximate correlation of data.

A significant difference between the two instruments lies in the basis of reasoning. As such, the FES is based on the algorithms and deductions, while the ANN is based on the inference from simulating the learning mechanisms of specialized neurons. Based on the techniques used for processing information, the ESF uses sequential methods of processing while ANN has parallel processing, that is, each neuron performs functions in parallel with other neurons in the network.

In the case of learning processes and reasoning in the FES, learning is made outside of the system and the knowledge is obtained from outside and then coded in the knowledge base. For ANN, the knowledge accumulates in the form of weights of the connections between the nodes (neurons), the learning process being internal, permanently adjusting the knowledge deployments as new examples. The FES is based on the method of deductive reasoning, unlike the ANN, in which the methods are inductive. The algorithms of inference of the FES are based on the logic of the sequence "forward or backward" method in the knowledge base, and the ANN uses the approximate correlation of the components of the knowledge base in order to return to items previously learned. The ANN may acquire knowledge through direct learning from examples, which constitutes an advantage, on the basis of algorithms of specific learning with the possibility to learn from the incomplete or partially incorrect or contradictory input data, having the capacity to generalize. On the other hand, the FES has the advantage of a friendly user interface with the possibility of incorporating elements of heuristic reasoning.

One of the basic paradigms of artificial intelligence, with applications in the medical field, is to find a tool which will make it possible to the representation of a large number of meta-knowledge, consistent, and usable for the user. There are two approaches of a computerized system based on knowledge: the first approach is one in which the field of knowledge representation is based on the rules. This involves the necessity that human experts extract rules from its experience and express them in the form of explicit and comprehensible rules. The system has the explanatory and perfect skills and performs well with incomplete information and inaccurate (fuzzy) using the factors of trust, but the construction of such base of knowledge is a difficult task.

The second approach has a connection with the development of the theory of the neuronal networks which is automatically created by a learning algorithm from a variety of inference examples. The knowledge representation is based on the weights of the connections between the neurons. Due to the default representation of knowledge, there is no possibility to identify a problem at the level of the singular neuron. In this case, both working with incomplete information and the provision of evidence of the inference are limited.

From these considerations, combining fuzzy expert system with the neuronal networks will lay the base for the construction of a practical application for strategic decisions, (especially medical decisions), both tactical and operative, and will integrate the advantages of both types of information systems (neuro-fuzzy system expert) [10].

The main challenge in the integration of these two approaches is the creation of the knowledge base when they are only available the rules and examples of data. Additional problems may also occur when incomplete and unreliable information is encoded in neuronal networks. Therefore, it is necessary that the "learning" network is able to work with incomplete information during training in place of using of special heuristic inference.

The inputs and outputs values in a neuro-fuzzy expert system are coded using the analog statuses of neuronal values. An inference is a pair consisting of a vector of the typical inputs and the vector to the corresponding outputs obtained by the expert answers to these questions. Knowledge base of the neuro-fuzzy expert system is a multilayer neuronal network.

To solve the problems raised by the irrelevant values and unknown inputs and outputs of the expert system, the range neuron should be created. The value of the irrelevant or even unknown input and output of the expert system is coded using the full range of status of neurons.

The expert systems become effective and efficient not only to resolve problems of high complexity but also for the decision-making problems, which contain a high degree of uncertainty.

More recently, a hybrid system that includes fuzzy logic, neuronal networks, and genetic algorithms has been developed this required inclusion of additional techniques. The fundamental concept of these hybrid systems consists in complementarity and addresses the weaknesses of each other. The fuzzy expert systems are appropriate especially in the case of systems that have a mathematical model that is difficult to comprehend, for example, when the values of the inputs and of the parameters are vague, imprecise, and/or incomplete. It facilitates the decision-making process in the case of use of the estimated values for the inaccurate information (if the decision is not correct, it may be modified later when more information becomes available). Fuzzy models allow us to represent the descriptive phrases/ qualitative, which are subsequently incorporated in the symbolist instructions (fuzzy rules).

Neuro-fuzzy expert system has the following two functions: (i) the generalization of the information derived from the training data processed by the entries with fuzzy learning and incorporation of knowledge in the form of a neuronal fuzzy network; (ii) the extraction of fuzzy rules "IF THEN" using the importance of linguistic relative diversity of each sentence in a prerequisite ("IF" part), using for this purpose a trained neuro-fuzzy network. The neural network is similar to the standard multilayer network, having in addition, direct connections between the input and output nodes. Activation of nodes is muted, taking the values of +1, 0, or -1.

To work with various fuzzifications in the input and the output layers of the system, it is necessary to interpret the subjective input data. The neuronal network may include groups of fuzzy neurons and groups of non-fuzzy neurons involving shades and accurate data. The output layer will contain only fuzzy neurons.

By incorporating the factor of certainty (groups of non-fuzzy neurons) extends the traditional logic in two ways: (i) sets are labeled from the point of view of quality, and the elements in the same set are assigned different degrees of membership; (ii) any action which results from a valid premise will be executed with a weighting in order to reflect the degree of certainty.

The entrances of the system "suffer" three transformations to become exits: (i) fuzzification of the inputs which consists in the calculation of a value to represent the factor of membership in the qualitative groups; (ii) assessing the rules that consists in the elaboration of a set of rules type "IF THEN"; (iii) outputs defuzzification in order to describe the significance of vague actions through the functions of membership and to resolve the conflicts between competing actions which may trigger [10].

The factor of membership is determined by the function of membership, which is defined on the basis of intuition or experience. To implement a fuzzy system, the following data structure is required: (i) the entries in the system; (ii) the functions of the input membership; (iii) the previous values; (iv) a basis for the rules; (v) the weightings of the rules; (vi) the functions of the output membership; and (vii) exits from the system.

The use of fuzzy logic leads to finding answers and allows drawing conclusions on the basis of vague, ambiguous, and inaccurate information. Fuzzy techniques adopt reasoning similar to human, which allows a quick construction of technical, feasible, and robust systems. The application of the fuzzy methods involves less space of memory and a lot of calculation power in comparison with conventional methods. This fact leads to less expensive systems. The fuzzy expert systems should be constructed in such manner that the overall results are able to change in a way that is smooth and continuous, regardless of the type of inputs. Artificial neural networks have the advantage that it can be included in the fuzzy expert systems, becoming parts of it in the framework of a hybrid neuro-fuzzy expert system. In the majority of the medical applications, the ANN can be used for quick identification of the conditions on the base of FES rules, laying down quickly the rules that should be applied for a given set of conditions.

In conclusion, the specialized literature presents several models of integrating the FES with ANN in the hybrid systems (neuro-fuzzy expert systems), with medical applications. In the strategy of the human expert (programmer), the ANN is driven to solve a problem, and then, the responses are analyzed in order to extract a set of rules. The integrated systems jointly use the data structures and knowledge. Communication between the two components is carried out with both the symbolic and heuristic information, FES characteristics, and with their ANN structures, that is, using weighted coefficients.

5. Results and discussion

To solve issues related to classification, the objects should be grouped in clusters (in our case patients with speech disorders) based on their characteristics (feature vectors) in predefined classes. Classifiers are then built from examples of correct classification by a supervised learning process as opposed to unsupervised learning, where categories are not predefined.

For the classifier design, based on examples of classification, we grouped data into three main sets:

- Training data: data used in the training process to determine the classifier parameters (for example, in the case of the artificial neural networks, it is necessary to determine the weights of connections between neurons) (1).

- Validation data: data used to analyze the behavior during learning algorithm; the performance on the validation set during the learning process is used to decide whether or not learning should be continued (2);

- Test data: used to analyze the performance of a trained classifier (3).

ANN is composed of simple elements operating in parallel. Knowledge of ANN is stored as numerical values that are associated with connections between artificial neurons, named weights. ANN training means changing and/or adjusting the weights values. Most often, ANNs are trained so that for a given input, output returns a value as close to the desired output, a process exemplified in **Figures 8** and **9**.

For this process, a set of training data (pairs input–output) is required. To solve classification problems, we used the tools package offered by Matlab R2014, specifically the neural network Matlab package (nntool—the tool for classification).

We used a feedforward architecture characterized in [37]:

- An entry level that has as many units (attributes) as the input data;

- One or more hidden levels (the higher the number of hidden units, the greater the complexity of the model extracted from the network; however, this can be a disadvantage leading to decreased network capacity to generalization process);

- A level of output with as many units as the number of classes.

There are two main types of artificial neural networks:

- feedforward—with progressive propagation; the main characteristic of these networks is that a neuron receives signals only from neurons located in previous layer(s).

- feedback—with recurrent or regressive propagation; these networks are characterized by the fact that there is a feedback signal from the higher-order neurons, for those on lower layers or even for themselves.

We used a feedforward network for illustration (see **Figure 9**).

To design a simple Matlab neural network for classification ("Pattern Recognition"), we used "*nprtool*" tool that opens a graphical interface that allows specification of a network element characterized by the following:

- a level of hidden units (the number of hidden units can be chosen by the user);

- the logistics activation (logsig) for both hidden units and for the output [(output values ranged between (0.1)];

- the backpropagation training algorithm based on minimization method of conjugate gradient.

The artificial neural networks have the ability to learn, but the concrete way by which the process is accomplished is dictated by the algorithm used for training. A network is considered trained when application of an input vector leads to a desired output, or very close to it. Training consists of sequential application of various input vectors and adjusting the weights of the network in relation to a predetermined procedure. During this time, weights of the connections gradually converge toward certain values so that each input vector produces the desired output vector. Supervised learning involves the use of an input–output vector pair desired [37].

After input setting, the output is calculated by comparing the calculated output with the desired output, and then, the difference is used to change the weights in order to minimize the error to an acceptable level. In a backpropagation neural network, learning algorithm has two stages: the training patterns for the input layer and the updated error propagation. The ANN propagates the training pattern layer by layer, until it generates the output pattern. If this is different from the desired target pattern, it will calculate the error and will be backpropagated from the output to the input. The weights are updated simultaneously with error propagation [37].

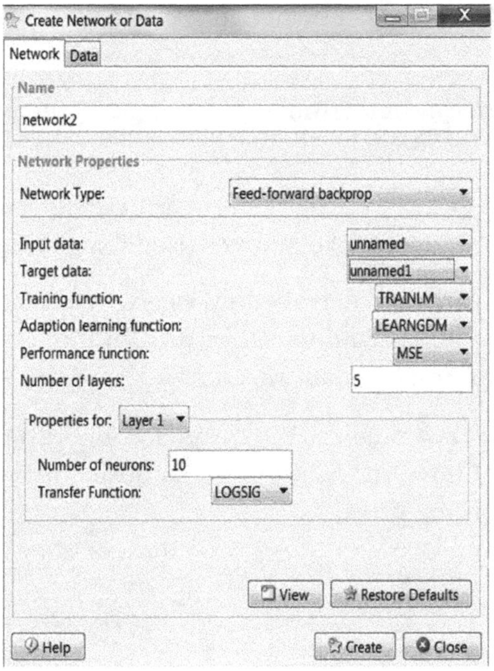

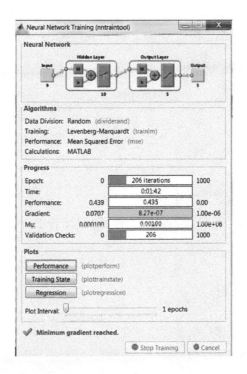

Figure 8. Create network using Matlab.

Figure 9. Neural network design and training.

The proposed artificial neural network uses supervised learning with two rules (see **Figures 10** and **11**):

1. extraction of a subset from the training dataset for testing dataset (not used during setting network parameters)

2. maintaining an acceptable level of error in the training set to avoid over learning (learning insignificant details of examples used for training).

The training process is controlled by means of a technique of cross-validation, which consists in splitting the initial random set of data in three subsets: for actual training (training); for controlling learning (validation); and for classifier's quality assurance (testing).

We used backpropagation as the correction algorithm (regressive propagation of errors) with propagation of the error signal in the opposite direction compared to how the signal travels during the working phase.

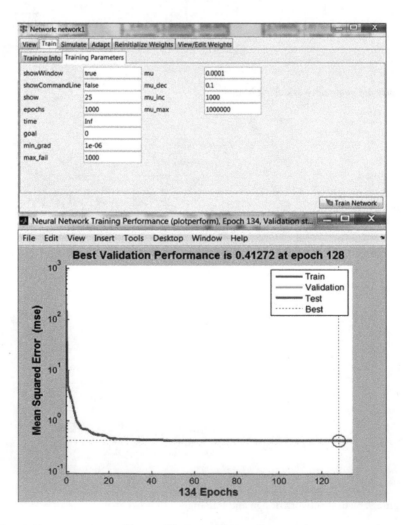

Figure 10. Network training parameters and best validation performance.

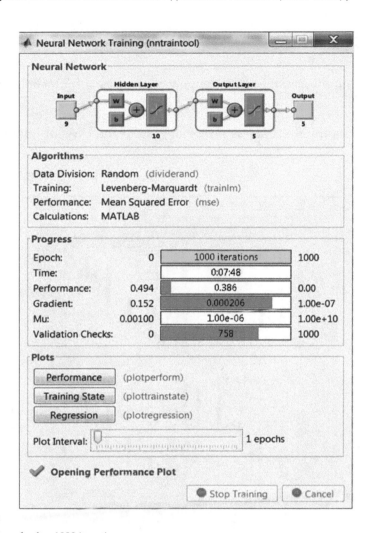

Figure 11. Neural network after 1000 iterations.

The training of the neural network lasted 1000 epochs. Matlab interface allows us to display graphs of the statistical parameters, for example, the mean square error, regression (the correlation between desired values and targets, and the values ??obtained; The R correlation close to 1 means a value very close?? to the desired one). Mean values ??for MSE and R are available after training in the main window, under Results section. Identification of classes of subjects from the dataset tested with ANN was achieved with high specificity and accuracy (see **Figures 12** and **13**).

One of the trivial artificial neural network is SOM—self-organizing map, which is mainly used for data clustering and feature mapping (see **Figures 14** and **15**).

The quality of a classifier in terms of correct identification of a class is measured using information from confusion matrix that contains the following:

- The number of data correctly classified as belonging to the class interests: true positive cases (TP);

- The number of data correctly classified as not belonging to the class of interest: true negative cases (TN);

- The number of data misclassified as belonging to the class of interest: false positive cases (FP);

- The number of data misclassified as not belonging to the class of interest: false negative cases (FN).

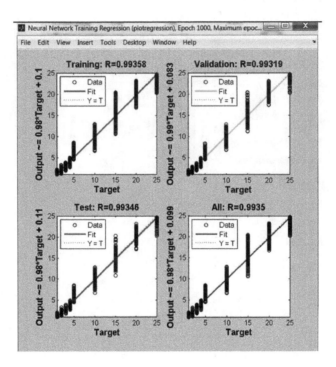

Figure 12. Neural network training regression.

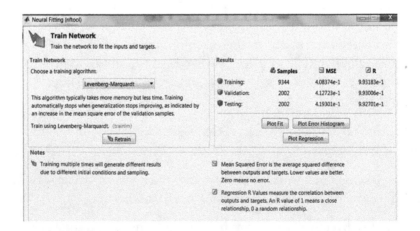

Figure 13. Train the network to fit the input and targets.

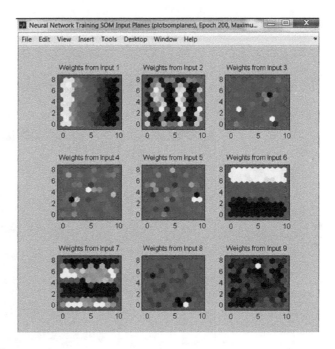

Figure 14. Neural network training self-organizing map (SOM) Input Planes, epoch 200.

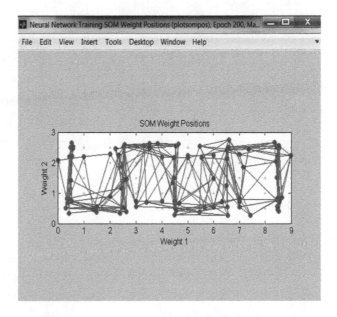

Figure 15. Neural network training Self-Organizing Map (SOM) Weight Positions, epoch 200.

Based on these values, we calculated the following measures:

Sensitivity = TP/(TP + FN)

Specificity = TN/(TN + FP)

Precision = TP/(TP + FP)

Recall = TP/(TP + FN)

F = 2 × precision × recall/(precision + recall)

Model Name	Training			Cross Validation			Testing		
	RMSE	r	MAE	RMSE	r	MAE	RMSE	r	MAE
MLPR-1-O-M (Regression MLP)	0.508933	1.402201	0.409704	0.322604	0.922972	0.255361	0.358704	0.96404	0.290742
MLPC-1-O-M (Classification MLP)	0.327037	1.220537	0.244729	0.321762	1.156201	0.219466	0.40723	1.18764	0.282503
LinR-0-B-R (Linear Regression)	0.392882	1.147459	0.321291	0.436575	1.334644	0.352292	0.55806	1.462276	0.455368
LinR-0-B-L (Linear Regression)	0.392851	1.145372	0.321291	0.436507	1.329756	0.352205	0.557872	1.453303	0.455158
LogR-0-B-R (Logistic Regression)	0.392077	1.238948	0.325784	0.428968	1.46138	0.322088	0.527981	1.59547	0.390729
LogR-0-B-L (Logistic Regression)	0.39111	1.230656	0.327396	0.423441	1.447031	0.322429	0.519991	1.579243	0.3882
MLPR-1-B-L (Regression MLP)	0.387056	1.198567	0.317948	0.421741	1.419294	0.335343	0.519126	1.529009	0.411309
MLPC-1-B-L (Classification MLP)	0.38846	1.141375	0.319109	0.394126	1.255082	0.311733	0.487495	1.489909	0.383896
PNN-0-N-N (Probabilistic Neural Network)	0.085338	0.456856	0.04353	0.271987	1.451648	0.11348	0.280823	1.952781	0.10972
RBF-1-B-L (Radial Basis Function)	0.662088	1.442092	0.534637	0.650547	1.28424	0.540903	0.616498	1.289826	0.504839
GFFR-1-B-L (Reg Gen Feedforward)	0.271436	1.084635	0.219762	0.303184	1.088514	0.240272	0.415099	1.284186	0.334125
GFFC-1-B-L (Class Gen Feedforward)	2.311805	11.90048	1.371521	4.419387	11.95021	2.995643	5.125515	13.28726	3.688224
MLPRPC-1-B-L (Reg MLP with PCA)	0.881967	2.045036	0.720389	0.813134	2.04216	0.673859	0.836139	2.042751	0.688616
MLPCPC-1-B-L (Class MLP with PCA)	0.542446	1.381137	0.477375	0.545818	1.408567	0.499732	0.593192	1.471763	0.531133
SVM-0-N-N (Classification SVM)	0.978216	3.46208	0.775134	0.57077	1.854557	0.461521	0.37726	1.215167	0.319964
TDNN-1-B-L (Time-Delay Network)	0.379655	2.001422	0.316254	0.407738	1.357801	0.318339	0.492179	1.460222	0.374016
TLRN-1-B-L (Time-Lag Recurrent Network)	0.471094	1.868466	0.393253	0.495184	1.631292	0.411436	0.547943	1.703328	0.44724
RN-1-B-L (Recurrent Network)	0.425129	1.325358	0.351005	0.398425	1.612961	0.298228	0.478658	1.58024	0.350892
MLPR-2-B-L (Regression MLP)	0.320861	1.233744	0.265915	0.331135	1.207313	0.26449	0.357926	1.260343	0.284382
MLPC-2-B-L (Classification MLP)	0.315982	1.167649	0.247558	0.357427	1.399602	0.242102	0.459333	1.542289	0.307155
MLPR-1-B-R (Regression MLP)	0.301484	1.14782	0.229342	0.33914	1.300022	0.233399	0.436376	1.420916	0.29758
MLPC-1-B-R (Classification MLP)	0.329803	1.479794	0.266462	0.33202	1.113177	0.250788	0.399761	1.220224	0.297668
MLPR-2-O-M (Regression MLP)	0.221099	1.074964	0.120141	0.113037	0.961053	0.054785	0.151261	0.932933	0.064494
MLPC-2-O-M (Classification MLP)	0.348334	1.121105	0.268159	0.318955	0.867087	0.223579	0.369996	0.924195	0.258641
MLPR-2-B-R (Regression MLP)	0.203215	0.933993	0.137048	0.231383	0.966788	0.141672	0.246501	1.069248	0.143614
MLPC-2-B-R (Classification MLP)	0.384336	1.4615	0.321085	0.432656	1.692839	0.343492	0.523127	1.739074	0.407794
MLPRPC-1-O-M (Reg MLP with PCA)	0.945582	1.954717	0.778937	0.666084	1.83967	0.536057	0.712878	1.839316	0.576275
MLPCPC-1-O-M (Class MLP with PCA)	0.545546	1.582078	0.484669	0.521149	1.344116	0.495434	0.553071	1.412793	0.514216
MLPRPC-1-B-R (Reg MLP with PCA)	0.54491	1.34828	0.46731	0.557591	1.428227	0.475297	0.613538	1.527512	0.504508
MLPCPC-1-B-R (Class MLP with PCA)	0.540359	1.434408	0.479016	0.546114	1.337124	0.501908	0.571789	1.370814	0.517757
GFFR-1-O-M (Reg Gen Feedforward)	0.454291	1.575135	0.374846	0.375064	1.214175	0.291732	0.420285	1.159984	0.329084
GFFC-1-O-M (Class Gen Feedforward)	0.324176	1.029036	0.253448	0.313517	0.903713	0.226223	0.396962	1.007077	0.281022
GFFR-1-B-R (Reg Gen Feedforward)	0.338294	1.11053	0.282375	0.391334	1.27208	0.313176	0.519232	1.459908	0.4269
GFFC-1-B-R (Class Gen Feedforward)	0.380846	1.311824	0.315969	0.418067	1.516297	0.310688	0.517929	1.633733	0.37983
RBF-1-O-M (Radial Basis Function)	0.894092	1.921294	0.741068	0.621811	1.60236	0.516025	0.665073	1.605045	0.552353
RBF-1-B-R (Radial Basis Function)	0.653407	1.435348	0.532607	0.636503	1.28597	0.533418	0.603007	1.287842	0.500127
TDNN-1-O-M (Time-Delay Network)	0.533729	1.451931	0.396164	0.340023	1.162859	0.209211	0.402151	1.168537	0.254628
TDNN-1-B-R (Time-Delay Network)	0.295563	1.069168	0.253161	0.283278	0.960019	0.233299	0.297115	0.964466	0.249916
RN-1-O-M (Recurrent Network)	0.394225	1.378934	0.319767	0.323742	1.351473	0.241807	0.385874	1.635519	0.275718
RN-1-B-R (Recurrent Network)	0.397754	1.582702	0.322333	0.428865	1.776686	0.313778	0.521978	1.855299	0.380998
TLRN-1-O-M (Time-Lag Recurrent Network)	0.294567	1.088781	0.23422	0.25323	0.93366	0.174036	0.304505	0.991213	0.210027
TLRN-1-B-R (Time-Lag Recurrent Network)	0.346775	1.28851	0.276559	0.407926	1.355195	0.291143	0.506161	1.658579	0.360642

Figure 16. A multilayer perceptron network (MLP) best performance.

The results show that the best performance was obtained using a multilayer perceptron network (MLP). MLP is a feedforward neural network comprising one or more hidden layers. Like any neural network, a network with backpropagation is characterized by the connections between neurons (forming the network architecture), activation of functions used by neurons and learning algorithm that specifies the procedure used to adjust the weights. Usually, a backpropagation neural network is a multilayer network comprising three or four layers fully connected [37].

Each neuron computes its output similar to perceptron. Then, input value is sent to the activation function. Unlike perceptron, in a backpropagation neural networks, the neurons have sigmoid-type activation functions. Derivative function is very easy to calculate and ensure the output range [0, 1]. Each layer of a MLP neural network performs a specific function. The input layer accepts input signals and computational rarely contains neurons that do not process input patterns. Output layer supports output signals (stimuli coming from the hidden layer) and lays it out on the network. Detects hidden layer neurons traits and their weight is hidden patterns of input traits. These characteristics are then used to determine the output layer to the output pattern.

The backpropagation algorithm is a supervised learning algorithm named generalized delta algorithm. This algorithm is based on minimizing the difference between the desired output and actual output by descending gradient method. The gradient tells us how the function varies in different directions. The idea of the algorithm is finding the minimum error function in relation to relative weights of connections. The error is given by the difference between the desired output and the actual output of the network. The most common error function is the mean square error (**Figures 16** and **17**).

RMSE is the mean square error and is used to characterize the scattering of the data in relation to the average. In our case, in all three stages of ANN testing, we obtained RMSE values below 0.5, with 100% identification of classes as shown in **Figure 18**.

Performance Metrics

Model Name	Training RMSE	r	Correct	Cross Validation RMSE	r	Correct	Testing RMSE	r	Correct
MLPR-1-O-M (Regression MLP)	0.193136	0.504298	100.00%	0.40441	1.276899	100.00%	0.411551	0.828285	94.44%
MLPC-1-O-M (Classification MLP)	0.292957	0.659528	100.00%	0.423566	0.766415	100.00%	0.360862	0.77623	100.00%
LinR-0-B-R (Linear Regression)	0.334444	0.771683	100.00%	0.36981	0.774197	100.00%	0.378221	0.679267	94.44%
LinR-0-B-L (Linear Regression)	0.320609	0.723112	100.00%	0.382431	0.899123	100.00%	0.373497	0.713072	94.44%
LogR-0-B-R (Logistic Regression)	0.323498	0.802886	100.00%	0.411873	0.883485	100.00%	0.429729	0.777518	100.00%
LogR-0-B-L (Logistic Regression)	0.320243	0.756819	100.00%	0.399313	0.862804	100.00%	0.406476	0.735547	100.00%
MLPR-1-B-L (Regression MLP)	0.321919	0.701325	100.00%	0.448925	1.193378	100.00%	0.338979	0.690299	94.44%
MLPC-1-B-L (Classification MLP)	0.29544	0.929712	100.00%	0.504155	1.517705	100.00%	0.524958	1.351233	100.00%
PNN-0-N-N (Probabilistic Neural Network)	4.27E-06	2.41E-05	100.00%	0.578235	1	100.00%	0.522295	1	100.00%
RBF-1-B-L (Radial Basis Function)	0.391416	0.896709	100.00%	0.370999	0.691104	100.00%	0.468485	0.883554	100.00%
GFFR-1-B-L (Reg Gen Feedforward)	0.230875	0.608818	100.00%	0.513599	1.403539	100.00%	0.492597	1.227754	94.44%
GFFC-1-B-L (Class Gen Feedforward)	2.631665	11.12665	29.85%	2.33251	5.953767	42.11%	3.168973	10.87653	16.67%
MLPRPC-1-B-L (Reg MLP with PCA)	0.539245	1.436432	100.00%	0.505726	1.220976	100.00%	0.450536	0.946967	100.00%
MLPCPC-1-B-L (Class MLP with PCA)	0.604741	1.112989	100.00%	0.631973	1.093975	100.00%	0.440293	0.863168	100.00%
SVM-0-N-N (Classification SVM)	0.278716	0.667789	95.52%	0.324384	0.573036	94.74%	0.326516	0.558213	100.00%
TDNN-1-B-L (Time-Delay Network)	0.341169	0.862838	100.00%	0.721197	1.834166	100.00%	0.531575	0.985912	100.00%
TLRN-1-B-L (Time-Lag Recurrent Network)	1.009541	1.902801	100.00%	0.707728	1.619331	100.00%	0.906855	1.618652	100.00%
RN-1-B-L (Recurrent Network)	0.378266	0.882711	100.00%	0.465783	1.180841	100.00%	0.390453	0.773721	100.00%
MLPR-2-B-L (Regression MLP)	0.310913	0.896222	100.00%	0.476074	1.445478	100.00%	0.536759	1.04037	100.00%
MLPC-2-B-L (Classification MLP)	0.276627	0.854803	100.00%	0.497293	1.247617	100.00%	0.475513	1.028863	100.00%
MLPR-1-B-R (Regression MLP)	0.287202	0.768005	100.00%	0.406402	1.018289	100.00%	0.364087	0.870826	100.00%
MLPC-1-B-R (Classification MLP)	0.258878	0.717773	100.00%	0.414439	1.198915	100.00%	0.32167	0.687884	100.00%
MLPR-2-O-M (Regression MLP)	0.320195	0.69593	100.00%	0.445851	1.09194	100.00%	0.325504	0.728061	100.00%
MLPC-2-O-M (Classification MLP)	0.665406	1.262284	100.00%	0.586722	1.249546	100.00%	0.505312	1.243577	100.00%
MLPR-2-B-R (Regression MLP)	0.232608	0.747501	100.00%	0.410747	0.847326	100.00%	0.329586	0.68689	94.44%
MLPC-2-B-R (Classification MLP)	0.266694	0.745959	100.00%	0.344822	0.973972	100.00%	0.322039	0.714744	100.00%
MLPRPC-1-O-M (Reg MLP with PCA)	0.507237	1.213724	100.00%	0.477877	1.059424	100.00%	0.570024	1.198079	100.00%
MLPCPC-1-O-M (Class MLP with PCA)	0.57946	1.458307	100.00%	0.506006	1.161431	100.00%	0.445815	1.024323	100.00%
MLPRPC-1-B-R (Reg MLP with PCA)	0.49895	1.472917	100.00%	0.481242	0.966154	100.00%	0.555227	1.320027	100.00%
MLPCPC-1-B-R (Class MLP with PCA)	0.532171	1.479628	100.00%	0.440814	0.816954	100.00%	0.453173	0.812813	100.00%
GFFR-1-O-M (Reg Gen Feedforward)	0.270117	0.819621	98.51%	0.477297	0.929855	100.00%	0.458854	1.079618	94.44%
GFFC-1-O-M (Class Gen Feedforward)	0.3695	1.101388	100.00%	0.391954	0.822629	100.00%	0.319803	0.552367	100.00%
GFFR-1-B-R (Reg Gen Feedforward)	0.26564	0.766449	100.00%	0.486714	1.097254	100.00%	0.483942	1.302634	94.44%
GFFC-1-B-R (Class Gen Feedforward)	0.319684	0.808798	100.00%	0.37662	0.763517	100.00%	0.401291	0.794602	100.00%
RBF-1-O-M (Radial Basis Function)	0.551233	1.150324	100.00%	0.542021	0.974906	100.00%	0.393073	0.868909	100.00%
RBF-1-B-R (Radial Basis Function)	0.382085	0.841063	100.00%	0.37343	0.862982	100.00%	0.420303	0.819838	100.00%
TDNN-1-O-M (Time-Delay Network)	0.193776	0.849372	100.00%	0.541533	0.976413	100.00%	0.478553	0.881798	100.00%
TDNN-1-B-R (Time-Delay Network)	0.343269	1.009517	100.00%	0.489615	1.053666	100.00%	0.542653	0.973057	100.00%
RN-1-O-M (Recurrent Network)	0.566416	1.428649	100.00%	0.602502	1.37504	100.00%	0.653149	1.362624	100.00%
RN-1-B-R (Recurrent Network)	1.002518	2.107082	80.60%	1.266936	2.103606	73.68%	0.96296	1.911124	61.11%
TLRN-1-O-M (Time-Lag Recurrent Network)	0.403019	1.071385	100.00%	0.539168	1.007768	100.00%	0.40355	0.952376	100.00%
TLRN-1-B-R (Time-Lag Recurrent Network)	0.416302	0.921486	100.00%	0.589876	1.371814	100.00%	0.400352	0.779646	100.00%

Figure 17. Performance metrics. A multilayer perceptron network (MLP) best classification results (100% for training data vs. 100% for validation data vs. 100% for testing data).

Performance Metrics

	Training	Cross Val.	Testing
# of Rows	9344	2002	2002
RMSE	0.47151	0.281644	0.321151
Correlation (r)	1.538889	0.826787	0.84907
# Correct	9344	2002	2002
# Incorrect	0	0	0
% Correct	100.00%	100.00%	100.00%

Figure 18. Performance metrics.

In medical applications, it is required to use a neuro-fuzzy hybrid system that can be fitted with a neural network that presents many advantages such as: flexibility, speed, adaptability. The structure of a hybrid system is represented in **Figure 19**:

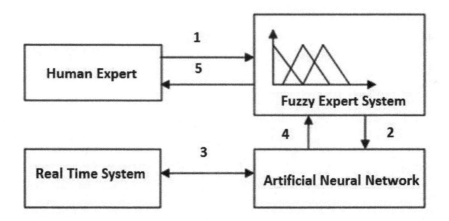

Figure 19. Hybrid neuro-fuzzy expert system [37].

The human expert knowledge is translated as symbolic (1) and is used for ANN initialization (2). The network is trained on a real inputs and outputs system (3). The knowledge obtained using ANN (4) is processed in a fuzzy manner for the determination of fuzzy rule, which are finally communicated to the human expert (5) [37]. These hybrid systems are suitable for the acquisition of knowledge and learning, and they can achieve inclusive process using weighting of the fuzzy neural network connections. Using a simple learning algorithm, such as backpropagation, neuro-fuzzy hybrid systems can identify fuzzy rules and then learn the associated functions of inferences. In summary, the hybrid system can also learn linguistic rules (fuzzy) as well as optimizing existing rules.

During generation and validation of expert system rules, we observed a positive correlation between speech disorders and eating disorders (obesity), so that a higher Body Max Index (BMI) exacerbated learning and speech difficulties in children. This is consistent with previous work demonstrating that risk of being obese in young adulthood was increased if the child had learning difficulties, scholastic proficiency below the class average, received special education, or had scholarly difficulties in childhood [38]. Therefore, our future studies will address the causal relationship between overweight, obesity, and various functions related to speech disorders and learning abilities during a longer period of time.

6. Conclusions

Each decision technique has specific advantages and drawbacks when it is used in medical field. Thus, a FES is able to make inferences with approximate data and, more importantly, it can track the decision-making process (i.e., the chain of activated rules). However, the rules must be written and, eventually, modified by human expert only. On the other hand, the artificial neural networks are the best choice when dealing with a large quantity of data and wish to obtain the related pattern but unable to provide useful information on how a specific conclusion is reached.

Due to the complementarity of expert system and artificial neural networks, several attempts to integrate these techniques have emerged. For example, combining qualitative modeling (based on fuzzy if-then rules) with quantitative modelling (used when all we have is chunks of already classified data) represents a major step forward. The hybrid neuro-fuzzy expert system is able to both learn by examples and organize knowledge and meta-knowledge in the form of fuzzy rules. For this type of system, we first fuel neural network with symbolic information and then adapt the raw model using individual examples. At the end of the process, we are able to extract symbolic information from trained neural network.

To the best of our knowledge, there are few, if any, studies based on the utilization of above-mentioned hybrid techniques in speech and language therapy of children. In this chapter, we have proposed and validated this original approach using Logomon, the first CBST for Romanian language. We have demonstrated that it is possible to use the equivalent relation between a fuzzy expert system and an artificial neural network in order to capitalize on the advantages of both techniques. The results are very encouraging and provide strong impetus to continuc these studies by extending rules database and by optimizing integration between the two parts of inferential system.

Acknowledgements

These authors contributed equally to this book chapter, and the work was supported by the Romanian National Program PN-II-ID-PCE-2012–4-0608 no. 48/02.09.2013, "Analysis of novel risk factors influencing control of food intake and regulation of body weight".

Author details

Ovidiu Schipor[1], Oana Geman[2*], Iuliana Chiuchisan[3] and Mihai Covasa[2,4]

*Address all correspondence to: oana.geman@usm.ro

1 Computers Department, Integrated Center for Research, Development and Innovation in Advanced Materials Nanotechnologies, and Distributed Systems for Fabrication and Control, "Stefan cel Mare" University of Suceava, Suceava, Romania

2 Department of Health and Human Development, "Stefan cel Mare" University of Suceava, Suceava, Romania

3 Computers, Electronics and Automation Department, "Stefan cel Mare" University of Suceava, Suceava, Romania

4 Department of Basic Medical Sciences, Western University of Health Sciences, Pomona, California, USA

References

[1] Verya E. Logopaedics Compendium. Humanitas Publisher: Bucharest, Romania; 2003.

[2] Schipor OA, Pentiuc SG, Schipor MD. Improving computer based speech therapy using a fuzzy expert system. Computing and Informatics—Slovak Academy of Sciences. 2010; 29(2):303–318.

[3] Schipor OA, Pentiuc SG, Schipor MD. Knowledge base of an expert system used for dyslalic children therapy. In: Proceedings of Development and Application System International Conference (DAS'08). Suceava, Romania; 2008, pp. 305–308.

[4] Schipor MD, Pentiuc SG, Schipor OA. End-user recommendations on LOGOMON—a computer based speech therapy system for Romanian language. Advances in Electrical and Computer Engineering. 2010; 10(4):57–60.

[5] Giza FF, Pentiuc SG, Schipor OA. Software Exercises for Children with Dyslalia. In: Proceedings of the Sixth International Scientific and Methodic Conference. Vinnytsia, Ukraine; 2008, pp. 317–326.

[6] Schipor OA, Schipor DM, Crismariu E, Pentiuc SD. Finding key emotional states to be recognized in a computer based speech therapy system. Journal of Social and Behavioral Sciences. 2011; 30:1177–1183.

[7] Badiru AB, Cheung JY. Fuzzy Engineering Experts Systems with Neural Network Application. John Wily & Sons: New York; 2002.

[8]   Zaharia MH, Leon F. Speech therapy based on expert system. Advances in Electrical and Computer Engineering. 2009; 9(1):74–77. ISSN:1582–7445.

[9]   Sikchi SS, Sikchi S, Ali MS. Design of fuzzy expert system for diagnosis of cardiac diseases. International Journal of Medical Science and Public Health. 2013; 2(1):56–61.

[10] Teodorescu HN, Zbancioc M, Voroneanu (Geman) O. Knowledge-based system applications. Performantica Publisher: Iasi; 2004, 293 p. ISBN: 973-730-014-9.

[11] Geman O. A fuzzy expert systems design for diagnosis of Parkinson's disease. In: Proceedings of the E-Health and Bioengineering Conference (EHB'11). Iasi, Romania: IEEE; 2011, pp. 122–126.

[12] Geman O. Nonlinear dynamics, artificial neural networks and neuro-fuzzy classifier for automatic assessing of tremor severity. In: Proceedings of the E-Health and Bioengineering Conference (EHB'13). Iasi, Romania: IEEE; 2013, p. 112–116.

[13] Geman O, Turcu CO, Graur A. Parkinson's disease screening tools using a fuzzy expert system. Advances in Electrical and Computer Engineering. 2013; 13(1):41–46.

[14] Geman O, Costin HN. Automatic assessing of tremor severity using nonlinear dynamics, artificial neural networks and neuro-fuzzy classifier. Advances in Electrical and Computer Engineering. 2014; 14(1):133–138.

[15] Sikchi S, Sikchi S, Ali MS. Fuzzy expert systems (FES) for medical diagnosis. International Journal of Computer Applications. 2013; 63(11):7–16. ISSN: 0975-8887.

[16] Al-Shayea QK. Artificial neural networks in medical diagnosis. IJCSI International Journal of Computer Science. 2011; 8(2):150–154. ISSN: 1694-0814.

[17] Hui C-L. Artificial Neural Networks–Application. InTech Publisher US; 2011; 586p, ISBN: 9–7895–3307–1886.

[18] Catalogna M, Cohen E, Fishman S, Halpern Z, Nevo U, Ben-Jacob E. Artificial neural networks based controller for glucose monitoring during clamp test. Plos One. 2012; 7:e44587.

[19] Fernandez de Canete J, Gonzalez-Perez S, Ramos-Diaz JC. Artificial neural networks for closed loop control of in silico and ad hoc type 1 diabetes. Computer Methods and Programs in Biomedicine. 2012; 106:55–66.

[20] Er O, Temurtas F, Tanrıkulu A. Tuberculosis disease diagnosis using artificial neural networks. Journal of Medical Systems. 2008; 34:299–302.

[21] Elveren E, Yumusak N. Tuberculosis disease diagnosis using artificial neural network trained with genetic algorithm. Journal of Medical Systems. 2011; 35:329–332.

[22] Dey P, Lamb A, Kumari S, Marwaha N. Application of an artificial neural network in the prognosis of chronic myeloid leukemia. Analytical and Quantitative Cytology and Histology. 2012; 33:335–339.

[23] Das R, Turkoglu I, Sengur A. Effective diagnosis of heart disease through neural networks ensembles. Expert Systems with Applications. 2009; 36(4):7675–7680.

[24] Higuchi K, Sato K, Makuuchi H, Furuse A, Takamoto S, Takeda H. Automated diagnosis of heart disease in patients with heart murmurs: application of a neural network technique. Journal of Medical Engineering & Technology. 2006; 30(2):61–68.

[25] Lin R. An intelligent model for liver disease diagnosis. Artificial Intelligence in Medicine. 2009; 47(1):53–62.

[26] Er O, Yumusak N, Temurtas F. Chest disease diagnosis using artificial neural networks. Expert Systems with Applications. 2010; 37(12):7648–7655.

[27] Gil D, Johnsson M, Garicia Chemizo JM, Paya AS, Fernandez DR. Application of artificial neural networks in the diagnosis of urological dysfunctions. Expert Systems with Applications. 2009; 36(3):5754–5760.

[28] Altunay S, Telatar Z, Erogul O, Aydur E. A new approach to urinary system dynamics problems: evaluation and classification of uroflowmeter signals using artificial neural networks. Expert Systems with Applications. 2009; 36(3):4891–4895.

[29] Barbosa D, Roupar D, Ramos J, Tavares A, Lima C. Automatic small bowel tumor 15 diagnosis by using multiscale wavelet based analysis in wireless capsule endoscopy 16 images. Biomed Eng Online. 2012; 17p, 11(3). doi:10.1186/1475-925X-11-3.

[30] Saghiri M, Asgar K, Boukani K, Lotfi M, Aghili H, Delvarani A, Karamifar K, Saghiri A, Mehrvarzfar P, Garcia-Godoy F. A new approach for locating the minor apical foramen using an artificial neural network. International Endodontic Journal. 2012; 45:257–265.

[31] Barwad A, Dey P, Susheilia S. Artificial neural network in diagnosis of metastatic carcinoma in effusion cytology. Cytometry Part B: Clinical Cytometry. 2012; 82:107–111.

[32] Moein S, Monadjemi SA, Moallem P. A novel fuzzy-neural based medical diagnosis system. International Journal of Biological & Medical Sciences. 2009; 4(3):146–150.

[33] Zhang G, Yan P, Zhao H, Zhang X. A computer aided diagnosis system in mammography using artificial neural networks. International Conference on BioMedical Engineering and Informatics, Sanya, China. 2008; 2:823–826. ISSN: 978–0–7695–3118–2.

[34] Amato F, Lopez A, Pena-Mendez EM, Vanhara P, Hampl A, Havel J. Artificial neural networks in medical diagnosis. Journal of Applied Biomedicine. 2013; 11:47–58.

[35] Monadjemi SA, Moallem P. Automatic diagnosis of particular diseases using a fuzzy-neural approach. International Review on Computers & Software. 2008; 3(4):406–411.

[36] Abraham A. Neuro fuzzy systems: state-of-the-art modelling techniques. In: International Work Conference on Artificial and Natural Neural Networks: Connectionist

Models of Neurons, Learning Processes and Artificial Intelligence; Granada, Spain, 2001, pp. 269–276. ISBN: 3540422358.

[37] Dosoftei C. Using computational intelligence in process management [thesis]. Romania; 2009.

[38] Lissau I, Sorensen TI. School difficulties in childhood and risk of overweight and obesity in young adulthood: a ten year prospective population study. International Journal of Obesity and Related Metabolic Disorders. 1993; 17(3):169–175.

6

Analyzing the Impact of Airborne Particulate Matter on Urban Contamination with the Help of Hybrid Neural Networks

Daniel Dunea and Stefania Iordache

Additional information is available at the end of the chapter

Abstract

In this study, particulate matter (PM), total suspended particulate (TSP), PM_{10}, and $PM_{2.5}$ fractions) concentrations were recorded in various cities from south of Romania to build the corresponding time series for various intervals. First, the time series of each pollutant were used as inputs in various configurations of feed-forward neural networks (FANN) to find the most suitable network architecture to the PM specificity. The outputs were evaluated using mean absolute error (MAE), mean absolute percentage error (MAPE), root mean square error (RMSE), and Pearson correlation coefficient (r) between observed series and output series. Second, each time series was decomposed using Daubechies wavelets of third order into its corresponding components. Each decomposed component of a PM time series was used as input in the optimal feed-forward neural networks (FANN) architecture established in the first step. The output of each component was re-included to form the modeled series of the original pollutant time series.

The final step was the comparison of FANN outputs with wavelet-FANN results to retrieve the wavelet utilization outcomes. The last section of the study describes the ROkidAIR cyberinfrastructure that integrates a decision support system (DSS). The DSS system uses artificial intelligence techniques and hybrid algorithms for assessing children's exposure to the pollution with particulate matter, in order to elaborate PM forecasted values and early warnings.

Keywords: air pollution, wavelet transformation, batch-learning algorithm, respiratory health, cyberinfrastructure

1. Air pollution with particulate matter in urban areas

Quantifying the human exposure to air pollutants is a challenging task because air pollution is characterized by high spatial and temporal variability. The atmospheric physicochemical parameters of interest from the point of view of air pollution in urban areas are carbon monoxide (CO), sulfur dioxide (SO_2), nitric oxide (NO), nitrogen dioxide (NO_2), various fractions of particulate matter (PM_{10}, $PM_{2.5}$, PM_1, and UFPs or ultrafine particles), ozone (O_3), volatile organic compounds (VOCs), and polycyclic aromatic hydrocarbons (PAHs). The levels of these parameters are significantly influenced by meteorological factors (such as speed and direction of wind, precipitations, temperature, relative humidity, and solar radiation), seasonal and diurnal fluctuations, geographical factors (e.g., local topography, buildings), emission sources i.e., industrial activities and traffic in the area, as well as the air mass trajectories (e.g., long-range transport of pollutants).

Class	Description	Size (in diameter)
TSP	Airborne particles or aerosols that constantly enter the atmosphere from many sources having below 100 µm are collectively referred to as total suspended particles (TSP). TSP is assessed with high-volume samplers.	Below 100 microns (<100 µm)
Large particulates	Particles are retained by the nasopharynx area.	Over 10 microns (>10 µm)
PM_{10}	Particulates that can be inhaled below the nasopharynx area (nose and mouth) and are thus called inhalable particulates (coarse fraction).	Below 10 microns (0–10 µm)
$PM_{2.5}$	Fine particulates travel down below the tracheobronchial region, that is, into the lungs (fine fraction).	below 2.5 microns (0–2.5 µm)
UFP	Ultrafine particulates can penetrate into the deepest parts of lungs and can be dissolved into blood (ultrafine fraction).	below 0.1 microns (0–0.1 µm)

The most hazardous size classes to humans are $PM_{2.5}$ and UFP as they penetrate into the lungs and can even be dissolved into the blood.

Table 1. Airborne particulate matter classification depending on particle size [8].

In many urban agglomerations around Europe, the concentrations of airborne particles, NO_x, and O_3 exceed at least occasionally the limit or target values. Therefore, air pollution control focuses mostly on the surveillance of the above-mentioned pollutants [1]. Urban agglomerations are areas of increased emissions of anthropogenic pollutants into the atmosphere having adverse health effects on population.

Consequently, a major issue of environmental policy at regional level is the reduction of their concentrations in the ambient air [2].

Particle sizes range from a few nanometers up to more than 100 µm, and depending on particle size, there are several classes of particles (**Table 1**). However, epidemiological studies have shown that the most hazardous size classes to human health are $PM_{2.5}$ and UFP, as they penetrate into the lungs and can even enter into the blood following the gas exchange. Diseases caused by UFP exposure primarily relates to lung cancer and heart disorders. Since the measurement of UFP is a difficult task requiring sophisticated equipment, one can monitor the submicrometric fraction that includes UFP using a reliable optical system, for example, Dusttrak DRX 8533 [3].

In the recent years, the most common size fraction that is usually monitored in the national air quality infrastructures at large scales in urban areas is $PM_{2.5}$. Recent long-term studies show the associations between PM and mortality at levels significantly below the current annual WHO air quality guideline level for $PM_{2.5}$, that is, 10 $\mu g/m^3$ (WHO, 2013).

The issue of studying the fine particulate matter is very complex and has many unknown variables mainly due to the multitude of sources from which it directly originate, as well as due to the physicochemical transformations that occur in the atmosphere, resulting in the formation of secondary $PM_{2.5}$ particulates [4–6]. Other major setbacks are the difficulties of compliance assessment and the setup of measurement methods equivalence. Furthermore, the methods of $PM_{2.5}$ measurement are still in the development period and the reference method was recently revised in EN 12341: 2014 standard [7].

2. Forecasting of particulate matter using neural networks

The analysis of environmental processes involves highly complex phenomena, random variations of parameters, and difficulty to perform accurate measurements in certain situations. In these conditions, the available data are incomplete, imprecise, and current applied models require further improvements.

Measuring and forecasting of atmospheric conditions is important for understanding the processes of formation, transformation, dispersion, transport, and removal of the pollutants. Reliable overall estimates regarding the identification of sources, effects on mixing, transformation, and transportation support the control of air quality and the implementation of preventive actions to reduce the anthropogenic emissions [8].

The performance of environmental management can be improved using forecasting tools of the potential pollution episodes that can affect the population from inner and surrounding areas where the episode might occur. Prediction of the evolution of an atmospheric parameter can be done for short term (1 h, 1 day, 1 month) or long term (1 or more years).

The interest in improving the forecasting performances of time series algorithms and models in air pollution studies has considerably grown. The applied methods may vary from statistical methods, artificial intelligence (AI) techniques, and probabilistic approaches to hybrid algorithms and complex models. The final purpose is to supplement monitored data and/or to complete the missing values in the time series of air pollutants.

The field of statistics, which deals with the analysis of time dependent data, is called time series analysis (TSA). One of the most widespread types of processing is the *time series forecasting*.

Many of these techniques are used in practice. We can mention, for example, random walks, moving averages, trend models, seasonal exponential smoothing, autoregressive integrated moving average (ARIMA) parametric models, Boltzmann composite lattice, etc.

Some of the traditional statistical models such as the moving average, exponential smoothing, and ARIMA model are linear techniques, which have been in the past the main research and application tools in air pollution research. Predictions of future values are constrained to be linear functions of past observations, under the assumption that the data series is stationary [9]. The general model ARIMA introduced by Box and Jenkins [10] involves the autoregressive and moving averages parameters, and explicitly includes differentiations in the formulation of the model. Three types of parameters are required in the model as follows: autoregressive parameter; differentiation passes, and moving averages parameters [10]. The ARIMA model assumes that a parametric model relating the most recent data value to previous data values and previous noise gives the best forecast for future data. However, one weakness of the ARIMA model resides in the assumption that the examined time series is stationary and linear, and therefore has no structural changes [9].

Air pollutants have a random evolution, which requires non-deterministic approaches. Advantages of neural computing techniques over conventional statistical approaches rely on faster computation, learning ability, and noise rejection [11]. Artificial neural networks (ANN), for example, succeeded to give good results for time series processing when the data present noise and nonlinear components. Their capacity of learning and generalization recommend them as valuable tools in a wide area of applications. The most popular architecture used in practice is the multilayer feed-forward neural network. Their processing units (neurons) are organized in layers and there exist only forward connections (i.e., their orientation is from the input layer toward the output). This type of networks started to be extensively used in the late 1980s when the standard back-propagation algorithm was introduced. Since that time, the multilayer feed-forward ANNs had a large applicability in various domains, that is, financial, health, meteorology, environmental protection, etc.

The research has been oriented to find faster algorithms for training the network and to provide algorithms to automate the design of an optimal network topology for a specific problem. We can mention the standard back-propagation with momentum or with variable learning rate, the adaptive Rprop, or algorithms based on the standard numerical optimization techniques (Fletcher-Powel, conjugate gradient, quasi-Newton algorithm, Levenberg-Marquardt, etc.).

Rprop algorithm introduced by Riedmiller and Braun [12] is a supervised batch learning which accelerates the training process in the flat regions of the error function and when the iterations get nearby a local minimum. This algorithm allows different learning rates for each weight. These rates are changed adaptively with the change of sign in the corresponding partial derivative of the error function. They change progressively but without getting out of an initially prescribed interval. The algorithm is described by four parameters denoted by η^+, η^-, Δ_{max} and Δ_{min}. The first two parameters give the increasing and decreasing factor for adjusting the update size and they are chosen such that $0 < \eta^- < \eta^+ < 1$. The size step of the update is bounded by Δ_{min} and Δ_{max}. The following values of the parameters were used in our tests: $\eta^+ = 1.25, \eta^- = 0.5, \Delta_{max} = 50, \Delta_{min} = 0$ [13].

Quickprop is a batch training algorithm introduced by Fahlman [14], which takes in consideration the information about the second-order derivative of the performance error function. Literature showed that Quickprop is a particular case of the multivariate generalization of the secant method for nonlinear equation [15]. The local minimum of the batch error function reached a critical point that is a zero of the gradient [13]. In practice, Newton's iteration is replaced by a quasi-Newton iteration, which uses an approximate of the Jacobian and saves the involved amount of computation. The approximation of the Jacobian by a diagonal matrix with its entries computed with finite difference formulas proves that Quickprop belongs to this category of quasi-Newton iterations. Its convergence is not anymore quadratic, but it remains linear in the vicinity of the solution. We have used the same value (equal to 1.75) for the maximum growth factor denoted by μ in [14], in all our tests with Quickprop algorithm.

3. Experimental setup

We used the resources of an AI forecasting system called RNA-AER [13] for the domain of air pollution forecasts in urban regions. RNA-AER stands for the Romanian abbreviation of ANN for air pollution. This is a part of a complex system for $PM_{2.5}$ forecasting based on various techniques of artificial intelligence (multi-agents, knowledge base system, ANNs, and neuro-fuzzy) and that is designed to analyze the pollution level of air within ROkidAIR system (http://www.rokidair.ro/en) [16]. A feed-forward neural network with a single hidden layer was used to perform the tests presented in this work (**Figure 1**).

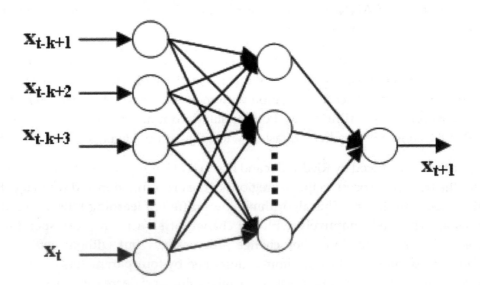

Figure 1. Example of feed-forward artificial neural network with one hidden layer.

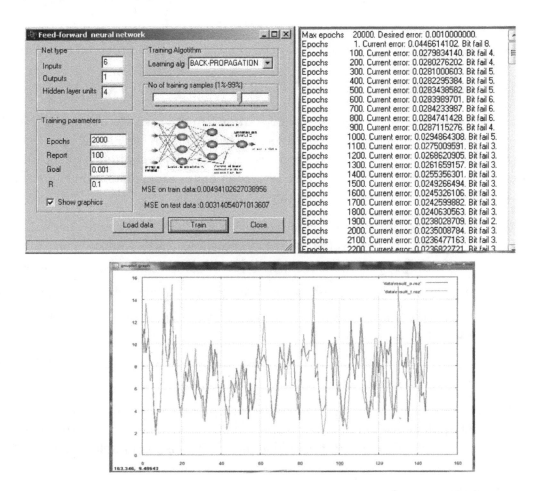

Figure 2. Front panel of the RNA-AER software with the feed-forward ANN configuration settings, error analysis, and observed and simulated time series.

The activation function used for the hidden and output layers was the symmetric sigmoid function (*tanh*). Since this function transforms the real axis into the range of (-1,1), the data were normalized before their use and transformed back in their real values after simulation.

In the training stage, we used various learning algorithms, but the most satisfactory results were obtained with Rprop and Quickprop. The application offers a friendly user interface from which one may choose various parameters that describe the network and the training algorithm. The program takes the raw data from one column text file and applies the necessary transformations in the preprocessing stage. After training, the application tests the network on the validation set of samples and shows the error. Then, the user is able to see the graphics for the evolution of the error in the training process and the observed and forecasted data (**Figure 2**). Best results were obtained with 4 or 6 units in the input layer, 6 neurons in the hidden layer and 1 output neuron. The output represents the one value ahead forecasted data. The network training comprised four learning algorithms. The first two were given by the batch and incremental implementations of the standard back-propagation learning [17]. These standard algorithms were tested with different values of the learning rate and momentum.

The other two algorithms were the resilient back-propagation Rprop and Quickprop. In this study, we present only the Rprop and Quickprop algorithms, which provided better results.

3.1. Steps for the development of a feed-forward neuronal model (FANN)

The use of raw data may rarely give satisfactory outputs. In this case, the training of the ANN will catch only general properties of the data series without being able to identify characteristics that are more refined. Therefore, a preprocessing step is often required in which the initial data are transformed such that the new data series eliminates some redundant characteristics from the analysis (e.g., interpolation, smoothing, wavelet decomposition, etc.).

The resulted series is then used to extract the required samples for training the network. Since our goal was to obtain one value ahead forecasting, each sample had the form $\left(x_{t-k+1}, x_{t-k+2}, ..., x_t, x_{t+1}\right)$, and the whole set of samples was obtained by moving window technique. Here, x_{t+1} represents the forecasting data while the other numbers are the corresponding inputs. Three-fourth of this set was used for training, while the rest was used in the validation process.

Inputs: particulate matter measurements of various PM fractions made in a certain default time window; outputs: one-step-ahead forecast of the PM pollutant.

Step 1. *Data preprocessing*. This stage involves the data processing, elimination of incomplete records, data interpolation to complete the missing values in the time series, data normalization validated by experts, and their redirection so that the database is compatible with the software used for forecasting.

Step 2. *Establishing the method of avoiding the overtraining of the ANN*. A common method is to divide the database into three sets of data: one for training (e.g., 75%), one for validation (e.g., 15%) and another one for testing (e.g., 15%). In some cases, the proportions that include the data in one of the datasets differ slightly around the value of 70–80% for the training set, 18–28% for the validation, and about 2% for the testing set. Alternatively, the cross-validation with 10 sets—9 sets used for training and the 10th for validation might be considered. This process is repeated until each of the 10 sets is used for validation.

Step 3. *Setting the ANN architecture*. This involves the establishing of the number of nodes in the input layer (optimal window time for the next value forecast of the pollutant), the number of nodes in the hidden layer, activation functions, etc.

Step 4. *Adjustment of training parameters*. The optimal number of epochs for network training, the learning rate, and momentum parameter are established experimentally, avoiding the overtraining of the network or an undertrained situation.

Step 5. *Network training* taking into account the parameters established in step 4 and step 5.

Step 6. *Validation of the resulted network architecture*.

Step 7. *Testing of the ANN*.

Step 8. *Analysis of the ANN performances.* At this stage, statistical parameters can be used such as the correlation coefficient between variables, mean absolute error (MAE), root mean square error (RMSE), the training error (MSE), and mean absolute percentage error (MAPE). The values of these parameters can be compared with the conventional limits established in the literature and those obtained with other models developed for forecasting the amount of particulate matter fractions.

The following tests present how different parameters, which describe the neural network model, affect the accuracy of the forecasted data. The topology of the neural network is denoted as $n_1 - n_2 - n_3$, where n_1 is the number of nodes in the input layer, n_2 is the number of nodes in the hidden layer, and n_3 is the number of nodes in the output layer. Since the training is sensitive to the initial values of the weights, 10 tests for each algorithm were performed and the mean of the resulted values was considered for all tables provided.

4. Results and discussion

4.1. Analysis of total suspended particulates time series

In the first test, we present the monthly average concentrations values of total suspended particulate (TSP) recorded between 1995 and 2006 in Targoviste, Romania. During that period, TSP often exceeded the limit value (75 µg/m³) and the city was considered as a PM risk area at national level due to emissions from metallurgical industries. Later on, Romanian technical norms replaced the earlier TSP air quality standard with a PM_{10} standard.

We compared various (p, d, q) setups of ARIMA model [10] to identify the statistical model with the smallest magnitude of the errors during the estimation period. ARIMA (4,0,3) presented the smallest MAE and MAPE. A significant relationship ($p < 0.001$) with a correlation coefficient of 0.8 was noticed between the ARIMA (4,0,3) forecasted variables and observed data [9].

The tests performed with the feed-forward neural network using the TSP observed series provided good forecasting results with the Quickprop (4,6,1) algorithm. The correlation coefficient of ANN Quickprop (4,6,1) indicated a strong relationship between the forecasted variables and observed data (**Table 2**).

Indicator	ARIMA statistical model (4,0,3)	ANN model (4,6,1) Quickprop	ANN model (4,6,1) Incremental	ANN model (6,6,1) Rprop
r	0.801	0.946	0.779	0.652

Table 2. Correlation coefficients of forecasted/observed series of the ARIMA model and ANN algorithms using the time series of total suspended particulates (TSP) concentrations in Targoviste city.

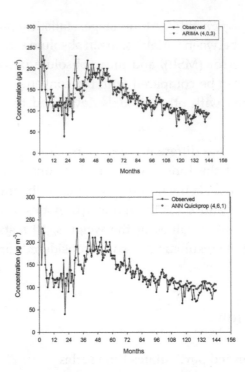

Figure 3. Comparison of monthly averages of total suspended particulates observations vs. the ARIMA (4,0,3) and Quickprop (4,6,1) simulations in Targoviste city (1995–2006) [9].

The ANN Quickprop (4,6,1) model presented a higher correlation coefficient ($r = 0.94$) than ARIMA (4,0,3) model. The neural network prediction algorithm provided a better fit to the TSP measured time series (**Figure 3**). Consequently, we observed that the use of a proper configuration of ANN could provide better results for TSP prediction than linear statistical models [9].

4.2. Analysis of PM_{10} time series

In the next test, we used daily time series of PM_{10} recorded by an optical analyzer in Targoviste city. We present a case with a time series of 101 values to test the influence of a short time series on the efficiency of the training.

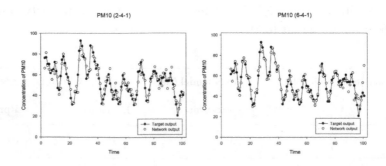

Figure 4. Observed and forecasted concentrations of PM_{10} (2-4-1) and PM_{10} (6-4-1) ANN configurations [13].

ANN	Rprop		Quickprop	
Network configuration	MSE	MSE	MSE	MSE
	Training data	Validation data	Training data	Validation data
2-4-1	0.00993	0.01095	0.01153	0.00866
4-4-1	0.00498	0.01659	0.00957	0.00950
6-4-1	0.00412	0.02069	0.00881	0.00949
8-4-1	0.00314	0.02285	0.00738	0.01368

Table 3. Dependence of training and validation errors with various topologies of feed-forward artificial neural network using short PM_{10} time series.

Figure 4 presents the graphics for the utilization of 2 and 6 neurons in the input layer.

We observed that the number of network inputs has a major influence over the forecasting performances. **Table 3** shows how the training error depends on the number of network inputs. For each case, we used the same number of values, that is, 80. Increasing the number of network inputs results in the decrease in the number of testing samples. Yet, the table shows an increase in the MSE of the validation data. This suggests that increasing the number of input neurons will improve the capability of the network to have a better response for the data close to ones used in the training process. On the other hand, the network loses its generalization abilities.

Table 4 shows how the network training and testing depend on the number of training samples. The selected network topology was 2-4-1.

The error of training data decreases with the increase in the number of samples, while the error of validation data increases for both tested algorithms.

ANN	Rprop		Quickprop	
No of training samples	MSE	MSE	MSE	MSE
	Training data	Validation data	Training data	Validation data
70	0.01060	0.00968	0.01242	0.00748
80	0.00991	0.01093	0.01151	0.00864
90	0.00962	0.01306	0.01075	0.01270

Table 4. Dependence of training and validation errors with the number of samples used in training a feed-forward artificial neural network (2-4-1).

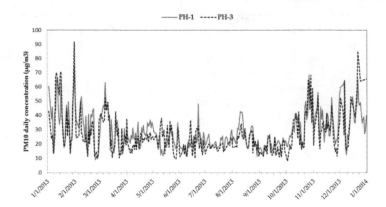

Figure 5. Plots of observed PM_{10} time series with daily averages from two automated stations i.e. PH-1 and PH-3 located in Ploieşti city in 2013.

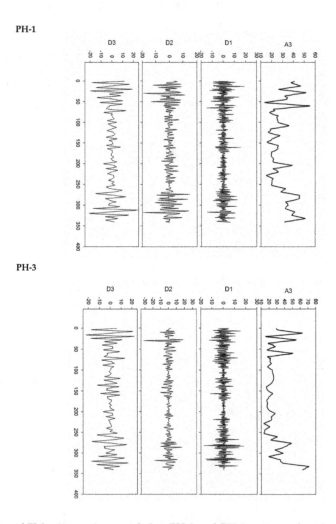

Figure 6. Decompositions of PM_{10} time series recorded at PH-1 and PH-3 automated stations in four components i.e. A3, D1, D2, and D3 using Daubechies wavelets of third order.

4.3. Analysis of PM_{10} time series

In this test, the daily averaged PM_{10} time series recorded at two automated stations located in Ploieşti city in 2013, that is, PH-1 and PH-3 were analyzed using the method of wavelet processing described in [11]. Data gaps (missing values 4 at PH-1 and 15 at PH-3) were interpolated based on existing measured values (**Figure 5**). Each air pollutant series (n = 365 values) was decomposed using the MATLAB Wavelet Toolbox in four components, that is, A3, D1, D2, and D3 using Daubechies wavelets of third order (**Figure 6**).

Automated station for monitoring air quality	PH-1 (F)	PH-1 (WF)	PH-3 (F)	PH-3 (WF)
Training data MSE	0.0098	A3: 0.00099	0.0067	A3: 0.00096
		D1: 0.00355		D1: 0.00289
		D2: 0.00099		D2: 0.00104
		D3: 0.00099		D3: 0.00099
Validation data MSE	0.0312	A3: 0.00053	0.0498	A3: 0.00263
		D1: 0.00677		D1: 0.01225
		D2: 0.00335		D2: 0.00238
		D3: 0.00274		D3: 0.00214
RMSE	7.7	3.4	9.9	4.4
MAE	5.5	2.5	6.8	3.2
Pearson coefficient (r)	0.78	0.96	0.75	0.95
Forecasted value ($\mu g\ m^{-3}$)	33.2	36.7	56.8	61.5
Observed value ($\mu g\ m^{-3}$)	39.9		65.6	
Studentized residuals >3.0	6	4	10	5

Table 5. Averages of 10 validation tests resulted from the Rprop (6-4-1) application to PM_{10} time series recorded in Ploiesti vs. Daubechies db3 wavelet—Rprop (6-4-1) results after recomposing the series; F—Rprop FANN, WF—Daubechies db3 wavelet—Rprop FANN.

The components resulted from decomposition of time series (A3, D1, D2, and D3) was used as input in an optimal FANN architecture established prior to this analysis, that is, Rprop (6-4-1). The simulated FANN output of each component was recomposed to form the modeled series of the original pollutant time series and the network performance was analyzed using MSE, MAE, RMSE, and r. The comparison of outputs when FANN is solely used with wavelet-FANN results allowed the evaluation of wavelet contribution to the improvement of forecasting abilities [11].

The application of Daubechies db3 wavelet as a decomposing preprocessor of daily averages time series has significantly improved the out-of-sample forecasted values (**Table 5**). The results showed that the exclusive use of Rprop (6-4-1) configuration was less fitted to the observed data at both stations. Wavelet preprocessing followed by the individual training of resulted components has substantially increased the r coefficient from 0.7 to 0.9 and decreased the error indicators for both time series as compared to the exclusive use of FANN. Furthermore, the forecasted values were closer to the corresponding real observations.

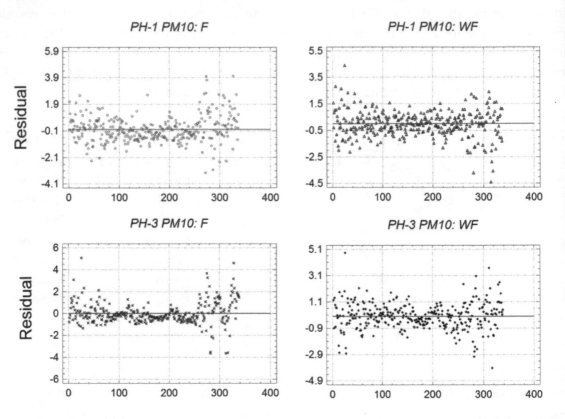

Figure 7. Plots of residuals resulted after correlating the daily averages of PM_{10} ($\mu g\ m^{-3}$) and Rprop FANN (6-4-1) modeled data, and Daubechies db3 wavelet—Rprop WFANN (6-4-1) data, respectively, recorded at two automated monitoring stations in Ploiesti.

A reduction of Studentized residuals number greater than 3.0 was observed using the wavelet processing of data from both stations compared to FANN (**Figure 7**), that is, from 6 Studentized residuals to 4 (PH-1), and from 10 to 5 (PH-3).

These aspects suggested that wavelet integration in processing of daily averages of PM_{10} series provided significant improvements of the forecasting ability recommending the use of the hybrid model. Compared to these results, the application of the hybrid model to hourly recorded PM_{10} time series at other Romanian stations showed also the improvements of correlation coefficient. However, the wavelet processing increased errors and provided more potential outliers [11]. Wavelet integration did not provide computational benefits taking into account the increase in time required for data processing. On the other hand, application of Rprop FANN to hourly recorded PM_{10} produced overfitting. For improved results when neural network is solely used, overfitting is required to be adjusted by using additional techniques, for example, early stopping [18], dropout [19], etc.

We observed in our study that wavelet integration diminished the overfitting tendencies.

4.4. Analysis of PM$_{2.5}$ time series

The section presents the results of Daubechies db3 wavelet—Rprop neural network (6-4-1) modeling using PM$_{2.5}$ time series of 24-h daily averaged concentrations recorded in Râmnicu Vâlcea city, south-west of Romania at VL-1 monitoring station. We selected this station for tests because VL-1 station was one of the two stations that recorded a substantial exceeding of the annual limit value (25 µg/m^3) at national level in 2012. The maximum value reached 149.13 µg/m^3 and the annual geometric mean was 23.8 µg/m^3.

Automated monitoring station in Ramnicu Valcea city (VL-1)	2012 (F)	2012 (WF)
RMSE	6.3	26.1
MAE	3.8	16.3
MAPE	31.6	50.4
Pearson coefficient (r)	0.86	0.93
Studentized residuals > 3.0	7	7

Table 6. Averages of 10 validation tests resulted from the Rprop (6-4-1) application to PM$_{2.5}$ time series recorded at VL-1 station vs. Daubechies db3 wavelet—Rprop (6-4-1) results after recomposing the series; F—Rprop FANN, WF—Daubechies db3 wavelet—Rprop FANN.

A significant increasing of the r coefficients was observed after the application of wavelet preprocessing. RMSE, MAE, and MAPE showed higher values compared to the exclusive use of Rprop configuration (**Table 6**). Both models overestimated the forecasted values in the last quarter of time series. However, the fluctuations observed in the original time series were simulated better by using Daubechies wavelets [11].

These results suggest that other models or algorithms with noise-filtering/smoothing properties may be applied in various stages of the simulation in conjunction with the Daubechies db3 wavelet—Rprop FANN utilization. The expected outcome would be a superior refining of the initial PM$_{2.5}$ forecasted values [11].

5. A cyberinfrastructure for the protection of children's respiratory health by integrating hybrid neural networks for PM forecasting—ROkidAIR

ROkidAIR cyberinfrastructure is currently developed in a European Economic Area (eea-grants.org) research project to facilitate the protection of children's respiratory health in two Romanian cities, that is, Targoviste and Ploiesti.

Recent developments in the management of urban atmospheric environment demonstrated the imperative need to ensure quick, efficient, and easy-to-understand information regarding the status of air quality. The negative impact of air pollution on human health requires improvements of contemporary systems for air quality management to reduce the human exposure to various pollutants. Providing full and comprehensive information concerning the air quality is regarded as a mandatory service for citizens in the current air quality management systems. The authorities should establish an appropriate framework, especially in urban areas, where adverse health effects caused by poor air quality are more pronounced, to ensure the integration of relevant data regarding the maintaining of air quality at required standards. The systems for air quality management need to be adapted to decision makers' requirements (in order to reduce the ambient air quality issues through adequate policies) and citizens (for early warning and for providing useful recommendations). Aiming to reduce their exposure, citizens should receive adequate information on the spatiotemporal variation of air quality or the forecasts on short, medium, and long term. To achieve this goal, it is necessary to collect, integrate, and analyze data from multiple sources. Air quality forecast is one of the essential elements of modern air quality management in urban areas. However, the efficiency of the used forecasting methods is limited by the complex relationships between air quality, meteorological parameters, and specific characteristics of each study area. In addition, an important issue that needs to be considered in choosing the forecasting method is the variation of the input data quality. The methods to be used should be less sensitive to this factor [20]. Information related to air quality in urban areas is obtained by using specific methods and tools for processing the time series recorded by the monitoring stations. Mathematical methods and tools can provide air quality forecasting, so that decision makers can act with preventive measures that would "mitigate" or change the results of a foreseen critical pollution episode. There is an increasing demand regarding the development of cyber-platforms that may facilitate the air quality management providing real health benefits to the end user (e.g., ROkidAIR, *http://www.rokidair.ro*).

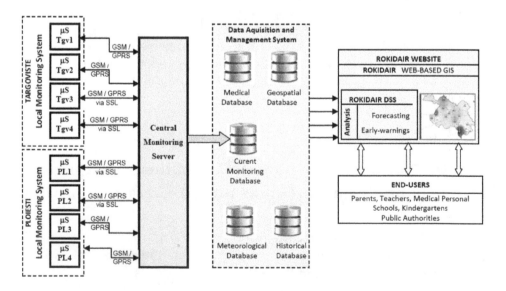

Figure 8. The architecture of the ROkidAIR system.

The main goal of the ROkidAIR project is to develop and deploy a monitoring network system and an adjacent early warning structure that provide synthesized data concerning the $PM_{2.5}$

levels obtained from simplified but reliable monitoring micro-stations and AI forecasting algorithms developed within the project . The architecture of the ROkidAIR system is presented in **Figure 8**. The ROkidAIR cyberinfrastructure is a pilot system, which is focused on fine particulate matter effects on children's health in two towns of Romania, that is, Targoviste and Ploiesti. It provides early warnings concerning the PM levels, tailored to the end-user requirements via several communication channels [3]. Collected time series obtained from the self-developed monitoring network system, based on PM micro-stations, are preprocessed and adapted to feed the forecasting module based on AI algorithms. All data are presented in a dedicated geo-portal adapted to be used by smartphones and other portable equipment. The main stream of information is transmitted both to the responsible authorities and to the sensitive persons, who are registered in the system. The expert advises and recommendations are transmitted via e-mails and SMSs to the registered users providing support for children's health management under the impact of air quality stressors and pressures. Early warnings are developed in cooperation with pediatric specialists, which synthesize the most relevant information concerning the protection of children's health against air pollution threats. The early warning data packages are also transmitted to the authorities (e.g., local EPAs—Environmental Protection Agencies and DPH—Public Health Protection Directions) for informational purposes. The monitoring network comprises eight PM micro-stations (four in each city), which are developed during the implementation of ROkidAIR project. These micro-stations provide continuous PM monitoring data that are processed to be used as inputs in forecasting algorithms based on AI. The raw data obtained from the eight micro-stations are also used in other modules of the cyber-platform: the ROkidAIR web-based geographic information systems (GIS) geoportal, and the decision support system (DSS) including the early warning module. The DSS system uses artificial intelligence techniques (ANNs and predictive data mining) and hybrid algorithms and models (Neuro-fuzzy ANFIS, and wavelet neural network, WNN) for assessing children's exposure to the pollution with particulate matter, in order to elaborate forecasted values and early warnings [16].

In ROkidAIR AI model, forecasting knowledge is extracted by using ANFIS (generating the fuzzy rules set), and other methods (e.g., a combination between some machine learning techniques) on the specific datasets (continuous monitoring data, historical data, meteorological data, and medical data). All the extracted forecasting rules and knowledge are included in a forecasting knowledge base that provide expert knowledge (heuristics) for a faster and optimal air pollution forecasting in a critical polluted area [21].

6. Conclusions

The contribution of artificial intelligence to the air quality monitoring systems under development relates to evolutionary computing, which provides stochastic search facilities that can efficiently assess complex spaces described by mathematical, statistical, neural network, or fuzzy inference models applied to assess the population exposure to air pollution in urban environments. Machine-learning techniques are currently contributing to the *online* air quality monitoring and forecasting. Statistical and neural modeling techniques can also provide approximations to supplement results from computationally expensive analytic methods.

Significant results for PM data forecasting were obtained with Rprop ($PM_{10}10$ and $PM_{2.5}$), and Quickprop (TSP) algorithms. The exclusive use of the ANN algorithms showed difficulties in predicting pollutant peaks and limitations due to limited continuous observations and large local-scale variations of concentrations. WNNs is an alternative to overcome these drawbacks related to time series predictions by integrating a proper wavelet in the hidden nodes of WNNs or as a preprocessing step. The results of numerical tests provided that the application of wavelet transformation is a significant factor for improving the accuracy of forecasting. Further investigations are required using hourly, daily, and monthly air-quality data from other locations and regional level, by assessing and verifying the reliability, relevance, and adequacy of ANN data forecasting. An important step for reliable air quality forecasting is the optimal selection of ANN learning algorithm. The automation of this component is required to optimize the informational fluxes and to facilitate the decision-making process.

Acknowledgements

This study received funding from the European Economic Area Financial Mechanism 2009–2014 under the project ROkidAIR *Towards a better protection of children against air pollution threats in the urban areas of Romania* contract no. 20SEE/30.06.2014

Author details

Daniel Dunea* and Stefania Iordache

*Address all correspondence to: dan.dunea@valahia.ro

Valahia University of Târgoviste, Aleea Sinaia, Târgoviste, Romania

References

[1] Ianache C., Dumitru D., Predescu L., Predescu M. (2015), Relationship between airborne particulate matter and weather conditions during cold months, In Proceedings of 15th International Multidisciplinary Scientific Geoconference SGEM 2015, June 18–24, 2015, Albena, Bulgaria, 1017–1024, DOI: 10.5593/SGEM2015/B41/S19.131

[2] Langner M., Draheim T., Endlicher W. (2011), Particulate matter in the urban atmosphere: concentration, distribution, reduction—results of studies in the Berlin metro-

politan area, In W. Endlicher et al. (eds.), Perspectives in Urban Ecology, Berlin, Heidelberg, Springer-Verlag, 15–41. DOI: 10.1007/978-3-642-17731-6_2

[3] Iordache St., Dunea D., Lungu E., Predescu L., Dumitru D., Ianache C., Ianache R. (2015), A cyberinfrastructure for air quality monitoring and early warnings to protect children with respiratory disorders, In Proceedings of the 20th International Conference on Control Systems and Computer Science (CSCS20-2015), Bucharest, 789–796.

[4] Dunea D., Iordache St., Alexandrescu D.C., Dincă N. (2014), Screening the weekdays/ weekend patterns of air pollutant concentrations recorded in southeastern Romania, Environmental Engineering and Management Journal, 14(12), 3105–3115.

[5] WHO (2014), World Health Organization, Ambient (outdoor) air quality and health—Fact sheet N°313, Updated March 2014, http://www.who.int/mediacentre/factsheets/fs313/en, Accessed 10 February 2016.

[6] AQEG (2012), Fine Particulate Matter (PM2.5) in the United Kingdom, Defra, London.

[7] Dunea D., Iordache St. (2015), Time series analysis of air pollutants recorded from Romanian EMEP stations at mountain sites, Environmental Engineering and Management Journal, 14(11), 2725–2735.

[8] Vaisala (2016), Weather monitoring and urban air quality, Application note, http://www.vaisala.com/Vaisala%20Documents/Application%20notes/Urban%20air%20application%20note%20B210959EN-A.pdf, Accessed 10 February 2016.

[9] Dunea D., Oprea M., Lungu E. (2008), Comparing statistical and neural network approaches for urban air pollution time series analysis. In L. Bruzzone (ed.), Proceedings of the 27th IASTED International Conference on Modelling, Identification and Control, Acta Press, Innsbruck, Austria, February 11–13, 93–98.

[10] Box G.E.P., Jenkins G.M. (1970), Time Series Analysis: Forecasting and Control, Holden-Day, San Francisco, CA.

[11] Dunea D., Pohoață A., Iordache St. (2015), Using wavelet—feed forward neural networks to improve air pollution forecasting in urban environments, Environmental Monitoring and Assessment, 187, 477, 1–6.

[12] Riedmiller M., Braun H. (1993), A direct adaptive method for faster backpropagation learning: The RPROP algorithm, In H. Ruspini (ed.), Proceedings of the IEEE International Conference on Neural Networks, San Francisco, 586–591.

[13] Lungu E., Oprea M., Dunea D. (2008), An application of artificial neural networks in environmental pollution forecasting, In Proceedings of the 26th IASTED International Conference on Artificial Intelligence and Applications, Acta Press, Innsbruck, Austria, February 11–13, 187–193.

[14] Fahlman S.E. (1988), Faster learning variations on back-propagation: an empirical study, In D.S. Touretzky, G.E. Hinton, and T.J. Sejnowski (eds.), Proceedings of the 1988 Connectionist Models Summer School, Morgan Kaufmann, San Mateo, CA, 38–51.

[15] Vrahatis M.N., Magoulas G.D., Plagianakos V.P. (1999), Convergence analysis of the Quickprop method, In Proceedings of the International Joint Conference on Neural Networks (IJCNN'99), Washington DC, 848, Session: 5.3.

[16] Oprea M., Ianache C., Mihalache S., Dragomir E., Dunea D., Iordache Şt., Savu T. (2015), On the development of an intelligent system for particulate matter air pollution monitoring, analysis and forecasting in urban regions, In 19th International Conference on System Theory, Control and Computing (ICSTCC), 711–716.

[17] Oprea M. (2005), A case study of knowledge modelling in an air pollution control decision support system, AiCommunications, 18(4), 293–303.

[18] Guo X. (2010), Learning gradients via an early stopping gradient descent method, Journal of Approximation Theory, 162(11), 1919–1944.

[19] Srivastava N., Geoffrey H., Krizhevsky A., Sutskever I., Salakhutdinov R. (2014), Dropout: a simple way to prevent neural networks from overfitting, Journal of Machine Learning Research, 15, 1929–1958.

[20] Zhang Y., Bocquet M., Mallet V., Seigneur C., Baklanov A. (2012), Real-time air quality forecasting, part I: history, techniques, and current status, Atmospheric Environment, 60, 632–655.

[21] Mihalache S.F., Popescu M., Oprea M. (2015), Particulate matter prediction using ANFIS modelling techniques, In 19th International Conference on System Theory, Control and Computing (ICSTCC), 895–900.

7

Neural Networks for Gas Turbine Diagnosis

Igor Loboda

Additional information is available at the end of the chapter

Abstract

The present chapter addresses the problems of gas turbine gas path diagnostics solved using artificial neural networks. As a very complex and expensive mechanical system, a gas turbine should be effectively monitored and diagnosed. Being universal and powerful approximation and classification techniques, neural networks have become widespread in gas turbine health monitoring over the past few years. Applications of such networks as a multilayer perceptron, radial basis network, probabilistic neural network, and support vector network were reported. However, there is a lack of manuals that summarize neural network applications for gas turbine diagnosis.

A monitoring system comprises many elements, and many factors influence the final diagnostic accuracy. The present chapter generalizes our investigations that are devoted to the enhancement of this system by choosing the best option for each element. In these investigations, a diagnostic process is simulated on the basis of neural networks, and we focus on reaching the highest accuracy by choosing the best network and its optimal tuning to the issue to solve. Thus, helping with enhancement of a whole monitoring system, neural networks themselves are objects of investigation and optimization. As a result of the conducted investigations, the chapter provides the recommendations on choosing and tailoring the network for a particular diagnostic task.

Keywords: gas turbines, gas path diagnosis, fault classification, pattern recognition, artificial neural networks

1. Introduction

As complex and expensive mechanical systems, gas turbine engines benefit a lot from the application of advanced diagnostic technologies, and the use of monitoring systems has become a standard practice. To perform effective analysis, there are different diagnostic approaches that cover all gas turbine subsystems. The diagnostic algorithms based on measured gas path variables are considered as principal and pretty complex. These variables (air and gas pressures and temperatures, rotation speeds, fuel consumption, etc.) carry valuable information about an engine's health condition and allow to detect and identify different engine abrupt faults and deterioration mechanisms (for instance, foreign object damage, fouling, erosion, tip ribs, and seal wear). Malfunctions of measurement and control systems can be diagnosed as well. Thousands of technical publications devoting to the gas path diagnosis can be found. They can be arranged according to input information and mathematical models applied.

Although advancement of instrumentation and computer science has enabled extensive field data collection, the data with gas turbine faults are still infrequent because real faults rarely appear. Some intensive and practically permanent deterioration mechanisms, for example, compressor fouling, allow their describing on the basis of real data. However, to describe the variety of all possible faults, mathematical models are widely used. These models and the diagnostic methods that use them fall into two main categories: physics-based and data-driven.

A thermodynamic engine model is a representative physics-based model. This nonlinear model is based on thermodynamic relations between gas path variables. It also employs mass, energy, and momentum conservation laws. Such a sophisticated model has been used in gas turbine diagnostics since the work of Saravanamuttoo H.I.H. (see, e.g., [1]). The model allows to simulate the gas path variables for an engine baseline (healthy engine performance) and for different faults embedded into the model through special internal coefficients called fault parameters. Applying system identification methods to the thermodynamic model, an inverse problem is solved: Unknown fault parameters are estimated using measured gas path variables. During the identification, such parameters are found that minimize the difference between the model variables and the measured ones. Besides the better model accuracy, the simplification of the diagnosing process is reached because the fault parameter estimates contain information of current engine health. The diagnostic algorithms based on the model identification constitute one of two main approaches in gas turbine diagnostics (see, for instance, [1–4]).

The second approach uses a pattern recognition theory. Since model inaccuracy and measurement errors impede a correct diagnosis, gas path fault localization can be characterized as a challenging recognition issue. Numerous applications of recognition tools in gas path diagnostics are known, for instance, genetic algorithms [5], correspondence and discrimination analysis [6], k-nearest neighbor [7], and Bayesian approach [8]. However, the most widespread techniques are artificial neural networks (ANNs). The ANNs applications are not limited by the fault recognition, they are also applied or can be applied at other diagnostic stages: feature extraction, fault detection, and fault prediction.

At the feature extraction stage, differences (a.k.a. deviations) between actual gas path measurements and an engine baseline are determined because they are by far better indicators of engine health than the measurements themselves are. To build the necessary baseline model, the multilayer perceptron (MLP), also called a back-propagation network, is usually employed [9, 10]. To filter noise, an auto-associative configuration of the perceptron is sometimes applied to the measurements [11].

At the fault localization stage, fault classes can be presented by sets of the deviations (patterns) induced by the corresponding faults. Such a pattern-based classification allows to apply the ANNs as recognition techniques, and multiple applications of the MLP (see, e.g., [4, 5]) as well as the radial basis network (RBN) [5], the probabilistic neural network (PNN) [12, 13], and support vector machines (SVM) a.k.a. Support vector network (SVN) [7, 12] were reported. In spite of many publications on gas turbine fault recognition, comparative studies, which allow to choose the best technique [4, 5, 7, 12], are still insufficient. They do not cover all of the used techniques and often provide differing recommendations.

The fault detection stage can also be presented as a pattern recognition problem with two classes to recognize: a class of healthy engines and a class of faulty engines. If the classification for the fault localization stage is available, it does not seem a challenge to use the patterns of this classification for building the fault detection classification. However, the studies applying recognition techniques, in particular the ANNs, for gas turbine fault detection are absent so far. Instead, the detection problem is solved by tolerance monitoring [14, 15].

The fault prediction stage is less investigated than the previous stages, and only few ANNs applications are known. Among them, it is worth to mention book [16] analyzing the ways to predict gas turbine faults and study [17], comparing a recurrent neural network and a nonlinear auto-regressive neural network. We can see that in total for all stages, the perceptron is by far the highest demand network. It is used for filtering the measurements, approximating the engine baseline, and recognizing the faults.

Thus, a brief observation of the neural networks applied for gas turbine diagnosis has revealed that the multiple known cases of their use need better generalization and recommendations to choose the best network. The areas of promising ANNs application were also found. In the present chapter, we generalize our investigations aimed at the optimization of a total diagnostic process through the enhancement of each of its elements. On the one hand, the neural networks help with process realization being its critical elements. On the other hand, the networks themselves are objects of analysis: For known applications, they are compared to choose the best network, and one new application is proposed. During the investigations, the rules of proper network usage have also been established.

The rest of the chapter describes these investigations and is structured as follows: description of the networks used (Section 2), network-based diagnostic approach (Section 3), diagnostic process optimization (Section 4), feature extraction stage optimization (Section 5), fault detection stage optimization (Section 6), and fault localization stage optimization (Section 7).

2. Artificial neural networks

The four networks mentioned in the introduction have been chosen for investigations: MLP, RBN, PNN, and SVN. The PNN is a realization of the Parzon Windows and has the important property of probabilistic outputs, that is, the gas turbine faults are recognized on the basis of their confidence probabilities. These probabilities are computed through numerical estimates of probability density of fault patterns. For the purpose of comparison, a similar recognition tool, the K-nearest neighbor (K-NN) method has been involved into the investigations. Foundations of the chosen techniques can be found in many books on classification theory, for example, in [18, 19, 20]. The next subsections include only a brief description of techniques required to better understand the present chapter.

2.1. Multilayer perceptron

The perceptron can solve either approximation or classification issues. The scheme shown in **Figure 1** illustrates structure and operation of the MLP [18, 19]. We can see that the perceptron presents a feed-forward neural network in which no feedback is observed, and all signals go only from the input to the output.

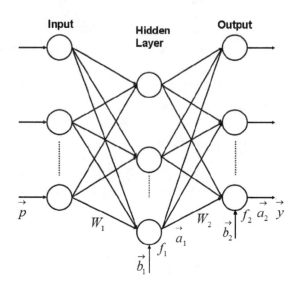

Figure 1. Multilayer perceptron.

To determine a hidden layer input vector, the product of a weight matrix W_1 and a network input vector (pattern) $\vec{p}$ is summed with a bias vector $\vec{b_1}$. A hidden layer transfer function f_1 transforms this vector in an output vector $\vec{a_1}$. A network output $\vec{a_2}$ is computed similarly considering the vector $\vec{a}_1$ as an input. In this way, perceptron operation can be expressed by $\vec{y} = \vec{a_2} = f_2\{W_2f_1(W_1\vec{p} + \vec{b_1}) + \vec{b_2}\}$. When we apply the MLP to classify patterns, elements of the vector $\vec{a_2}$ show how close the pattern $\vec{p}$ is to the corresponding classes. The nearest class is chosen as a class to which the pattern belongs, and such classifying can be considered as deterministic.

To find unknown matrixes W_1 and W_2 and vectors $\vec{b_1}$ and $\vec{b_2}$, a back-propagation learning algorithm distributes a network output error on these unknown quantities. In every learning iteration (epoch), they vary in the direction of error reduction. The iterations continue unless the minimum error has been reached. This algorithm requires differentiable transfer functions, and a sigmoid type is commonly used.

2.2. Radial basis network

Figure 2 illustrates operation of an RBN. It includes two layers: a hidden radial basis layer and an output linear layer. Operation of radial basis neurons is different from the perceptron neurons operation [18, 19, 20]. The neuron's input n is formed as the Euclidean norm $\|\|$ of a difference between a pattern vector $\vec{p}$ and a weight vector $\vec{w}$, multiplied by a scalar b (bias). In this way, $n = \|\vec{w} - \vec{p}\|b$. Using this input, a radial basis transfer function determines an output $a = \exp(-n^2)$. Where there is no distance between the vectors, the function has the maximum value $a=1$, and the function decreases when the distance increases. The bias b allows changing the neuron sensitivity. The output layer transforms the radial basis output $\vec{a}_1$ to a network output $\vec{a}_2$. Operation of this layer does not differ from the operation of a perceptron layer with a linear transfer function. The radial basis layer usually needs more neurons than a comparable perceptron hidden layer because the radial basis neuron covers a smaller region compared with the sigmoid neuron.

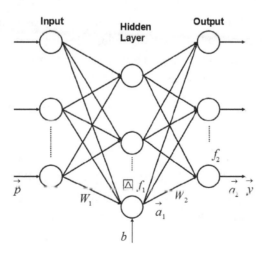

Figure 2. Radial basis network.

2.3. Probabilistic neural networks

The PNN is a specific variation of radial basis network [18]. It is used to solve classification problems. **Figure 3** presents the scheme of this network and helps to understand its operation. Like the RBN, the probabilistic neural network has two layers.

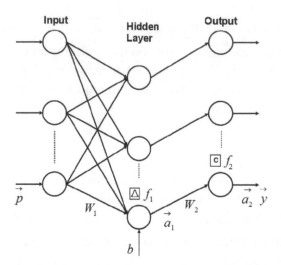

Figure 3. Probabilistic neural network.

The hidden layer is formed and operates just like the same layer of the RBN. It is built from learning patterns united in a matrix W_1. Elements of an output vector $\vec{a}_1$ indicate how close the input pattern is to the learning patterns.

The output or classification layer differs from the RBN output layer. Each class has its output neuron that sums the radial basis outputs a_j corresponding to the class patterns. To this end, a weight matrix W_2 formed by 0- and 1-elements is employed. A vector $W_2\vec{a}_1$ contains probabilities of all classes. A transfer function f_2 finally chooses the class with the largest probability. In this way, the probabilistic network classifies input patterns using a probabilistic measure that is more realistic than the perceptron classifying. The PNN is the most used realization of a Parzen Windows (PW) [18], a nonparametric method that estimates probability density in a given point (pattern) $\vec{Z}$ using the nearby learning patterns.

2.4. k-Nearest neighbors

Like the Parzen Windows (PNNs), the k-nearest neighbors is a nonparametric technique [18]. For a given class and point (pattern) $\vec{p}$, it counts the number k of class patterns in a nearby region of volume V and estimates the necessary probability density in accordance with a simple formula

$$\rho = \frac{k/n}{V} \tag{1}$$

where n stands for a total number of class patterns.

To ensure the convergence of the estimate ϱ, we need to satisfy the following requirements

$$\lim_{n \to \infty} V = 0; \lim_{n \to \infty} k = \infty; \lim_{n \to \infty} k/n = 0. \tag{2}$$

To this end, we increase n and can let V be proportional to $1/\sqrt{n}$.

In contrast to the Parzen Window method that fixes the volume V and looks for the number k, the K-nearest neighbor method specifies k and seeks for the sphere of volume V. Since the PW uses constant window size, it may not capture patterns when the actual density is low. The density estimate will be equal to zero, and the classification decision confidence will be underestimated. A solution to this problem is to use the window that depends on learning data. Using this principle, the K-NN increases a spherical window individually for each class until k patterns (nearest neighbors) fall into the window. A sphere radius will change class by class. The greater the radius is, the lower probability density estimate will be according to Eq. (1).

2.5. Support vector network

Any hyperplane can be written in the space R^P as the set of points $\vec{p}$ satisfying:

$$\vec{p}^T \vec{w} + b = 0 \tag{3}$$

where $\vec{w}$ is a vector perpendicular to the hyperplane and b is the bias. Let us present learning data of two classes as pattern vectors $\vec{p}_i \in R^P, i = 1, N$ and their corresponding labels $y_i \in (-1, 1)$, indicating the class to which the pattern $\vec{p}$ belongs.

If the learning data are linearly separable, two parallel hyperplanes without points between them can be built to divide the data. The hyperplanes can be given by $\vec{w}^T \vec{p}_i + b = 1$ and $\vec{w}^T \vec{p}_i + b = -1$. The margin is defined to be the distance between them and is equal to $2/\|\vec{w}\|$ (**Figure 4**). Intuitively, it measures how good the separation between the two classes is. The points divided in this manner satisfy the following constraint:

$$y_i(\vec{w}^T \vec{p}_i + b) \geq 1 \tag{4}$$

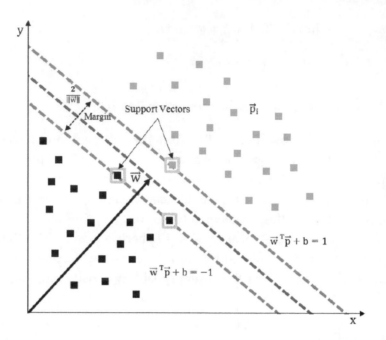

Figure 4. SVN: hyperplanes and separation margin.

The objective of the SVN is to find the hyperplanes that produce the maximal margin or minimum vector $\vec{w}$ [19, 20]. In this way, SVN needs to solve the following primal optimization problem:

$$\min \frac{1}{2}\vec{w}^T \vec{w} \tag{5}$$

subject to $y_i(\vec{w}^T \vec{p}_i + b) \geq 1$, for $i = 1, ..., N$

Introducing the Karush-Kuhn-Tucker (KKT) multipliers $\alpha_i \geq 0$, objective function (5) can be transformed to:

$$\min_{w,b} \max_{\alpha} \frac{1}{2}\vec{w}^T \vec{w} - \sum_{i-1}^{N} \alpha_i (y_i(\vec{w}^T \vec{p}_i + b) - 1) \tag{6}$$

As can be seen, expression (6) is a function of $\vec{w}$, b, and α. This function can be transformed into the dual form:

$$L = \min_{\alpha} \frac{1}{2}\sum_{i=1}^{N} \sum_{j=1}^{N} y_i y_j \alpha_i \alpha_j \vec{p}^T_i \vec{p}_j - \sum_{i=1}^{N} \alpha_i \tag{7}$$

subject to $\alpha_i \geq 0$ and $\sum_{i=1}^{N} \alpha_i y_i = 0$ for i = 1, ..., N

It can be also expressed as:

$$L = \min_{\alpha} \frac{1}{2} \vec{\alpha}^T \, Q\vec{\alpha} - 1^T \vec{\alpha} \qquad (8)$$

where **Q** is the matrix of quadratic coefficients. This expression is minimized now only as a function of $\vec{\alpha}$, and the solution is found by Quadratic Programming.

In SVM classification problems, a complete separation is not always possible, and a flexible margin is suggested in reference [21] that allows misclassification errors while tries to maximize the distance between the nearest fully separable points. The other way to split not separable classes is to use nonlinear functions as proposed in reference [22]. Among them, radial basis functions are recommended [23].

SVMs were originally intended for binary models; however, they can now address multi-class problems using the One-Versus-All and One-Versus-One strategies.

A gas turbine diagnostic process using the techniques above described is simulated according to the following approach.

3. Neural networks-based diagnostic approach

The approach described corresponds to the diagnostic stages of feature extraction and fault localization and embraces the steps of fault simulation, feature extraction, fault classification formation, making a recognition decision, and recognition accuracy estimation.

3.1. Fault simulation

Within the scope of this chapter, faults of engine components (compressor, turbine, combustor, etc.) are simulated by means of a nonlinear gas turbine thermodynamic model

$$\vec{Y}(\vec{U}, \, \vec{\Theta}) \qquad (9)$$

The model determines monitored variables $\vec{Y}$ as a function of steady-state operating conditions $\vec{U}$ and engine health parameters $\vec{\Theta} = \vec{\Theta}_0 + \Delta\vec{\Theta}$. Each component is presented in the model by its performance map. Nominal values $\vec{\Theta}_0$ correspond to a healthy engine, whereas fault parameters $\Delta\vec{\Theta}$ imitate fault influence by shifting the component maps.

3.2. Feature extraction

Although gas turbine monitored variables are affected by engine deterioration, the influence of the operating conditions is much more significant. To extract diagnostic information from raw measured data, a deviation (fault feature) is computed for each monitored variable as a difference between the actual and baseline values. With the thermodynamic model, the deviations Z_i i=1,m induced by the fault parameters are calculated for all m monitored variables according to the following expression

$$Z_i = \left(\frac{Y_i\left(\vec{U},\vec{\Theta}_0 + \Delta\vec{\Theta}\right) - Y_{0i}\left(\vec{U},\vec{\Theta}_0\right)}{Y_{0i}\left(\vec{U},\vec{\Theta}_0\right)} + \varepsilon_i\right)/a_i \qquad (10)$$

A random error ε_i makes the deviation more realistic. A parameter a_i normalizes the deviation errors, resulting that they will be localized within the interval [−1, 1] for all monitored variables. Such normalization simplifies fault class description.

Deviations of the monitored variables united in an (m×1) deviation vector $\vec{Z}$ (feature vector) form a diagnostic space. Every vector $\vec{Z}$ presents a point in this space and is a pattern to be recognized.

3.3. Fault classification formation

Numerous gas turbine faults are divided into a limited number q of classes $D_1, D_2, ..., D_q$. In the present chapter, each class corresponds to varying severity faults of one engine component. The class is described by component's fault parameters $\Delta\Theta_j$. Two types of fault classes are considered. The variation of one fault parameter results in a single fault class, while independent variation of two parameters of one gas turbine component allows to form a class of multiple faults.

To form one class, many patterns are computed by expression (10). The required parameters $\Delta\Theta_j$ and ε_i are randomly generated using the uniform and Gaussian distributions correspondingly. To ensure high computational precision, each class is typically composed from 1000 patterns. A learning set **Z1** uniting patterns of all classes presents a whole pattern-based fault classification. **Figure 5** illustrates such a classification by presenting four single fault classes in the diagnostic space of three deviations.

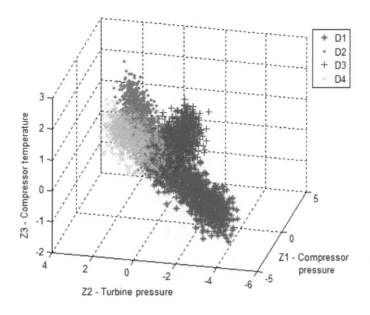

Figure 5. Pattern-based fault classification.

3.4. Making a fault recognition decision

In addition to the given (observed) pattern $\vec{Z}$ and the constructed fault classification **Z1**, a classification technique (one of the chosen networks) is an integral part of a whole diagnostic process. To apply and test the classification techniques, a validation set **Z2** is also created in the same way as set **Z1**. The difference between the sets consists in other random numbers that are generated within the same distributions.

3.5. Recognition accuracy estimation

It is of practical interest to know recognition accuracy averaged for each fault class and a whole engine. To this end, the classification technique is consequently applied to the patterns of set **Z2** producing diagnoses d_l. Since true fault classes D_j are also known, probabilities of correct diagnosis (true positive rates) $P(d_j/D_j)$ can be calculated for all classes resulting in a probability vector $\vec{P}$. A mean number $\overline{P}$ of these probabilities characterizes accuracy of engine diagnosis by the applied technique. In this chapter, the probability $\overline{P}$ is employed as a criterion to compare the techniques described in Section 2.

4. Optimization of the neural networks-based diagnostic process

The structure and efficiency of a diagnostic algorithm depend on many factors and the options that can be chosen for each factor. The classification of these factors and options is given in

Figure 6, where the factors are shown in the first line. On the basis of accumulated knowledge and experience, every research center (even a single researcher) chooses an appropriate option for each factor and develops its own diagnostic algorithm. To be optimal, this algorithm should take into account all peculiarities of a given engine, its application, and other diagnostic conditions. Thus, it is not likely that the algorithm be optimal for other engines and applications. As a result, every monitoring system needs an appropriate diagnostic algorithm.

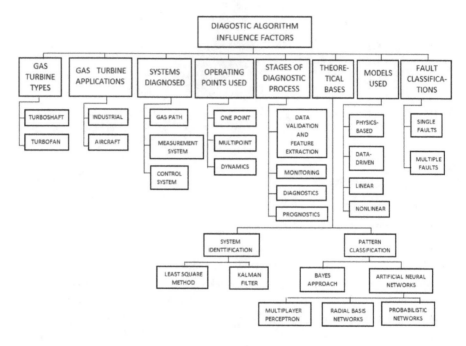

Figure 6. Factors that influence structure and efficiency of gas path diagnostic algorithms.

Thus, comparing complete diagnostic algorithms does not seem to be useful. Instead, comparing options for each above factor and choosing the best option are proposed. When options of one factor are compared, the other factors (comparison conditions) are fixed forming a comparison case. To draw sound conclusions about the best option, the comparison should be repeated for many comparison cases. To form these cases, each comparison condition varies independently according to the theory of the design of experiments. Since every new condition drastically increases the volume of comparative calculations, the most significant conditions are considered first.

To perform the comparative calculations, a test procedure based on the above-described approach has been developed in Matlab (MathWorks, Inc.). For each compared option, the procedure executes numerous cycles of gas turbine fault diagnosis by the chosen technique and finally computes a diagnosis reliability indicator, which is used as a comparison criterion.

Three gas turbine engines (Engine 1, Engine 2, and Engine 3) of different construction and application have been chosen as test cases. Engine 1 and Engine 2 are free turbine power plants. Engine 1 is a natural gas compressor driver; it is presented in the investigations by its thermodynamic model and field data recorded. Engine 2 is intended for electricity production and is given by field data. Engine 3 is a three-spool turbofan for a transport aircraft; its thermody-namic model is used. The field data called hourly snapshots present filtered and averaged steady-state values recorded every hour during about one year of operation of Engine 1 and Engine 2. Since the data include periods of compressor fouling and points of washing, they are very suitable for testing diagnostic techniques.

Using the network-based approach described in Section 3 and the information about the test case engines, many investigations have been conducted to improve the diagnostic process at the stages of feature extraction, fault detection, and fault localization. The results achieved for the feature extraction stage are described in the next section.

5. Feature extraction stage optimization

As stated in Section 3, the deviations are useful diagnostic features. Although the thermody-namic model can be used as a baseline model for computing the deviations, it is too complex for real monitoring systems and has intrinsic inaccuracy. As mentioned in the introduction, to build a simple and fast data-driven baseline model, only neural networks, in particular the MLP, are applied. On the other hand, in the previous studies we successfully used a polynomial type baseline model. It was therefore decided [24] to verify whether the application of such a powerful approximator as the MLP instead of polynomials yields higher adequacy of the baseline model and better quality of the corresponding deviations.

Given a measured value Y_i^* and data-driven baseline model $\vec{Y}_0(\vec{U})$, the deviation is written as

$$\delta Y_i^* = \frac{Y_i^* - Y_{0i}(\vec{U})}{Y_{0i}(\vec{U})} \tag{11}$$

For one monitored variable, a complete second-order polynomial function of four arguments (operating conditions) is written as

$$\vec{Y}_0(\vec{U}) = a_0 + a_1 u_1 + a_2 u_2 + a_3 u_3 + a_4 u_4 + a_5 u_1 u_2 + a_6 u_1 u_3 + a_7 u_1 u_4 +$$
$$a_8 u_2 u_3 + a_9 u_2 u_4 + a_{10} u_3 u_4 + a_{11} u_1^2 + a_{12} u_2^2 + a_{13} u_3^2 + a_{14} u_4^2 \tag{12}$$

For all m monitored variables and measurements at n operating points, equation (12) is transformed to a linear system $\mathbf{Y=VA}$ with matrixes $\mathbf{Y}$ ($n\times m$) and $\mathbf{V}$ ($n\times k$) formed from these data, where $k=15$ is number of coefficients. To enhance coefficient estimates (matrix $\mathbf{A}$), great volume of input data ($n>>k$) is involved and the least-squares method is applied.

As to the perceptron, its typical input is formed by four operating conditions, and the output consists of seven monitored variables. Hidden layer size determines a network's capability to approximate complex functions and varies in calculations. As a result of MLP tuning, we chose 12 nodes at this layer. Thus, the perceptron structure is written as 4×12×7. Since the MLP has tan-sigmoid transfer functions, and the output varies within the interval (−1, 1), all monitored quantities are normalized.

Many cases of comparison on the simulated and real data of Engines 1 and 2 were analyzed. The MLP was sometimes more accurate at the learning step. At the validation step, the deviations computed with the MLP had a little worse accuracy for Engine 1. For Engine 2, the best MLP validation results are illustrated in **Figure 7** . As can be seen here, both polynomial deviations dTtp and network deviations dTtn reflect the fouling and washing effects equally well. However, in many other cases the polynomials outperformed. Why does the network approximate well a learning set and frequently fail on a validation set? The answer seems to be evident because of an overlearning (overfitting) effect. Due to a greater flexibility, the network begins to follow data peculiarities induced by measurement errors in the learning set and describes worse a gas turbine baseline performance for the validation set.

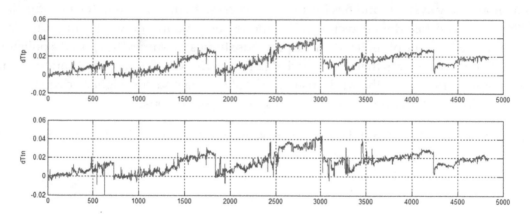

Figure 7. EGT deviations computed on the Engine 2 real data validation set (dTtn—network-based deviation; dTtp—polynomial-based deviation).

Although the MLP as a powerful approximation technique promised better gas turbine performance description, the results of the comparison have been somewhat surprising. No manifestations of network superiority were detected. When comparing these techniques, it is also necessary to take into consideration that an MLP learning procedure is more complex because it is numerical in contrast to an analytical solution for polynomials. Thus, a polynomial baseline model can be successfully used in real monitoring systems along with neural networks. At least, it seems to be true for simple cycle gas turbines with gradually changed performance, like the turbines considered in this chapter.

6. Fault detection stage optimization

As mentioned in the Introduction, the fault detection is actually based on tolerances (thresholds). However, it seems reasonable to present it as a pattern recognition problem like we do at the fault recognition stage. Classification $D_1, D_2, ..., D_q$ created for the purpose of fault localization and presented in **Figure 5** corresponds to a hypothetical fleet of engines with different faults of variable severity. To form the classification for fault detection, we can reasonably accept that the engine fleet and the distributions of faults are the same. Paper [25] explains how to use patterns of the existing classification $D_1, D_2, ..., D_q$ for two new classes of healthy and faulty engines. The boundary between these classes corresponds to maximal error of the normalized deviations and is determined as a sphere of radius $R = 1$. The patterns, for which a vector of true deviations (without errors) is situated inside the sphere, form the healthy engine class; the others create the faulty engine class. It is clear that the patterns (deviation vectors with noise) of these two classes are partly intersected, resulting in α- and β-errors during the detection. **Figure 8** illustrates the new classification; the intersection is clearly seen. Two variations of the new classification based on single and multiple original classes have been prepared.

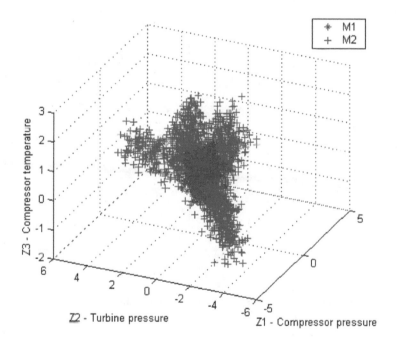

Figure 8. Patterns-based classification for monitoring.

Since new patterns-based classification (learning and testing sets) is ready, we can use any recognition technique to perform fault detection, and the MLP has been selected once more. It conserved sigmoid transfer functions and the hidden layer size of 12. Given that a threshold-based approach, which classifies pattern vectors according to their length, is traditionally used in fault detection, the algorithm with a distance measure (r-criterion) was also developed and compared with the MLP. Since the consequences of α- and β-errors are quite different (α-error is always considered as more dangerous), reduced losses $\bar{c} = P_\beta + \dfrac{c_\alpha}{c_\beta} P_\alpha$ were introduced to quantify monitoring effectiveness, where P_α and P_β are probabilities of α- and β-errors, c_α and c_β denote the corresponding losses, and $\dfrac{c_\alpha}{c_\beta}$ are equal to 10.

Figure 9 shows the plots of the reduced losses versus the radius r. For the MLP the change of r was simulated by the corresponding change of the boundary radius R during pattern separation in the learning set. It can be seen that the introduction of an additional threshold r, which is different from the boundary, reduces monitoring errors for both techniques. The best results correspond to the minimums of the curves. By comparing them, we can conclude that the network (MLP) provides better results for single classes, and the techniques are equal for multiple classes. In general for all comparison cases, the MLP slightly outperforms the r-criterion-based technique. Thus, the perceptron can be successfully applied for real gas turbine fault detection.

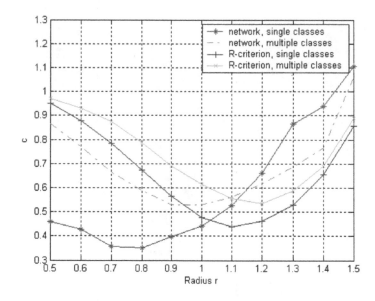

Figure 9. Reduced losses due to monitoring errors versus the threshold radius r.

7. Fault localization stage optimization

To draw sound conclusions about the ANN applicability for gas turbine fault localization, the comparison of the chosen networks was repeated for many comparison cases formed by independent variation of the main influencing factors: engines, operating modes, simulated or real information, and class types. In this way not only the best network is chosen but also the influence of these factors on diagnosis results is determined helping with the optimization of a total diagnostic process. For the purpose of correct comparison, the networks were tailored to a concrete task to solve.

7.1. Neural network tuning

We started to use ANNs applications and their tuning with the MLP [26]. The numbers of monitored variables and fault classes unambiguously determine the size of input and output layers of this network. As to the hidden layer, the number of 12 nodes was estimated as optimal using the probability $\overline{P}$ as a criterion. To choose a proper back-propagation algorithm, 12 variations were compared by accuracy and execution time. The resilient back-propagation ("rp"-algorithm) provided the best results and has been chosen. It was also found that 200 batch mode training epochs are sufficient for good learning; however, a learning stop by an Early Stopping Option may be useful as well.

Figure 10 illustrates other example of the tuning. Averaged probabilities computed for the PNN are plotted here against spread b, unique PNN tuning parameter. To determine this probability that has high precision of about ±0.001, calculations of $\overline{P}$ were repeated 100 times for each spread value, each time with a different seed (quantity that determines a consequence of random numbers), and an average value was computed. Such computations to find the best value b were repeated for two operating modes of Engine 1 and for two fault class types. It can be seen in the figure that the highest values of probability $\overline{P}_{av}$ does not depend on operating mode. These values are b=0.35 for the single fault type and b=0.40 for the multiple one.

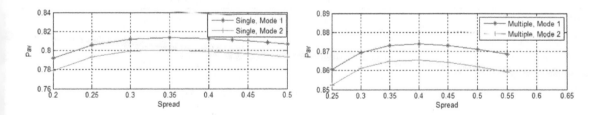

Figure 10. Probabilities versus spread parameter.

For all networks, the value 1000 simulated patterns per fault class has been selected as tradeoff between the required computer resources and the accuracy of the probabilities $\overline{P}$ and $\overline{P}_{av}$.

It is worth mentioning that the networks tuning is very time consuming. A tuning time can occupy up to 80% of a total investigation time, leaving 20% for the calculations related to final learning and validation of the networks.

7.2. Neural network comparison

The comparison of three tuned networks: MLP, RBN, and PNN, was firstly performed in reference [27], then the SVN was also evaluated. The variations of comparison conditions embraced independent changes of two engines, two operating modes, and two classification variations. The resulting probabilities $\overline{P}_{av}$ are given in **Table 1**. We can see that all networks are practically equal in accuracy for all comparison cases.

Paper [28] provides some additional results extending the comparison on the K-NN technique. The data given in **Table 2** confirm the conclusion about equal performances, now for five different techniques.

Class type	ANN	Engine 1		Engine 3	
		Mode 1	Mode 2	Mode 1	Mode 2
Single	MLP	0.8184	0.8059	0.7338	0.7470
	RBN	0.8186	0.8058	0.7349	0.7485
	PNN	0.8134	0.8004	0.7287	0.7456
	SVN	0.8190	0.8064	-	-
Multiple	MLP	0.8765	0.8686	0.7749	0.7596
	RBN	0.8783	0.8701	0.7787	0.7643
	PNN	0.8739	0.8653	0.7730	0.7617
	SVN	0.8770	0.8698	-	-

Table 1. Results of the network comparison (probabilities computed for Engine 1 and Engine 3).

Technique	Class type	
	Single	Multiple
PNN	0.8134	0.8739
K-NN	0.8154	0.8735
MLP	0.8193	0.8765

Table 2. Additional results of the technique comparison (probabilities for Engine 1).

The PNN and K-NN have probabilistic output, and every pattern recognition decision is accompanied with a confidence probability. This is an important advantage for gas turbine diagnosticians and maintenance staff. It can be taken into account for choosing the best technique when mean diagnosis reliability $\bar{P}$ is equal for all techniques considered. The PNN and K-NN are nonparametric techniques that estimate a probability density for each fault class by counting the patterns that fall into a given volume (window). To accurately estimate the probability density in a multidimensional diagnostic space, the number 1000 of available patterns can be insufficient. To assess possible imprecision of the density and confidence probability estimation by the PNN and K-NN techniques, a more precise analytical density estimation (ADE) technique has been proposed and developed [28]. It analytically determines the density and is employed as a reference to assess imprecision of the PNN and K-NN. To verify the newly developed technique, it was firstly compared with the others by the criterion $\bar{P}_{av}$. The results were reasonably good: the performances of all the techniques remained very close, but the ADE had the highest probability with the increment of 0.366–0.771 relatively the others.

The results of comparison by the estimated confidence probability are illustrated in **Figure 11**, when the PNN, K-NN, and MLP errors are plotted for 100 patterns. One can see that the bias and scatter for the K-NN estimates are by far greater. As to the MLP outputs, these non-probabilistic quantities look by far more precise than the K-NN probability estimates and seem to have the same precision level as the PW-PNN estimates.

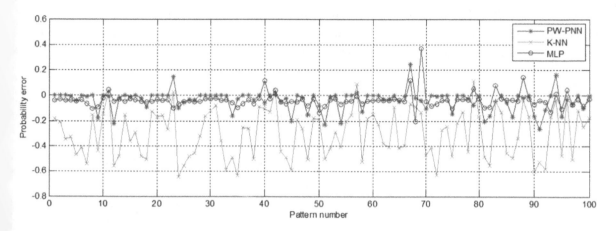

Figure 11. Errors of probability estimation by PW-PNN, K-NN, and MPL techniques (Engine 1, first 100 patterns of the first single fault class).

Table 3 presents the mean estimations errors for the case of the single fault classification. The table data confirm the above conclusion on the compared techniques: The bias and standard deviation of the K-NN errors are by far greater. The table also shows that on average the MLP outputs are even more exact than the PNN probabilities. It is one more argument to apply the perceptron in real gas turbine monitoring systems.

	Bias			σ	
PNN	K-NN	MLP	PW-PNN	K-NN	MLP
0.0444	-0.3293	-0.0419	0.0845	0.2020	0.0791

Table 3. Mean errors of confidence probability estimation (Engine 1, single fault classification).

7.3. Fault classification extension

In the investigations previously described, only two rigid classifications were maintained: one formed by single fault classes and the other constituted from multiple fault classes created by two fault parameters. However, the classification can vary a lot in practice even for the same engine, and it is difficult to predict what classification variation will be finally used in a real monitoring system. To verify and additionally compare the networks for different classification variations, the test procedure was modified for easily creating any new fault classification, more complex and more realistic than the classifications previously analyzed.

Twelve classification variations have been prepared and three networks: MLP, RBN, and PNN, were examined in reference [29]. These classifications have from 4 to 18 gas path and sensor fault classes, 1 to 4 fault parameters to form each class, positive and negative fault parameter changes. All the networks operated successfully for all fault classifications. **Table 4** shows the resulting averaged probabilities of correct diagnosis. Analyzing them, one can state that the differences between the networks within the same classification remain not great (except variation 6), about 0.015 (1.5%), while the difference between the variations can reach the value 0.10. Thus, these results reaffirm once more the conclusion drawn before that many recognition techniques may yield the same gas turbine diagnosis accuracy.

Variation	MLP	RBN	PNN
1	0.8172	0.8169	0.8099
2	0.8732	0.8759	0.8720
3	0.8091	0.8072	0.8037
4	0.8490	0.8524	0.8474
5	0.8033	0.8080	0.8036
6	0.6805	0.7319	0.7316
7	0.7362	0.7616	0.7567
8	0.7828	0.7965	0.7910
9	0.9279	0.9280	0.9260
10	0.7909	0.8017	0.7930
11	0.8075	0.7867	0.7775
12	0.8209	0.8184	0.8076

Table 4. Technique comparison for new classification variations (probabilities $\bar{P}_{av}$ for Engine 1).

7.4. Real data-based classification

Gas path mathematical models are widely used in building fault classification required for diagnostics because faults rarely occur during field operation. In that case, model errors are transmitted to the model-based classification. Paper [30] looks at the possibility of creating a mixed fault classification that incorporates both model-based and data-driven fault classes. Such a classification will combine a profound common diagnosis with a higher diagnostic accuracy for the data-driven classes. Engine 1 has been chosen as a test case. Its real data with two periods of compressor fouling were used to form a data-driven class of the fouling. **Figure 12** illustrates simulated (without errors) and real data.

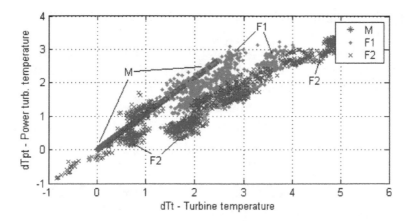

Figure 12. Simulated and real compressor fouling deviations (Engine 1: M—simulated deviations, F1 and F2—real deviations for the first and second fouling periods).

Different variations of the classification were considered and compared using the MLP. In spite of irregular distribution of real patterns, the MLP normally operated at the learning and validation steps. We also found that the perceptron trained on simulated data has 30% recognition errors when applied to real compressor fouling data. However, the use of mixed learning data allows to reduce these errors up to 3%. It was shown as well how to form a representative real fault class, which ensures minimal recognition errors.

Paper [31] presents another way to enhance gas turbine fault classification using real information. Diagnostic algorithms widely use theoretical random number distributions to simulate measurement errors. Such simulation differs from real diagnosis because the diagnostic algorithms work with the deviations, which have other error components that differ from simulated errors by amplitude and distribution. As a result, simulation-based investigations might result in too optimistic conclusions on gas turbine diagnosis reliability. To make error presentation more realistic, it was proposed in reference [31] to extract an error component from real deviations and to integrate it in fault description.

Using simulated and real data of Engine 1, six alternative variations of deviation error were integrated in the fault classification. Diagnosis was performed by the MLP, and the diagnosis reliability was estimated for each variation. Despite irregular real error distribution, the MLP successfully operated for all the variations. Experiments with error representation variations have shown what can happen when the classification formed with accurate simulated deviations is applied to classify less accurate real deviations. In that case, the diagnosis accuracy can fall from $\bar{P} \approx 92\%$ to $\bar{P} \approx 54\%$, but this low diagnostic accuracy can be considerably elevated by including real errors into the description of fault classes.

The fault classifications with integrated real errors were used in reference [32] to compare three networks: MLP, RBN, and PNN, one more time. All networks operated well and they differed in accuracy indicators $\bar{P}_{av}$ by less than 1%, thus confirming again the conclusion about equality of recognition techniques.

7.5. Different operating conditions

Many known studies show that grouping the data collected at different engine operating modes for making a single diagnosis (multipoint diagnosis) yields higher diagnostic accuracy than the accuracy provided by traditional one-point methods. But it is of a practical interest to know how significant the accuracy increment is and how it can be explained. The diagnosis of engines at dynamic modes poses the similar questions. To make one diagnosis, this technique combines data from successive measurement sections of a transient operation mode and in this regard looks like multipoint diagnosis.

Paper [33] analyzes the influence of the operating conditions on the diagnostic accuracy by comparing the one-point, multipoint, and transient options. The MLP is used as a pattern recognition technique. In spite of significant increase of the input dimensionality, the perceptron operated well for all options.

The calculations have revealed that the process of network training has peculiarities for multipoint diagnosis. They are illustrated in **Figure 13**, which shows the plots of the perceptron error versus training epochs for the cases of one-point and multipoint diagnosis. As can be seen, the curves of the error function for the training and validation processes almost coincide for the one-point option, they slow down along with training epochs, and a total epoch number 300 is relatively large. These are indications of no over-training effect. The behavior of the perceptron applied for the multipoint diagnosis is quite different. We can see that the validation curve falls behind the training curve after the 30th epoch, this gap rapidly increases, and the training process stops earlier (108 epochs) because of the over-training phenomenon. We can conclude that the Early Stopping Option is more required here. The differences indicated above can be explained by the ratio of input data volume to the unknown perceptron parameter number. For both cases, the volume of the training set is equal to 7000 patterns, but the numbers of unknown quantities significantly differ: 144 for the first case and 1540 for the second. Consequently, in the case of multipoint diagnosis, the trained network is much more flexible and the over-training becomes possible. An increase of the reference set volume can improve the training process; however, this increase is presently limited by the computation time.

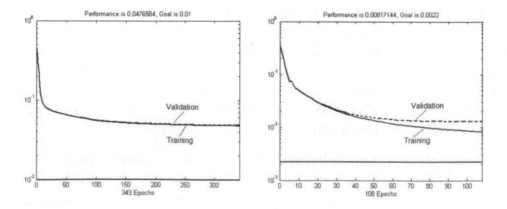

Figure 13. Training process (Engine 1, left plot—one-point diagnosis, right plot—multipoint diagnosis).

The results of the option comparison (probabilities $\bar{P}$) are grouped in **Table 5**. One can see that a total growth of diagnosis accuracy due to switching to the multipoint diagnosis and data joining from different steady states is significant: The diagnosis errors decrease by two to five times. The diagnosis at transients causes further accuracy growth, but it is not great. It has been found that this positive effect of the data joining is mainly explained by averaging the input data and smoothing the random measurement errors.

Option	Single fault classification	Multiple fault classification
One-point	0.7316	0.7351
Multipoint	0.8915	0.9444
Transient	0.9032	0.9561

Table 5. Comparison of the one-point, multipoint, and transient options (Engine 1).

8. Conclusions

A monitoring system comprises many elements, and many factors influence the final diagnostic accuracy. The present chapter has generalized our investigations aimed to enhance this system by choosing the best option for each element. In every investigation, a diagnostic process was simulated mainly on the basis of neural networks, and we focused on reaching the highest accuracy by choosing the best network and its optimal tuning to the issue to solve. As can be seen, all the examined techniques (MLP, RBN, PNN, SVN, and K-NN) use a pattern-based classification. Such a classification can be formed from complex classes in which faults are simulated by the nonlinear thermodynamic model. Moreover, this classification allows its description by real fault displays that completely exclude a negative effect of model inaccuracy. Thus, being objects of investigation and optimization, neural networks help with enhancement of a whole monitoring system. As a result of the conducted investigations, some methods to elevate diagnostic accuracy were proposed and proven. The chapter also provides the recommendations on choosing and tailoring the networks for different diagnostic tasks. For solving many tasks, the utility of the multilayer perceptron has been proven on simulated and real data.

Acknowledgements

The work has been carried out with the support of the National Polytechnic Institute of Mexico (research project 20150961).

Author details

Igor Loboda

Address all correspondence to: igloboda@gmail.com

National Polytechnic Institute, Mexico

References

[1] Saravanamuttoo, H.I.H., MacIsaac, B.D., 1983, Thermodynamic models for pipeline gas turbine diagnostics, *ASME Journal of Engineering for Power*, Vol. 105, pp. 875–884.

[2] Doel, D.L., 2003, Interpretation of weighted-least-squares gas path analysis results, *Journal of Engineering for Gas Turbines and Power*, Vol. 125, Issue 3, pp. 624–633.

[3] Aretakis, N., Mathioudakis, K., Stamatis, A., 2003, Nonlinear engine component fault diagnosis from a limited number of measurements using a combinatorial approach, *Journal of Engineering for Gas Turbines and Power*, Vol. 125, Issue 3, pp. 642–650.

[4] Volponi, A.J., DePold, H., Ganguli, R., 2003, The use of Kalman filter and neural network methodologies in gas turbine performance diagnostics: a comparative study, *Journal of Engineering for Gas Turbines and Power*, Vol. 125, Issue 4, pp. 917–924.

[5] Sampath, S., Singh, R., 2006, An integrated fault diagnostics model using genetic algorithm and neural networks, *ASME Journal of Engineering for Gas Turbines and Power*, Vol. 128, Issue 1, pp. 49–56.

[6] Pipe K., 1987, Application of advanced pattern recognition techniques in machinery failure prognosis for turbomachinery, *Condition Monitoring 1987 International Conference*, British Hydraulic Research Association, UK, pp. 73–89.

[7] Lokesh Kumar S., et al., 2007, Comparison of a few fault diagnosis methods on sparse variable length time series sequences, *IGTI/ASME Turbo Expo 2007*, Montreal, Canada, 8 p., ASME Paper GT2007-27843.

[8] Romessis, C., Mathioudakis, K., 2006, Bayesian network approach for gas path fault diagnosis, *ASME Journal of Engineering for Gas Turbines and Power*, Vol. 128, Issue 1, pp. 64–72.

[9] Fast, M., Assadi, M., De, S., 2008, Condition based maintenance of gas turbines using simulation data and artificial neural network: a demonstration of feasibility, *IGTI/ASME Turbo Expo 2008*, Berlin, Germany, 9 p., ASME Paper GT2008-50768.

[10] Palme, T., Fast, M., Assadi, M., Pike, A., Breuhaus, P., 2009, Different condition monitoring models for gas turbines by means of artificial neural networks, *IGTI/ASME Turbo
Expo 2009*, Orlando, Florida, USA, 11 p., ASME Paper GT2009-59364.

[11] Palme, T., Breuhaus, P., Assadi, M., Klein, A., Kim, M., 2011, Early warning of gas
turbine failure by nonlinear feature extraction using an auto-associative neural network
approach, *IGTI/ASME Turbo Expo 2011*, Vancouver, British Columbia, Canada, 12 p.,
ASME Paper GT2011-45991.

[12] Butler, S.W., Pattipati, K.R., Volponi, A., et al., 2006, An assessment methodology for
data-driven and model based techniques for engine health monitoring, ASME Paper
No. GT2006-91096.

[13] Romessis, C., Mathioudakis, K., 2003, Setting up of a probabilistic neural network for
sensor fault detection including operation with component fault, *Journal of Engineering
for Gas Turbines and Power*, Vol. 125, pp. 634–641.

[14] Jaw, L. C., Wang, W., 2006, Mathematical formulation of model-based methods for
diagnostics and prognostics, *IGTI/ASME Turbo Expo 2006*, Barcelona, Spain, 7 p., ASME
Paper GT2006-90655.

[15] Borguet, S., Leonard, O., Dewallet, P., 2015, Regression-based modelling of a fleet of
gas turbine engines for performance trading, *IGTI/ASME Turbo Expo 2015*, Montreal,
Canada, 12 p., ASME Paper GT2015-42330.

[16] Vachtsevanos, G., Lewis, F.L., Roemer, M., Hess, A., Wu, B., 2006, *Intelligent Fault
Diagnosis and Prognosis for Engineering Systems*, John Wiley & Sons, Inc., New Jersey,
434 p.

[17] Vatani, A., Korasani, K., Meskin, N., 2015, Degradation prognostics in gas turbine
engines using neural networks, *IGTI/ASME Turbo Expo 2015*, Montreal, Canada, 13 p.,
ASME Paper GT2015-44101.

[18] Duda, R.O., 2001, *Pattern Classification*, Wiley-Interscience, New York, 654 p.

[19] Haykin, S., 1994, *Neural Networks*, Macmillan College Publishing Company, New York.

[20] Bishop, C.M., 2006, *Pattern Recognition and Machine Learning*, Springer Science, New
York.

[21] Cortes, C., Vapnik, V., 1995, Support-vector networks, *Machine Learning*, Vol. 20, pp.
273–297.

[22] Boser, B.E., Guyon, I.M., Vapnik, V.N., 1992, A training algorithm for optimal margin
classifiers, Fifth Annual Workshop on Computational Learning Theory—COLT '92,
ACM Press, New York, USA, pp. 144–152.

[23] Hsu, C.W., Chang, C.C., Lin, C.J., 2010, A practical guide to support vector classification,
National Taiwan University. http://www.csie.ntu.edu.tw/~cjlin/papers/guide/
guide.pdf

[24] Loboda, I., Feldshteyn, Y., 2011, Polynomials and neural networks for gas turbine monitoring: a comparative study, *International Journal of Turbo & Jet Engines*, Vol. 28, Issue 3, pp. 227–236 (also see ASME paper GT2010-23749).

[25] Loboda, I., Yepifanov, S., Feldshteyn, Y., 2009, An integrated approach to gas turbine monitoring and diagnostics, *International Journal of Turbo & Jet Engines*, Vol. 26, Issue 2, pp. 111–126 (also see ASME paper GT2008-51449).

[26] Loboda, I., Yepifanov, S., Feldshteyn, Y., 2007, A generalized fault classification for gas turbine diagnostics on steady states and transients, *Journal of Engineering for Gas Turbines and Power*, Vol. 129, Issue 4, pp. 977–985.

[27] Loboda, I., Yepifanov, S., 2013, On the selection of an optimal pattern recognition technique for gas turbine diagnosis, *IGTI/ASME Turbo Expo 2013*, San Antonio, Texas, USA, 11 p., ASME Paper GT2013-95198.

[28] Loboda, I., 2014, Gas turbine fault recognition using probability density estimation, *ASME Turbo Expo 2014*, Dusseldorf, Germany, 13 p., ASME Paper GT2014-27265.

[29] Perez Ruiz, J.L., Loboda, I., 2014, A flexible fault classification for gas turbine diagnosis, *Aerospace Techniques and Technology*, Vol. 113, Issue 6, pp. 94–102.

[30] Loboda, I., Yepifanov, S., 2010, A mixed data-driven and model based fault classification for gas turbine diagnosis, *International Journal of Turbo & Jet Engines*, Vol. 27, Issue 3–4, pp. 251–264 (also see ASME Paper GT2010-23075).

[31] Loboda, I., Yepifanov, S., Feldshteyn, Y., 2013, A more realistic scheme of deviation error representation for gas turbine diagnostics, *International Journal of Turbo & Jet Engines*, Vol. 30, Issue 2, pp. 179–189 (also see ASME Paper GT2012-69368).

[32] Loboda, I., Olivares Robles, M.A., 2015, Gas turbine fault diagnosis using probabilistic neural networks, *International Journal of Turbo & Jet Engines*, Vol. 32, Issue 2, pp.175–192.

[33] Loboda, I., Feldshteyn, Y., Yepifanov, S., 2007, Gas turbine diagnostics under variable operating conditions, *International Journal of Turbo & Jet Engines*, Vol. 24, Issues 3–4, pp. 231–244 (also see ASME Paper GT2007-28085).

Permissions

All chapters in this book were first published in ANN, by InTech Open; hereby published with permission under the Creative Commons Attribution License or equivalent. Every chapter published in this book has been scrutinized by our experts. Their significance has been extensively debated. The topics covered herein carry significant findings which will fuel the growth of the discipline. They may even be implemented as practical applications or may be referred to as a beginning point for another development.

The contributors of this book come from diverse backgrounds, making this book a truly international effort. This book will bring forth new frontiers with its revolutionizing research information and detailed analysis of the nascent developments around the world.

We would like to thank all the contributing authors for lending their expertise to make the book truly unique. They have played a crucial role in the development of this book. Without their invaluable contributions this book wouldn't have been possible. They have made vital efforts to compile up to date information on the varied aspects of this subject to make this book a valuable addition to the collection of many professionals and students.

This book was conceptualized with the vision of imparting up-to-date information and advanced data in this field. To ensure the same, a matchless editorial board was set up. Every individual on the board went through rigorous rounds of assessment to prove their worth. After which they invested a large part of their time researching and compiling the most relevant data for our readers.

The editorial board has been involved in producing this book since its inception. They have spent rigorous hours researching and exploring the diverse topics which have resulted in the successful publishing of this book. They have passed on their knowledge of decades through this book. To expedite this challenging task, the publisher supported the team at every step. A small team of assistant editors was also appointed to further simplify the editing procedure and attain best results for the readers.

Apart from the editorial board, the designing team has also invested a significant amount of their time in understanding the subject and creating the most relevant covers. They scrutinized every image to scout for the most suitable representation of the subject and create an appropriate cover for the book.

The publishing team has been an ardent support to the editorial, designing and production team. Their endless efforts to recruit the best for this project, has resulted in the accomplishment of this book. They are a veteran in the field of academics and their pool of knowledge is as vast as their experience in printing. Their expertise and guidance has proved useful at every step. Their uncompromising quality standards have made this book an exceptional effort. Their encouragement from time to time has been an inspiration for everyone.

The publisher and the editorial board hope that this book will prove to be a valuable piece of knowledge for researchers, students, practitioners and scholars across the globe.

List of Contributors

Mohamad Mostafa
German Aerospace Center (DLR), Institute of Communications and Navigation, Wessling, Germany

Giuseppe Oliveri
Ulm University, Institute of Electron Devices and Circuits, Ulm, Germany

Werner G. Teich and Jürgen Lindner
Ulm University, Institute of Communications Engineering, Ulm, Germany

Dongsheng Guo and Laicheng Yan
College of Information Science and Engineering, Huaqiao University, Xiamen, China

Yunong Zhang
School of Data and Computer Science, Sun Yat-sen University, Guangzhou, China

Zbigniew Szadkowski, Dariusz Głas and Krzysztof Pytel
Department of Physics and Applied Informatics, University of Łódź, Łódź, Poland

Hayrettin Okut
Yüzüncü Yıl University, Faculty of Agriculture, Biometry and Genetic Branch, Van, Turkey
Wake Forest University, School of Medicine, Center for Diabetes Research, Center for Genomics and Personalized Medicine Research, Winston-Salem, NC, USA

Ovidiu Schipor
Computers Department, Integrated Center for Research, Development and Innovation in Advanced Materials Nanotechnologies, and Distributed Systems for Fabrication and Control

Oana Geman and Mihai Covasa
"Stefan cel Mare" University of Suceava, Suceava, Romania
Department of Health and Human Development, "Stefan cel Mare" University of Suceava, Suceava, Romania
Department of Basic Medical Sciences, Western University of Health Sciences, Pomona, California, USA

Iuliana Chiuchisan
Computers, Electronics and Automation Department, "Stefan cel Mare" University of Suceava, Suceava, Romania

Daniel Dunea and Stefania Iordache
Valahia University of Târgoviste, Aleea Sinaia, Târgoviste, Romania

Igor Loboda
National Polytechnic Institute, Mexico

Index